Beyond Great Powers and Hegemons

Beyond Great Powers and Hegemons

WHY SECONDARY STATES SUPPORT, FOLLOW, OR CHALLENGE

Edited by Kristen P. Williams, Steven E. Lobell,

and Neal G. Jesse

Stanford Security Studies
An Imprint of Stanford University Press
Stanford, California

Stanford University Press
Stanford, California

Printed in the United States of America on acid-free, archival-quality paper

Library of Congress Cataloging-in-Publication Data

Beyond great powers and hegemons : why secondary states support, follow or challenge /
edited by Kristen P. Williams, Steven E. Lobell, and Neal G. Jesse.
    pages cm
  Includes bibliographical references and index.
  ISBN 978-0-8047-7163-4 (cloth : alk. paper) —
  ISBN 978-0-8047-7164-1 (pbk. : alk. paper)
  1. Hegemony. 2. International relations. 3. States, Small. 4. Great powers.
5. World politics—1945–1989. 6. World politics—1989– I. Williams, Kristen P., editor
of compilation. II. Lobell, Steven E., editor of compilation. III. Jesse, Neal G., editor of
compilation.
  JZ1312.B49 2012
  327.1—dc23
  2011036721

Special discounts for bulk quantities of Stanford Security Studies are available to
corporations, professional associations, and other organizations. For details and discount
information, contact the special sales department of Stanford University Press. Tel: (650)
736-1782, Fax: (650) 736-1784

Typeset by Thompson Type in 10/14 Minion

CONTENTS

PREFACE

THIS BOOK EMERGED from a series of discussions that the editors initiated in 2003 about the limitations of hegemony resulting from challenges by secondary states. We recognized that the majority of the literature on great powers and hegemons focused on their motives and strategies for fending off other great power challengers and rivals. In adding a new dimension to the discussion, this book focuses on the responses to global and regional hegemons by secondary and tertiary powers, and particularly their motives, objectives, and interests. Unlike other authors, not only do we discuss the limitations of hegemony, but this volume also examines the domestic and international factors that motivate the rest of the powers. Secondary and tertiary states rarely challenge global and regional hegemons directly and must find other ways to respond. Our overarching question is: Why do states follow, or not, the hegemon? To explain the motivations and strategies of these states, we develop three explanatory frameworks and examine them in the case studies: realist arguments and the role of material power distributions (both global and regional), the role of domestic politics, and liberal institutionalist theories and the role of international organizations and global norms. We examine the strategies and motivations of the followers, which range from opposing the hegemon to accommodating it, and the specific strategies including hard balancing, soft balancing, blackmail, leash slipping, binding, bonding, and bandwagoning. In examining these responses to the hegemon, the chapters also highlight the process of negotiation and renegotiation of the relationship between hegemons and followers.

We focus on the Cold War and post–Cold War periods and on responses to global and regional hegemons. The cases in the volume examine the three explanatory variables that are developed in Chapter 1. The cases are: Romania's response to Soviet hegemony, Cuba's relations with the Soviet Union, Ireland's response to American and British hegemony, domestic divisions in Jordan's and America's response, the role of trade relations between the United States and Latin America, NATO allies' interaction with the United States after the end of the Cold War, Pakistan's cooperation with the United States, the response of Brazil's neighbors to its regional hegemonic aspirations, the balancing relationship between Russia and its new neighbors, the effect of India's emergence as a hegemonic power on South Asia, the relationship between China and its Asia-Pacific neighbors, and South Africa's interaction with other states in the region. The conclusion discusses American decline and the greater space it gives other powers in their region and on the global-international level.

The concepts, explanatory frameworks, and strategies of the rest of the powers in this volume were developed and refined during many conference calls and e-mails between Worcester, Salt Lake City, and Bowling Green, and during three conference presentations at the International Studies Association annual meetings (2004, 2007, and 2011). We were fortunate to have all the contributing authors participate on at least one of these panels.

We would like to thank three anonymous reviewers for their detailed comments and suggestions, which greatly strengthened this volume at different stages of the review process. We are fortunate to have Geoffrey Burn, director and acquisitions editor of the Security Studies series at Stanford University Press, as our editor, and we thank him for all his assistance and professionalism in helping us move this project from idea to completion. We extend our thanks to his editorial assistant, Jessica Walsh, for her help. We thank Todd Bailey for his research assistance and his eye for detail. We also thank Margaret Pinette for her meticulous copyediting. Funding for the index to the volume was generously provided by the Clark University Political Science Department's Francis A. Harrington Funds. Finally, we express our gratitude to our families for their support.

CONTRIBUTORS

Stephen F. Burgess is Professor, Department of International Security Studies, U.S. Air War College. His three books are *South Africa's Weapons of Mass Destruction* (with Helen Purkitt) (Indiana University Press, 2005), *Smallholders and Political Voice in Zimbabwe* (University Press of America, 1997), and *The United Nations under Boutros Boutros-Ghali, 1992–1997* (Scarecrow Press, 2001). He has published numerous articles and book chapters on African and South Asian security issues. Dr. Burgess has been a faculty member at Vanderbilt University, the University of Zambia, the University of Zimbabwe, and Hofstra University.

John R. Dreyer is Assistant Professor of Political Science at the South Dakota School of Mines and Technology. He research includes the hegemonic use of force, environmental security, and the military history of neutrality. Besides work on hegemonic malcontents, he is currently researching how military intervention might occur within the context of environmental security. A separate research project is focused on the relationship between social networking and hegemony.

Shale Horowitz is Professor of Political Science at the University of Wisconsin–Milwaukee. He is the author of *From Ethnic Conflict to Stillborn Reform: The Former Soviet Union and Yugoslavia* (Texas A&M University Press, 2005), and coeditor of four other books, including *Identity and Change in East Asian Conflicts: The Cases of China, Taiwan, and the Koreas* (Palgrave Macmillan,

2007). He is the author or coauthor of articles in *Comparative Political Studies*, *Comparative Politics*, *Comparative Studies in Society and History*, *International Interactions*, *International Studies Quarterly*, *Journal of Peace Research*, and other journals. His research focuses on ethnic and international conflict, economic policy making, and political institutions.

Jennifer D. Kibbe is Associate Professor of Government at Franklin & Marshall College. She has published articles on covert action and the militarization of intelligence in *Intelligence and National Security* and *Foreign Affairs* and has chapters in the edited volumes, *Strategic Intelligence* (Praeger Security International, 2007) and *The Oxford Handbook of National Security Intelligence* (Oxford University Press, 2010). Her research interests include covert action, congressional oversight of intelligence, foreign policy decision making, and the U.S.–Soviet conflict in the developing world during the Cold War.

Neal G. Jesse is Associate Professor of Political Science at Bowling Green State University. He has published in journals such as *Electoral Studies, International Political Science Review, International Studies Quarterly, Political Psychology, New Hibernia Review/Iris Éireannach Nua,* and *Representation* and contributed chapters to edited volumes, including: *Elections in Australia, Ireland and Malta under the Single Transferable Vote* (University of Michigan Press, 2000) and *Ethnic Conflict and International Politics: Explaining Diffusion and Escalation* (Palgrave Macmillan, 2004). His books include *Identity and Institutions: Conflict Reduction in Divided Societies* (SUNY, 2005) and *Ethnic Conflict: A Systematic Approach to Cases of Conflict* (CQ Press, 2011), both coauthored with Kristen P. Williams.

Nancy D. Lapp is Professor of Government at California State University, Sacramento. She is the author of *Landing Votes: Representation and Land Reform in Latin America* (Palgrave/Macmillan, 2004). Her research interests include the origins and effects of electoral institutions in Latin America, compulsory voting, and U.S.–Latin American relations.

Christopher Layne is Professor of International Affairs and Robert M. Gates Chair in National Security at the Bush School of Government and Public Service at Texas A&M University. He is author of *The Peace of Illusions: American Grand Strategy from 1940 to the Present* (Cornell University Press, 2006) and (with Bradley A. Thayer) *American Empire: A Debate* (Routledge, 2006). Layne's next book is *After the Fall: International Politics, U.S. Grand Strategy, and the End of the Pax Americana* (forthcoming, Yale University Press). He has published in such scholarly and policy journals as: *International Security, International History Review, Security Studies, Journal of Strategic Studies, The National Interest, Foreign Policy, The Washington Quarterly,* and *Orbis.*

Steven E. Lobell is Associate Professor of Political Science at the University of Utah. He is the author of *The Challenge of Hegemony: Grand Strategy, Trade, and Domestic Politics* (University of Michigan Press, 2003); *Ethnic Conflict and International Politics: Explaining Diffusion and Escalation* (Palgrave Macmillan, 2004) with Philip Mauceri; and *Neoclassical Realism, the State, and Foreign Policy* (Cambridge University Press, 2009) with Norrin M. Ripsman and Jeffrey W. Taliaferro. He has published journal articles in *Security Studies, International Studies Quarterly, International Interactions, Review of International Studies, Political Science Quarterly, Journal of Strategic Studies, The International Relations of the Asia Pacific, International Politics, Comparative Strategy, Chinese Journal of International Politics, International Journal,* and *World Affairs.*

Galia Press-Barnathan is a Senior Lecturer at the International Relations Department, Hebrew University at Jerusalem. Her publications include: *Organizing the World: The United States and Regional Cooperation in Asia and Europe* (Routledge, 2003) and *The Political Economy of Transitions to Peace: A Comparative Perspective* (Pittsburgh University Press, 2009). She has also published journal articles in *International Studies Review, Cooperation and Conflict, Security Studies* and the *Journal of Peace Research.*

Maria Sampanis teaches at California State University, Sacramento. She is the author of *Preserving Power through Coalitions* (Praeger, 2003). Her research interests include international political economy and U.S. foreign policy.

Srini Sitaraman is Associate Professor in the Department of Political Science and Director of the Asian Studies Program at Clark University and a Research Associate with the Fairbank Center for East Asian Research. He has published several articles and monographs on international regimes and has written about South Asian security issues. His book, *State Participation in International Treaty Regimes,* was published in 2009 (Ashgate Publishing).

Alexander C. Tan is Associate Professor of Political Science at the University of Canterbury (Christchurch, New Zealand). He is also Associate Director of the New Zealand Contemporary China Research Centre (Wellington, New Zealand), Senior Fellow at the John G. Tower Center for Political Studies at Southern Methodist University (Dallas, Texas), and an Associate of the Election Study Center at National Cheng Chi University (Taipei, Taiwan). He is coeditor of Ashgate Publishing's book series on *Paradigms from Asian Politics,* associate editor of *International Studies Perspectives,* and editorial board member of several academic journals such as *Electoral Studies, Political Science,* and *Open Political Science Journal.* He has published numerous books and academic articles in the areas of comparative political parties and elections, comparative political economy, East Asian politics, and European politics.

Michael D. Tyburski is a doctoral candidate in political science at the University of Wisconsin–Milwaukee. In addition to ethnic conflict, Tyburski writes on political corruption and is the author of a forthcoming journal article on corruption in Mexico in *International Studies Quarterly.*

Kristen P. Williams is Professor of Political Science at Clark University. She has published journal articles, chapters in edited books, and several books. Her books include: *Despite Nationalist Conflicts: Theory and Practice of Maintaining World Peace* (Praeger, 2001); *Identity and Institutions: Conflict Reduction in Divided Societies* (SUNY, 2005) and *Ethnic Conflict* (CQ Press, 2011) (both coauthored with Neal G. Jesse); *Women, the State and War: A Comparative Perspective on Citizenship and Nationalism* (Lexington Books, 2007) and *Women and War: Gender Identity and Activism in Times of Conflict* (Kumarian Press, 2010) (both coauthored with Joyce P. Kaufman), and *World Politics in a New Era,* 5th edition (Oxford University Press, 2012) (coauthored with Steven L. Spiegel, Jennifer Taw, and Elizabeth Matthews).

Beyond Great Powers and Hegemons

1 THE LEADER CAN'T LEAD WHEN THE FOLLOWERS WON'T FOLLOW

The Limitations of Hegemony

Neal G. Jesse, Steven E. Lobell, Galia Press-Barnathan, and Kristen P. Williams

U.S. HEGEMONY HAS DEFINED the post–Cold War world.[1] By virtue of its preponderant military and economic power relative to the other states in the system, the hegemon is able to exert power and influence over those states. Most of international relations (IR) theory and security studies, from Thucydides to Hans Morgenthau to John Mearsheimer, is about the study of the leading power of the day: great powers, superpowers, hegemons, and, most recently, überpowers.[2] This realist literature has vacillated between a portrayal of the world as one characterized by a balance of power between competing powers (for example, Waltz), and a portrayal of the world as characterized by periods of hegemonic control (for example, Gilpin). Reflecting this duality, IR scholars in the early post–Cold War years debated whether the American preponderance following the breakdown of the USSR was indeed the beginning of an era of U.S. hegemony or a "unipolar moment."[3] Consequently, one drawn-out policy discussion with the end of the Cold War among scholars was whether the United States should try to perpetuate and prolong its "unipolar moment" as the sole preponderant power.[4] Scholars debated whether preponderance was sustainable and durable (calling for a policy of primacy and unilateralism) or self-defeating, costly, and likely to provoke counterbalancing behavior (calling for a policy of selective engagement, offshore balancing, and buckpassing).[5] A second policy debate was how to perpetuate America's unipolar moment: whether the United States should use military power, self-restraint, trade, democracy, international institutions, or security communities to prevent, punish, coerce, or reassure secondary states not to counterbalance.[6]

1

These debates in the literature primarily focus on the motivations and strategies of the hegemon to exert its influence and power and in particular its attempt to stave off challengers. The literature shows that hegemons seek to ensure that the less powerful states follow, whether through coercion or benevolence.[7] Strategies and incentives include trade, direct aid, diplomacy, and military alliances. And yet it takes two to tango. The reaction of other states in the system is not fully contingent on the hegemon's own strategies. Nor can these reactions be neatly classified into a "followers" or "challengers" dichotomy.

Building on the work of others who have addressed the issue of responses to hegemons,[8] this book seeks to understand the *motivations, objectives,* and *interests of the followers*—why they follow, or not, the hegemon and whether they challenge the policies and strategies or the core position of the hegemon.[9] Some of these second-ranked (major powers) and tertiary states are relatively powerful, and others are weak; some are satisfied status quo powers, and others are dissatisfied.[10] This renewed interest in the "rest" of the states is reflected in the emerging debate over soft balancing as the common response by secondary powers to U.S. hegemony.[11] Scholars have discussed other strategies, including leash-slipping, hedging, and prebalancing.[12] The focus on soft balancing ignores the broader question of when and why states choose to support, follow, or challenge the hegemon and the tactics and grand strategies they employ. Using both historical and contemporary cases (in different issue areas—military, political and economic; different hegemons—global and regional; and different geographic regions—Europe, Latin America, Middle East, Africa, Asia, South Asia), this book, unlike much of the existing literature, examines the domestic and international factors that account for the motivations of the rest of the powers.

While also reviewing the literature on hegemonic leadership, specifically the strategies available to a hegemon to garner support from followers, the primary focus of the chapter, and thus the book, is to examine the strategies and motivations of the followers. Do followers follow (or not) because of external security threats (realism), coercion or cooptation by the hegemon, shared values about how the international system should be ordered, or domestic politics? This question is interesting and important both theoretically and for policy makers because it has direct implications for what the United States can and should do to generate followership as well as to the more fundamental question of whether this is really in U.S. hands.

The chapter begins with a brief overview of the literature on hegemons—namely the dominant theories in IR to account for how the hegemon is able to influence the behavior of secondary states. We then turn to a discussion of followers and an examination of the literature that explores the strategies they can take to challenge or resist the hegemon. Following this, we address the motivations of followers, pose several questions, and provide an explanatory framework for examination in the subsequent case study chapters: namely, domestic and international factors that account for the motivations of the followers in response to strategies of the hegemon. While not covered as a separate case chapter in the volume, as way of illustration, this chapter notes examples of followers and their motivations in looking at the historical case of the 1991 Gulf War and the contemporary example of responses to U.S. hegemony in the invasion of Iraq in 2003. Finally, we provide a brief overview of the organization of the book.

HEGEMONS, UNIPOLARITY, LEADERSHIP, AND IR THEORY

In assessing the distribution of power in the post–Cold War international system, one thinks immediately of the overarching dominance of the United States, whose power (economic, military, and technological) surpasses that of any other state in the system. As Stephen G. Brooks and William C. Wohlforth note, "What truly distinguishes the current international system is American dominance in all of them [power dimensions] simultaneously." Moreover, there is no state today that can rival the United States "in any critical dimension of power. There has never been a system of sovereign states that contained one state with this degree of dominance."[13] Both the capabilities and influence of the United States, according to Elke Krahmann, enable it to engage in policies deemed both hegemonic and imperialistic.[14] For the most part, scholars seem to be in agreement that the structure of the contemporary international system is unipolar.[15] But is it hegemonic?

While much has been written about hegemony, it is possible to make a rough distinction among three approaches to the concept. Put succinctly, they address the questions of what a hegemon has, what a hegemon wants, and what a hegemon does. The first is purely material, focusing on the necessary power capabilities needed to be called a hegemon (this approach nowadays compares hegemony to unipolarity). The second approach focuses on the state's motivation to exercise hegemony. A third, yet closely related, approach focuses on hegemony as a certain relationship between a preponderant state and other states in the system. This approach implies that hegemony is not a trait but rather a type of interaction or relationship. These approaches find their expression in various theoretical as well as policy debates among offensive realists, defensive realists, neoliberal institutionalists, and constructivists, all really arguing mostly about strategy and interaction rather than about hegemony as a condition.

Robert Keohane, in his formative work in *After Hegemony*, distinguished between the "basic force model," which identifies a hegemon by examining material power distribution in the system, and the "force activation model," which insists that a hegemon is not only a preponderant power but one that has the will to lead the system. A hegemon is thus a state "that is powerful enough to maintain the essential rules governing interstate relations, and is willing to do so."[16] This basic distinction runs through most of the discussion of hegemony to this day. The first definition, focusing on concentration of capabilities, is obviously appealing as it is more elegant and potentially more deterministic. Stephen Krasner's seminal work on state power and international trade discussed a hegemon as "a much larger and relatively more advanced state."[17] Robert Gilpin defined a hegemon as "a state that is politically the most powerful and economically the most efficient."[18] Military power is also seen as important, especially in its ability to guard economic resources. Keohane talked about "control over raw materials, sources of capital, markets and competitive advantage in the production of highly valued goods."[19] David Lake focused on the combination of relative size (each country's proportion of world trade) and relative labor productivity to define a hegemon as a large state with high labor productivity.[20]

All of these are what we can call "first-wave hegemony studies," focused mainly on the international political economy (IPE) arena and driven by the puzzle of explaining the openness of the international economic system and its prospects in face of perceived (or not) American decline.[21]

"Second-wave hegemony studies" emerged several years after the end of the Cold War, as the continued strengthening of the United States and the lack of balancing against it slowly gave way to an understanding that we do not live in a "unipolar moment" but rather a "unipolar system." The very discussion of "unipolarity" rather than "hegemony" highlights the focus on studying the impact first and foremost of material power capabilities, along the same lines Kenneth Waltz adopted in his characterization of bipolar and multipolar systems. This approach finds clear expression in Wohlforth's discussion of the United States as unipole, which focuses on various indicators of economic and military capabilities.[22] A similar focus on material power preponderance can be found in Barry Posen's work and in the recent work of Brooks and Wohlforth. While they note what they call the confusing use of the term *hegemony*, both as concentration of capabilities in one state and as political domination, they choose to focus on the distribution of capabilities.[23]

Equating unipolarity and hegemony thus offers us an elegant way to measure and define a hegemonic state, as well as to test more elegant hypotheses about how this unique power position shapes the hegemon's preferences and policies, as well as the preferences and policies of other states in the system. This solution, however, is more problematic on closer inspection. One reason has to do with the "will factor," to which we turn next. But, even on their own terms, capability-based definitions of hegemony fail to come to terms with the relative importance of various power capabilities across time and space. Whereas the United States today is perhaps a relatively easy case, given its preponderance across so many power indicators, it becomes much more complicated to assess other cases of possible hegemony, especially in a regional context. Throughout the 1980s experts debated as to whether Japan could be considered a hegemon in Asia, given its huge economic power preponderance but limited military and political capabilities. Today, scholars continue to debate whether China is becoming a regional hegemon in Asia and, if so, when that is likely to occur. These debates highlight the limitations of a power-as-resource approach to hegemony. Such an approach to hegemony could, however, be fine-tuned if we choose to assess it on either an issue-area or a regional basis. This way we can identify, for example, wider or narrower power disparities between the lead state and others across regions or issues and examine the extent to which such variations have an impact on how others treat the lead states.

The second basic approach to hegemony adds to the material capabilities a motivational element. Keohane stressed that a hegemon has both the power and willingness "to maintain the essential rules governing interstate relations."[24] Earlier, Charles Kindleberger emphasized that a hegemon is a strong state that is willing to assume responsibility for the system and to exercise leadership. A hegemon is measured in large part by its acts of leadership (serving as a lender of last resort, opening its markets to goods in distress, ensuring coordination of macroeconomic policies, and so on).[25] This focus on motivation, in turn, created a distinction between two types of hegemons: benevolent (Kindleberger) and malevolent (Gilpin).[26]

More recently, in the second wave of hegemony studies, this has found expression in discussions of U.S. motivation to continue leading the world and to remain engaged internationally. Layne argues that hegemons and hegemony can be described by five characteristics, most of which are material, but he brings in the motivational factor: "raw, hard power" and "economic supremacy"; "acts self interestedly to safeguard its security, economic, and ideological interests"; "is about polarity. . . . a hegemon is the only great power in the system, which is therefore, by definition, unipolar"; "is fundamentally about structural change"; and "is about will. A hegemon purposefully exercises its overwhelming power to impose order on the international system."[27] An important distinction between structural and motivational approaches is that structural approaches argue that the hegemon's preferences can be deduced from its material power preponderance, whereas a motivational approach gives room for other factors that may shape motivation to lead one way or another.

The third element defining hegemony in the literature is the nature of the lead state's interaction with others in the system. Hegemony is mainly about what a hegemon does. From Gilpin to G. John Ikenberry, hegemony is about creating a certain international order through the construction of various institutions. In *War and Change* Gilpin argued that a hegemon controls the processes of interactions among the elements of the system and seeks to organize political, territorial, and economic relations in terms of its respective security and economic interests.[28] Twenty years later, and from a different, neoliberal, theoretical perspective, Ikenberry elaborated on how great powers in general, but hegemons in particular, have used international institutions to build a favorable international order, as well as to reassure other states in the system.[29]

The discussion of strategy is also central in recent debates about whether to describe the United States as a hegemon or as an empire. While this distinction is perhaps not central here, much of it falls on the nature of the governance structure created by the powerful state in the system. A hegemonic order, according to Daniel Nexon and Thomas Wright, "involves the existence of at least some weak and sparse ties of authority between the hegemon and the lesser powers. These represent the minimal level of authority, or asymmetric influence, created by the hegemonic bargain." They are also characterized by a higher level of interdependence among states. This type of order combines anarchic and hierarchical elements.[30]

The recent debate about a U.S. empire, and the strong political undertones that accompany it, do raise an additional point worthy of consideration in a volume discussing followers. It seems that much of the debate on whether the United States is simply a great power, a hegemon, an empire, a hyperpower, or the like, is not a theoretical debate about the core elements of U.S. power or power more generally but rather a political-ideological debate about whether such power and influence are good or bad. This suggests an important point: The meaning of hegemony is often in the eyes of the beholder. Keeping this point in mind may be useful when we move to examine different reactions to American power preponderance.

Where does this review then lead us? Can we flesh out a basic working definition for hegemony that would be comprehensive yet clear enough to work with? Based on the preceding discussion we suggest that a hegemon is a state that is (a) significantly stronger than other states in the system on both economic and military dimensions; (b) aware of its power preponderance and willing to use it to shape its international environment according to its interests and values; and (c) active in the building, developing, and sustaining of various international institutions, which reflect the negotiation and renegotiation of hegemonic bargains with other states in the system (comprising varying trade-offs between provision of public goods and private goods for the followers and the hegemon). Thus, while unipolarity refers more narrowly to the nature of systemic power distribution, hegemony by definition implies a type of *relationship* between states.

There are two merits in this definition. First, it includes all three elements discussed in the hegemony literature. Secondly, it is useful for the purpose of this book as a basis for the development of a theory of followers. Each one of these three elements is fluid and can entail much variation: (a) Material power disparities can be wider or narrower (though still wide) and may be the same or different across various issues areas, across different power indicators, and vis-à-vis different states and regions; (b) the type of interests, values, and international order that hegemonic states may wish to advance can be different (for example, United States versus China); and (c) the extent to which the hegemon is involved in the institutional building of this order, as well as the strategies it uses in the process can also vary greatly (positive versus negative sanctions, multilateral versus unilateral, and so on). These variations can help explain different reactions by different states, in different regions, across time, and across issue areas. The three elements of hegemony also point to the different types of reactions by others. The power distribution element is more closely linked with traditional balancing or bandwagoning behavior. The ideational element can be linked to strategies of soft balancing. The relational element in turn opens up space for various types of reactions to hegemony, that is, operating through existing institutions to restrain it and creating new institutional arrangements to challenge the existing hegemonic order.

REGIONAL AND GLOBAL HEGEMONY

The question of the viability of a regional level of analysis, and our ability to apply to it similar structural arguments, is a broad and important question.[31] It is important for both empirical and methodological reasons, especially in light of the difficulty of expanding our database of comparable cases to test structural arguments. It would be very useful to examine not only reactions to U.S. hegemony but also regional reactions to Chinese or Brazilian regional hegemony at different times. The question then is whether we can use the same definition of global hegemony to discuss patterns of regional distribution of power and governance structures.

Many scholars adopt Waltz's global structural analysis to explore regional stability and security dynamics. The main question in this regard is the extent to which regional dynamics are independent from global political dynamics. Such variations between the complete "overlay" of great power politics and regional politics, which characterized the Cold War, and greater regional autonomy in the post–Cold War era, are discussed by David Lake and Patrick Morgan and by Barry Buzan and Ole Waever.[32] To the extent that we can identify a distinguished pattern of regional interaction among regional states, we can discuss regional power distribution and its regional implications. By adopting a qualitative method of investigation, as this study does, we can also closely monitor for extraregional interactions and assess the extent to which their impact is significant enough to undermine the value of a regional analysis.

We should also note that on the specific issue of hegemony there was some ambiguity regarding the relevant level of analysis. At the height of the first wave of hegemony studies on hegemonic stability theory, scholars were writing in broad global terms but in fact were discussing for the most part America's regional hegemony in Europe. This in turn was embedded in a global bipolar structure. Offensive realists like Mearsheimer argued quite clearly that while all great powers aspire for global hegemony, the best they can achieve is regional.[33] The scope of hegemony can also vary between global and regional across issue areas. Consequently, it seems very reasonable to try to apply the logic of hegemony both at the regional and at the global levels, as long as, as already noted, we remain sensitive to extraregional interactions.

HEGEMONS AND THEIR STRATEGIES

Having overwhelming power does not mean that hegemons always get their way. Rather, as Christopher Layne observes, a hegemon's "vast power will help it get its way with other states far more often than they will get their way with it."[34] Hegemony can lie anywhere on the spectrum from highly benevolent (that is, the hegemon shoulders the burden of providing the public good and creating international regimes, and thus the hegemon "gains relatively less than others") to highly coercive (that is, the hegemon forces others to contribute and participate to increase the relative gains of the hegemon, even to the point of shouldering "the entire burden"). According to Lake, the hegemon can use "negative sanctions (threats), positive sanctions (rewards), the restructuring of market incentives, ideological leadership, or simply success worthy of emulation."[35]

Consequently, in the same way that the hegemon can use strategies to force states to participate in the free trade system, the hegemon can also seek to remain dominant in the realm of security, and it does so by engaging in strategies to stave off challengers and ensure that followers follow. Neorealist theory asserts that, given the anarchic structure of the international system, states are concerned first and foremost with their security and therefore will take actions to ensure that security, including balancing against other states.[36] A state in a preponderant position relative to other states will pursue strategies, including preventive war, that increase the gap between itself and other states, namely potential challengers.[37] Thus, within realist theory there are two different approaches as to how to generate followership. Offensive realism stresses the importance of taking opportunities to increase the power gap, to expand and demonstrate might and resolve as the best way to get others to comply and follow. Conversely, defensive realism stresses the importance of moderate behavior and of reassuring others as the best means to cultivate followers and minimize the number of challengers.[38]

As Ikenberry and Kupchan argue, hegemons are able to assert their control over other states through manipulating material incentives. Coercion leads the secondary states to acquiesce to the hegemon—these states are faced with inducements and sanctions that lead them to calculate that they are better off cooperating with the hegemon than not. Hegemons can also socialize the secondary states into cooperating through getting the elites to "buy into and internalize the norms that are articulated by the hegemon and therefore pursue policies consistent with the hegemon's notion of international order."[39] Importantly, they assert that the hegemon is able to consolidate its power more readily if the socialization of elites is successful: "Rule based on might is enhanced by rule based on right." Moreover, they argue that socialization is less costly for the hegemon as it "can expend fewer economic and military resources to secure acquiescence because there is a more fundamental correspondence of values and interests."[40] To get states to follow, without having to use coercive power, the leading state must make credible commitments to agreements and institutions, as well as recognize limits to its own power. It is the institutions that hegemons create and maintain that enable hegemons to get other states to follow. These institutions, according to Ikenberry, "must bind the leading state when it is initially stronger and the subordinate states later when they are stronger."[41] Institutions allow for cooperation between states—the claims of neoliberal institutionalist theory.

Yet the hegemon's ability to lead is often difficult due to domestic factors. In essence what one finds is what Cronin calls the "paradox of hegemony." In asking the question of why hegemons often undermine the very institutions they create, he finds that hegemons are faced with the tension between their hegemonic ("defined as leadership") role as the dominant state in the system and the role of the hegemon as a great power. Secondary states expect the dominant state to play the leadership role in providing public goods, but domestic level factors within the hegemonic state push for policies that favor the national interest—investing scarce resources in domestic rather than international issues. He argues that "hegemons fail in part because they are unable or unwilling to resolve this dilemma."[42]

What does all this say about the continuation of the hegemon's dominance? Does such a structure lead to instability in the system as the leading state is faced with resistance to its power or even outright challenges to its dominant status? What does this say about followers? What does this say about the negotiation and renegotiation of the relationship between a hegemon and other states? The next section addresses the followers and their motivations.

FOLLOWERS: WHY THEY FOLLOW—OR NOT

In light of the preceding discussion, America's current power is unmatched by any others in terms of military, political, economic, and cultural power. One would assume, therefore, that in having such a vast range of power, the hegemon would be able and willing to act successfully and effectively on the international stage in dealing with a variety of challenges and threats, readily gaining the support of its allies and friends. And yet one can clearly see that U.S. foreign policy in the 1990s and early 2000s did not translate into an effortless ability to get other states to follow its lead. In fact, in the case of recent foreign policy goals, whether attempting to obtain U.N. Security Council support for the invasion of Iraq in 2003 or to persuade Iran to give up its nuclear program, the United States has been unable to garner the backing of many of its allies and friends. What we are witnessing instead is a resentment of, and resistance to, U.S. power. As Robert Kagan stated, "Europe's assaults on the legitimacy of U.S. dominance may also become an effective way of constraining and controlling the superpower."[43] In examining anti-Americanism globally, Peter W. Rodman asserts that "a common theme of European rhetoric, even of the friendliest of our allies, is that it is time for Europe to make itself an equal of the United States, to be a counterweight to it, to achieve greater autonomy from it, to lessen dependence on it, and so on."[44] He further notes that Russia's foreign policy is a "categorical rejection of American leadership."[45] China and Russia call for a multipolar world, and even Japan, a staunch supporter of its relationship with the United States, has sought more autonomy.[46] Posen suggests that the EU Security and Defense Policy is a response to U.S. hegemony.[47]

A hegemon's power and influence, therefore, is very much contingent on the policies of other states. Scholars have focused on strategies available to these states in response to the hegemon's dominance. Some strategies are outright opposition to the hegemon, seeking to challenge the hegemon's leadership and dominance. Others are more subtle—they do not seek to overthrow the hegemon but are forms of resistance to the hegemon's dominance.

Neorealism asserts that because the international system is anarchic and states are concerned about their security they will balance against a state seeking dominance. Balance-of-power theory, as Waltz asserted, "begins with assumptions about states: They are unitary actors who, at a minimum, seek their own preservation and, at a maximum, drive for universal domination." To counter those states seeking domination, other states balance either internally (arms buildup) or externally (form alliances with other states).[48] In building on Waltz's balance-of-power theory, Stephen Walt argues that states balance against threats (rather than capabilities only).[49]

Consequently, in considering the United States as the hegemon in the system today, states should balance against it. In fact, some scholars argue that in terms of U.S. policy toward Iraq, allies and nonallies did balance. Major states such as China, France, Germany, and Russia opposed U.S. military intervention. They expressed their opposition by arguing that the U.N. inspectors should have been able to conduct further inspections to determine whether the Iraqi regime possessed weapons of mass destruction. They also threatened to veto the U.N. Security Council resolution proposed by the United States, United Kingdom, and Spain that would call for intervention. Turkey (a NATO member and U.S. ally) opposed the use of its airbases by U.S. forces for the invasion.[50] The minute we open up the hard military balancing concept to various notions of soft balancing, many more allies or "others" can be seen as balancing.

Several scholars, therefore, have argued that what we are witnessing in the post–Cold War era is not hard balancing, in which other states increase their military capabilities and form alliances as a means to balance against the hegemon out of fear for their continued survival and security. Instead, states are engaging in a *soft balancing* strategy: Diplomacy, economic statecraft, international institutions, and international law are the mechanisms by which states attempt to constrain the actions of the hegemon.[51] States coordinate "their diplomatic positions to oppose U.S. policy and obtain more influence together." Seen in this light, one can argue that the opposition to the U.S. push for intervention in Iraq was a form of soft balancing. The major powers did not seek to overthrow U.S. power but rather to check it.[52]

In a further refinement of balancing behavior, Layne proposes the strategy of *leash slipping*: "States engaging in leash-slipping do not fear being attacked by the hegemon. Rather, they build up their military capabilities to maximize their ability to conduct an independent foreign policy."[53] Such a strategy is not hard balancing because other states do not view the hegemon as "an existential . . . threat." He notes that "at the same time, it is a form of insurance against a hegemon that might someday exercise its power in a predatory and menacing fashion."[54]

Other strategies of opposition, as described by Walt, include undermining the hegemon's power through contesting its legitimacy as the hegemon. States attempt to persuade other states that the hegemon's actions—in this case, those of the United States—are "selfish, hypocritical, immoral, and unsuited for world leadership, and that its dominance harms them." This strategy does not seek to challenge American power but rather "to resent and resist U.S. supremacy."[55]

In the case of *blackmail*, another strategy of resistance, states can try to gain concessions from the hegemon through the threats of "undesirable consequences." Both adversaries and allies can use this strategy. Walt notes that countries might blackmail the United States by threatening to spread nuclear weapons; allies might attempt to convince the United States that their regime will collapse without additional support. He cites the example of Afghan president Hamid Karzai, who pushed America to increase support for his regime from the threat of collapse.[56]

Using a strategy of *balking*, a state can ignore or refuse the hegemon's demands. This is a particularly effective strategy "because even a country as powerful as the United States cannot force every state to do its bidding all the time. And the more some states balk, the more overextended the United States becomes—making it easier for other states to balk as well." Examples include Russia's continued cooperation with Iran in building nuclear power plants and Turkey's refusal to allow the use of its airbases for the invasion of Iraq.[57]

States can also respond to the hegemon through various forms of accommodation. One strategy is to *bandwagon* with the stronger state.[58] States may be more concerned about regional threats than about any threat posed by the hegemon. As Walt notes, "states choose to ally themselves with the United States out of a desire for U.S. protection from a regional threat." Importantly, he claims that these states accommodate the hegemon with the expectation that American power will benefit them as well. Whereas bandwagoning assumes utilitarian support for the hegemon, regardless of one's own different immediate stakes in the situation at hand, accommodation may also stem from a real sense of shared interests. Thus, Blair's Britain actively supported the war in Iraq, also due to a genuine sense of shared interests and threats.[59]

A *bonding* strategy refers to the use of the close relationship between the hegemon and secondary states as a way to influence the hegemon. In looking at the United States, Walt notes the personal relationships that foreign leaders have forged with U.S. officials. In doing so, these foreign leaders are able "to gain greater influence over how the United States uses its power." The quintessential example is the "special relationship" between the United States and the United Kingdom.[60]

Because, in many cases, states have both shared and conflicting interests with the hegemon, they can constrain the hegemon's power through membership in institutions. According to the logic of liberal institutionalism, international institutions can provide the necessary conditions for states to reach cooperative agreements and arrangements.[61] The hegemon plays a role in creating these institutions and, as a way to maintain its power, is willing to bind itself to these institutions. The secondary states then get a voice and a means to influence the institution and perhaps the behavior of the hegemon as well.[62] Walt cautions, however, that *binding* the hegemon, namely the United States in the contemporary period, is more likely to be successful in the economic sphere than in the security sphere. For example, the United States did not pursue U.N. Security Council authorization for action in Kosovo in 1999. Instead, it acted through NATO. Moreover, the United States opposed the creation of the International Criminal Court. In the case of economics, the United States is dependent on the international trading order and thus cannot stop the World Trade Organization (WTO) from ruling against it.[63]

Finally, a state can also pursue a strategy of *neutrality*, choosing not to ally with other states and pursue an independent foreign policy. According to Efraim Karsh, those member states of the United Nations that pursued a neutral policy viewed such a position as a positive one.[64] During the Cold War, for example, smaller European countries such as Austria, Finland, Ireland, and Sweden joined the United Nations and, aside from the case of the Korean War, "were not called upon to participate in a collective military enforcement action." The U.N. Security Council resolution authorizing intervention in the Korean conflict was not a mandatory resolution but a recommendatory one. As a result, Sweden was able "to abstain from physical engagement in the war."[65] Neutrality, however, is an unlikely strategy for states already previously allied with the hegemon.

The preceding discussion considers various strategies that states can use as they attempt to check the power of the hegemon (see Table 1.1 for a continuum

Table 1.1. Continuum of responses to hegemony.

Opposition	↔		*Resistance*	↔	*Neutral*		↔	*Accommodation*
Hard balancing	Soft balancing	Balking	Blackmail	Leash slipping	Neutrality	Binding	Bonding	Bandwagoning

of responses). But what factors account for the decisions to follow or resist the hegemon?

THE MOTIVATIONS OF THE FOLLOWERS FOR PURSUING THEIR STRATEGIES

How is it that the leader is unable to get the followers to follow? In essence, what does this tell us about the limitations of hegemony? A compelling (and yet, in much of the literature, neglected) question revolves around the motivations of the followers. Why do states follow—or not? In this section, we explore the factors that may account for the strategies, noted in the previous section, that followers pursue in their efforts to respond to the hegemon's dominance. This discussion will serve as the analytical framework for application in the chapters that follow.

As Andrew Cooper and his coauthors note, the literature on hegemony has primarily focused on the leader. The "smaller states or the hegemon's followers do not occupy a position of prominence in these analyses."[66] In examining the literature on the motivations of followers, they found that followers follow for a variety of reasons. Followership occurs because of reciprocity: "Leadership and followership involve a transactional social exchange in which they give and receive benefits." Secondly, rather than a social exchange, a "transforming leadership" occurs in which the leader "transform[s] the interests, priorities, and expectations of would-be followers, and convince them to join in the pursuit of 'higher' moral goals articulated by the leader." Alternatively, followers might follow because of the perceived legitimacy of the leader and its leadership ability.[67]

In their analysis of the 1991 Gulf War, Cooper and his coauthors show that followers were not presented with a clear vision of President George H. W. Bush's New World Order to the extent that friends and allies would join the United States in undertaking a military response to Iraq's invasion of Kuwait. Rather, they assert, "since the alternatives to defection were so costly for all friends and allies of the United States, we should be wary of interpreting this cohesion as followership."[68] In fact, they argue that Italy and France bandwagoned with the United States as they expressed their support for the war after it had started, not before. Countries such as Japan, Germany, Canada, Pakistan, and Morocco were reluctant to follow the U.S. lead.[69] Andrew Bennet, Joseph Lepgold, and Danny Unger found that a mix of domestic and international factors accounted for the motivations of states to support the United States during this period. Military, economic, and diplomatic contributions depended on alliance dependence, as well as domestic autonomy and bureaucratic politics.[70]

More recent works have looked at contemporary cases of state responses to U.S. hegemony. In an examination of three Southeast Asian countries (Indonesia, Malaysia, and the Philippines), David Capie argues that a combination of domestic politics and international level factors explained the policy decisions of each of these states. While they were willing to support the United States, "subsequent bilateral relations have been predominantly influenced by domestic, not external, events." With the U.S. actions in Iraq and Afghanistan, bilateral ties between the United States and Malaysia and the United States and Indonesia became strained. U.S. policies contributed to "unrest within local Islamic communities." For these states, security of their regimes is paramount.[71] Moreover, to explain why Indonesia and Malaysia cooperated with the United States in intelligence and law enforcement, as well as by allowing the United States to use their airspace (at the same time criticizing U.S. policies and behavior), one needs to look at the systemic level. Concerned with their regional security and the regional balance of power, cooperation with the United States enables these countries to ensure maintenance of the regional balance of power.[72]

One can also look more closely at the motivations of the secondary states in the lead-up to the 2003 invasion of Iraq. In an analysis by Jurgen Schuster and Herbert Maier, many small European countries supported the United States, even when faced with public opinion that opposed the invasion. The concerns of these states are those of regional security—dominance by France and Germany, rather than fear of U.S. dominance. Alternatively, for the Western European countries, domestic politics, particularly party affiliation of the government, played a major role in determining whether the government supported or opposed the invasion. A realist explanation goes a long way to explain the bandwagoning behavior of the smaller states that joined the "coalition of the willing," as well as the balancing behavior of other states such as France, Russia, Germany, and China. Yet domestic politics better explains the motivations of other Western European countries because they are not confronted by serious external threats.[73] Galia Press-Barnathan suggests that allies' reactions will diverge given the degree of compatibility between their own and the hegemon's threat perceptions. These, in turn, depend on both systemic and domestic factors.[74]

QUESTIONS TO CONSIDER, EXPLANATORY FRAMEWORKS, AND METHODOLOGY

As the examples noted in the previous section indicate, it is not clear that when states follow the hegemon they are supporting the leadership role of the hegemon. States may follow the hegemon for other reasons and, in some cases, may not follow the hegemon at all. What is evident is that factors at the international and domestic levels can account for the motivations and the strategies of secondary states in their response to the hegemon. To reach significant conceptual conclusions based on comparative analysis about the relationship between hegemons and followers, this book seeks to address and answer a similar set of questions:

1. How can we characterize a state's response to the hegemon?
    a. How do states follow or support the hegemon?
    b. What form does opposition to the hegemon take? What strategies do states use to counter the hegemon?
2. What explains the reaction to the hegemon? In other words, why do states react to the hegemon?
    a. Is there a demand for leadership and to solve regional security dilemmas? Are states bandwagoning for profit and free-riding, seeking alliance with the hegemon to balance against regional or domestic primary threats, co-opted or restrained by grand bargains, or acting for nonpower reasons such as liberal transnationalism, interdependence, and commercial ties or shared identities and pluralistic security communities?
    b. When do states oppose the hegemonic power? Does opposition to the hegemon result from temporary windows of opportunity as the power of the hegemon declines, as expectations of future cooperation begin to wane, to renegotiate historic grand bargains, resentment and fear, or for greater autonomy and voice in the international system?

While most of the recent literature on followers is concerned with describing follower behavior and creating new behavioral typologies (our first question), a central goal of this book is to explore the sources of such behavior (our second question). The subsequent case chapters will address several explanatory variables for the choice of strategy:

1. What is the material power distribution, both global and regional, and can we deduce from it the degree of compatibility or conflict in the interests of the hegemon and the secondary and tertiary states?

2. To what extent is the policy toward the hegemon influenced by domestic factors?

3. To what extent do disagreements with the hegemon reflect normative disagreements?

In considering these questions, we propose three explanatory frameworks for consideration in the case chapters to account for the factors that determine a follower's motivations and strategies in responding to the hegemon. Realism would assert that external factors determine a state's response. In other words, when states perceive a threat, they will respond through balancing behavior against the greater threat. A hegemon, perceived as a threat to the distribution of power, will be challenged by other states, seeking to restore a balance of power in the system. Of course, states can also bandwagon with the hegemon. Regardless, it is external, international level factors that determine the state's motivation for responding,[75] though, as Walt notes, states balance against proximate threats. Therefore, a secondary or tertiary state's primary threat might come from a neighboring power rather than an extraregional hegemon. The consequences would be alliance with the hegemon against the regional power. Finally, in a tertiary state, the primary threat might come from internal challenges to the regime.[76] Thus, such a state might balance with a regional or global hegemon against these internal challengers.

> Explanatory Framework 1:
>
> *According to neorealist theory, states faced with security threats will balance against or bandwagon with the hegemon. Given the multiplicity of threats, states are more likely to balance the hegemon if and when they perceive it to be their primary threat. They will choose to bandwagon when they are faced with other primary threats.*

A state may attempt to respond to the hegemon by using its membership in international institutions. As liberal institutionalist theory asserts, secondary states can use the institutions to restrain the hegemon. Without the consent of other major states, the hegemon will find its freedom of action constrained.

Thus, a state's motivation can be found in its perceived ability to limit the hegemon's ability to take particular actions.

Explanatory Framework 2:

According to liberal institutionalist theory, states will attempt to bind the hegemon and thereby alter the hegemon's behavior through actions in an international institution.

The extent to which the hegemon signals its willingness to work via international institutions will influence other states' willingness to engage the hegemon via these institutions. The availability of institutional frameworks already engaging the hegemon will encourage using them to engage it.

Domestic-level factors may determine the strategy choice of states in response to the hegemon. For example, one could argue that economic interests explain Russia's continuing relationship with Iran in terms of assistance in building nuclear power plants, rather than as a response to U.S. hegemony.[77] Rather than concerns about U.S. relative power, states' motivations may be found at the domestic level. Domestic-level factors may also help to shape states' threat perceptions.

Explanatory Framework 3:

States will choose a strategy based on domestic-level factors, such as regime type, maintain the elites' power, political parties, public opinion, and interest groups.

Which explanatory framework best explains the strategies and motivations of followers? The subsequent chapters provide evidence for determining the factors that explain states' responses to the hegemon. We have selected cases based on the following criteria:

a. Variance in terms of types of hegemons—global (states that can project power and dominance around the globe) and regional (states that extend their power across the region they inhabit).

b. Variance on the power disparities with the hegemon—we examine both the behavior of secondary states (for example, France and Germany, NATO, Pakistan) and of tertiary states (for example, Cuba, Chile, Ireland, Jordan, Romania). The former are states with substantial regional power, be it economic, military, political, or any combination of these factors. The latter states typically are junior partners in all relations with a neighboring hegemon.

Table 1.2. Typology of hegemons and followers.

	Follower	
Hegemon	*Secondary*	*Tertiary*
Global	e.g., United States vs. Latin America	e.g., United States vs. Jordan; USSR vs. Cuba
Regional	e.g., India vs. Pakistan	e.g., Russia vs. Central Asian Republics

The combination of these first two factors provides an organizing typology in Table 1.2.

Most previous studies of hegemony deal with cases of a secondary state resisting a global hegemon and are mainly derived from European examples. This book expands the scope into the other three possible dyadic relationships:

c. Variance on geography. A key contribution of the volume is expanding the scope of inquiry beyond Europe. Chapters look at hegemonic relations in Africa, Europe, Latin America, the Middle East, South Asia, and Asia.

d. Variance in the nature of domestic politics and institutions and of regime type. Our cases explore democratic systems, Communist states, and authoritarian dictatorships.

e. Similar historic periods. The Cold War and Post–Cold War eras are considered, therefore controlling for the broad variable of system structure.

THE CASE CHAPTERS

The remainder of the book is divided into two parts, followed by a concluding chapter. Part I (Chapters 2 through 8) examines global hegemons (states with global reach) in the Cold War and post–Cold War periods. During the Cold War, states responded to the United States and the USSR in different ways. Both the United States and the USSR encountered intra-alliance politics, though these were much more serious in the latter case. In Chapter 2, Kristen Williams examines Romania's balking strategy in response to the Soviet hegemon. Reforms by the Czech leaders in early 1968 were perceived by the USSR as a threat to its dominance within the Communist bloc. As a result, Warsaw Pact troops invaded Czechoslovakia. Romania, a Warsaw Pact member, refused to send troops. Domestic politics, namely Ceausescu's drive for power and control in Romania, accounts for Romania's response.

In Chapter 3 Jennifer Kibbe looks at Cuba's decision to dispatch troops to Angola in 1975–1976 to help the MPLA (People's Movement for the Liberation of Angola) defend against the South African invasion. Fidel Castro's move, combined with Cuba's dependent relationship on the USSR and the nature of the Cold War, led Western policy makers to assume that he was merely doing Moscow's bidding. Soviet and, more recently, Cuban archives reveal that Castro's decision to intervene was his own and came after Brezhnev had turned down his previous request for Soviet help in doing so. Kibbe argues that Cuba's actions were driven by its deeply ingrained internationalist ideology and its domestic historical and cultural roots.

In contrast to Romania's and Cuba's dependence on their hegemonic supporter, in Chapter 4 Neal Jesse argues that Ireland did not bandwagon with the United States following the collapse of British hegemony. Instead, Ireland remained neutral in the face of U.S. hegemony, though it balanced against British hegemony. Domestic factors, such as public opinion and governmental decision-making institutions, provide an explanation for the continuing stance of neutrality.

Both Steven Lobell and Maria Sampanis argue that a hegemon can use trade and commercial relations to create followers. Lobell (Chapter 5) examines the domestic distributional consequence of America's Free Trade Agreement, Qualified Industrial Zones, and IMF and World Bank programs in Jordan. He argues that in tertiary states some domestic actors and interest groups will favor bandwagoning with the hegemon (moderate internationalists), while others will support balking against it (hard-line nationalists). The United States capitalized on this division by using trade and other commercial interests to strengthen the regime and increase the size of its moderate internationalist base and counter the domestic hard-line opposition.

In its trade relations, Sampanis (Chapter 6) assesses the lure for following. The United States has completed or is in the process of negotiating bilateral investment treaties, trade and investment framework agreements, and free trade agreements with trade partners that can be classified as developing, emerging, or in transition. She finds that, as the hegemon wanes, followers pursued soft balancing strategies as a form of opposition in multilateral agreements. In bilateral agreements, the followers pursued accommodation to seek extra gains.

Collective security and alliances can create dynamics between the hegemon and its allies, as examined in Chapter 7. Until the breakdown of the USSR, all NATO allies had a relatively clear and shared threat to cooperate against.

After the end of the Cold War, NATO allies found themselves within an alliance in which the United States, their senior partner in a common struggle against Communism, became a global hegemon and where threat perceptions became much more divergent. The allies face an alliance security dilemma: the threat of *entrapment* in the alliance and of *abandonment* by the United States. Galia Press-Barnathan argues that Western Europe has adopted both leash-slipping and binding strategies.

Waging war on a global scale involves the cooperation and participation of other states to assist the hegemonic power. The U.S. invasion and occupation of Afghanistan after 9/11 was no exception. Pakistan was transformed from a fringe state with an Islamist element to a reluctant ally in the War on Terror. In Chapter 8, John Dreyer demonstrates that, while Pakistan by and large cooperates with American wishes, this cooperation is opposed by elements within Pakistan. It walks a thin line between supporting U.S. policy and keeping its civil and political society in balance. The outcome is that Pakistan's reaction to American hegemony can best be categorized as alternating between compliance (bandwagoning) and resistance (balking and leash slipping).

The diminishing of U.S. extraregional hegemony has opened space for regional hegemons to assert themselves. In Part II, Chapters 9 through 13 explore regional hegemons and the motivations of followers. Regional hegemons are able to exert influence within a more limited geographic area, but their influence can be quite significant. Examples in this volume discuss the implications for regional hegemons and, more specifically, the followers of these hegemons, on four separate continents.

Brazil, an economic and political powerhouse occupying one-half of South America, has often dominated regional relations in Latin America. Nancy Lapp (Chapter 9) examines the responses of its neighbors to Brazil's hegemonic aspirations, emphasizing the importance of domestic factors over and above that of the power asymmetry in the region. She shows that the strategy of a smaller power was primarily determined by domestic factors.

Shale Horowitz and Michael Tyburski (Chapter 10) look at relations between Russia and the other former Soviet Republics. There are two major regime types in the post-Communist space: Western-oriented democracies and neo-Communist authoritarian regimes. Balance-of-power logic explains the basic reactions to Russian hegemony, although the form of the response is conditioned by the specific regime type. Liberal nationalist states defy Russia while neo-Communist states choose bandwagoning.

The South Asian Association for Regional Cooperation (SAARC) includes eight states, but South Asian politics, as addressed by Srini Sitaraman (Chapter 11), is and has been dominated by one singular dynamic—India's enduring rivalry with Pakistan and attempt to emerge as a hegemonic power within the subcontinent. Sitaraman looks at how Pakistan has used its relationship with the United States and China to undermine India (through hard balancing)—a tactic subsequently employed by Nepal, which has attempted to lean closer to China to stoke Indian insecurities.

Much of the post–Cold War research focuses on the challenge facing the United States from China. Alexander Tan (Chapter 12) looks at a different relationship, that of China and its neighbors in the Asia-Pacific region—Taiwan, Japan, and Australia. He argues that the reactions of China's neighbors are a complex and multivariate combination of realist and domestic factors. For example, Australia's view that it is not directly threatened by China, its close ties with the West, and the Australian public's negative view of China all combine in a foreign policy of leash slipping China's regional hegemony.

Stephen Burgess (Chapter 13) provides an analysis of South Africa. Given that its GDP is significantly larger than the other states in the Southern African region and that South African companies are investing in African states, South Africa is poised to play an important role as a regional leader. With the end of apartheid and emergence of black majority rule, it has not been eager to play this role, rather focusing on building consensus with the Southern African Development Community. He argues that states near South Africa bandwagon due to close relations with the African National Congress (ANC) and perceived help to develop their economies. Its enormous power imbalance effectively precluded other options.

While distinct from each other, all chapters address the same questions and explanatory frameworks presented before, thus providing a broad systematic comparison. By way of a conclusion, Christopher Layne (Chapter 14) incorporates the individual chapters in his analysis of U.S. hegemony today. In reviewing the post–Cold War debate about American hegemony, he argues that the era of U.S. dominance has now ended. He examines the implications for the future of the international system in light of the decline of U.S. hegemony, namely, the opening of space for secondary states, such as China, India, Brazil, and Russia, to challenge the hegemon and further limit the ability of the hegemon to maneuver.

CONCLUSION

In essence, this book addresses the issue of the limitations of hegemony. The literature has focused mostly on the hegemons and the strategies to get other states to follow and maintain the hegemon's dominant position in the system. Much of the literature focuses on the debate about the decline of hegemons in general and America specifically in the post–Cold War period. Our contribution to the literature is not just to examine the United States as a global hegemon in the Cold War and post–Cold War periods but also to examine the USSR as a global hegemon during the Cold War. In addition to looking at these two global hegemons, the book examines regional hegemons in the post–Cold War period and the challenges they face from followers.

Importantly, the relationship between hegemons and the secondary states in the system is a complex one. We argue that the complexity of the relationship is bound with understanding the strategies available to followers as well as their motivations for following or not. We put forward several questions and propose three explanatory frameworks to be tested to explain followers' motivations and strategies. The chapters that follow are case studies used to explore the followers' motivations. It may be the case that external factors motivate followers to pursue a particular strategy at some times, while domestic factors matter more in other times. Of course, both internal and external factors may matter in yet other cases. The relationship between hegemons and followers is dynamic and may ebb and flow over time in a continuing process of negotiation and renegotiation. An interesting aspect to be explored in each case is how and why the hegemon–follower relationship has changed or evolved.

We end with the observations of Robert Jervis:

> Great power also instills new fears in the dominant state. A hegemon tends to acquire an enormous stake in world order. As power expands, so does a state's definition of its own interests. Most countries are concerned mainly with what happens in their immediate neighborhoods; but for a hegemon, the world is its neighborhood, and it is not only hubris that leads lone superpowers to be concerned with anything that happens anywhere. However secure states are, they can never feel secure enough.[78]

Thus, it is the followers that matter for the hegemon, whether global or regional, to remain in its position of dominance.

NOTES

1. Robert J. Art, *A Grand Strategy for America* (Ithaca, NY: Cornell University Press, 2003); Stephen G. Brooks and William C. Wohlforth, *World out of Balance: International Relations and the Challenge of American Primacy* (Princeton, NJ: Princeton University Press, 2008); Melvyn P. Leffler and Jeffrey W. Legro, eds., *To Lead the World: American Strategy after the Bush Doctrine* (Oxford, UK: Oxford University Press, 2008); Michael E. Brown, Owen R. Cote Jr., Sean M. Lynn-Jones, and Steven E. Miller, eds., *Primacy and Its Discontents: American Power and International Stability* (Cambridge, MA: MIT Press, 2009); Joseph S. Nye Jr., "The Future of American Power: Dominance and Decline in Perspective," *Foreign Affairs* 89, 6 (November/December 2010): 2–12.

2. Josef Joffe, *Überpower: The Imperial Temptation of America* (New York: W. W. Norton, 2006).

3. Christopher Layne, "The Unipolar Illusion Revisited: The Coming End of the United States' Unipolar Moment," *International Security* 31, 2 (2006): 7–41.

4. Charles Krauthammer, "The Unipolar Moment," *Foreign Affairs* 70, 1 (1990/91): 23–33; Michael Mastanduno, "Preserving the Unipolar Moment: Realist Theories and U.S. Grand Strategy after the Cold War," *International Security* 21, 4 (1997): 49–88.

5. Barry R. Posen and Andrew L. Ross, "Competing Visions for U.S. Grand Strategy," *International Security* 21, 3 (1996/1997): 5–53.

6. Duncan Snidal, "The Limits of Hegemonic Stability Theory," *International Organization* 39, 4 (1985): 579–614; David A. Lake, "Leadership, Hegemony, and the International Economy: Naked Emperor or Tattered Monarch with Potential?" *International Studies Quarterly* 37, 4 (1993): 459–489; Daniel Byman and Matthew Waxman, *The Dynamics of Coercion: American Foreign Policy and the Limits of Military Might* (New York: Cambridge University Press, 2002); Stephen M. Walt, "Keeping the World 'Off Balance': Self-Restraint and U.S. Foreign Policy," in *America Unrivaled: The Future of the Balance of Power*, ed. G. John Ikenberry (Ithaca, NY: Cornell University Press, 2002): 121–154; Christopher Layne and Bradley A. Thayer, *American: Empire Debate* (New York: Routledge, 2007).

7. A number of scholars who have addressed the topic of hegemony include Robert Gilpin, *War and Change in World Politics* (Cambridge, UK: Cambridge University Press, 1981); G. John Ikenberry, *After Victory: Institutions, Strategic Restraint and the Rebuilding of Order after Major Wars* (Princeton, NJ: Princeton University Press, 2001); G. John Ikenberry and Charles A. Kupchan, "Socialization and Hegemonic Power," *International Organization* 44, 3 (Summer 1990): 283–315; Robert O. Keohane, *After Hegemony* (Princeton, NJ: Princeton University Press, 1984); Lake, "Leadership, Hegemony, and the International Economy"; Snidal, "The Limits of Hegemonic Stability Theory"; Bruce Russett, "The Mysterious Case of the Vanishing Hegemony; or, Is

Mark Twain Really Dead?" *International Organization* 39, 2 (Spring 1985): 207–231; Susan Strange, "The Persistent Myth of Lost Hegemony," *International Organization* 41, 4 (Autumn 1987): 551–574.

8. Andrew Fenton Cooper, Richard A. Higgott, and Kim Richard Nossal, "Bound to Follow? Leadership and Followership in the Gulf Conflict," *Political Science Quarterly* 106, 3 (1991): 391–410; Layne, "The Unipolar Illusion Revisited." On the importance of followers in the IPE field, see also Barry Eichengreen, *Elusive Stability: Essays in the History of International Finance, 1919–1939* (Cambridge, UK: Cambridge University Press, 1993).

9. Cooper et al., "Bound to Follow?"; Christopher Layne, "The Waning of U.S. Hegemony—Myth or Reality? A Review Essay," *International Security* 34, 1 (Summer 2009): 147–172; Stephen M. Walt, *Taming American Power: The Global Response to U.S. Primacy* (New York: W. W. Norton, 2005); Fareed Zakaria, *The Post-American World* (New York: W. W. Norton, 2008).

10. A. F. K. Organski, *World Politics* (New York: Alfred A. Knopf, 1968).

11. T. V. Paul, James J. Wirtz, and Michel Fortmann, *Balance of Power: Theory and Practice in the 21st Century* (Stanford, CA: Stanford University Press, 2004); Robert A. Pape, *Dying to Win: The Strategic Logic of Suicide Terrorism* (New York: Random House, 2005); Barry R. Posen, "European Union Security and Defense Policy: Response to Unipolarity?" *Security Studies* 15, 2 (April–June 2006): 149–186.

12. Christopher Layne, *The Peace of Illusions* (Ithaca, NY: Cornell University Press, 2006); Thomas J. Christensen, "Fostering Stability or Creating a Monster? The Rise of China and U.S. Policy toward East Asia," *International Security* 31, 1 (Summer 2006): 81–126; Walt, *Taming American Power*; Jeremy Pressman, *Warring Friends: Alliance Restraint in International Politics* (Ithaca, NY: Cornell University Press, 2008). See also the articles on unipolarity in *World Politics* 61, 1 (January 2009), especially Wohlforth, "Unipolarity, Status Competitions and Great Power War," and Stephen Walt, "Alliances in a Unipolar World."

13. Stephen G. Brooks and William C. Wolforth, "American Primacy in Perspective," *Foreign Affairs* 81, 4 (July/August 2002): 23. For a dissenting view, see John Mearsheimer, *Tragedy of Great Power Politics* (New York: W. W. Norton, 2001), who argues that the system is not unipolar but rather an unbalanced multipolar system.

14. Elke Krahmann, "American Hegemony or Global Governance? Competing Visions of International Security," *International Studies Review* 7 (2003): 539.

15. Krahmann, "American Hegemony or Global Governance?" 538. See also the articles in the 2009 special issue of *World Politics*.

16. Keohane, *After Hegemony*, chapter 3.

17. Stephen Krasner, "State Power and the Structure of International Trade," *World Politics* 28, 3 (April 1976): 317–347.

18. Gilpin, *War and Change in World Politics*.

19. Keohane, *After Hegemony*.

20. David Lake, *Power, Protection and Free Trade: International Sources of US Commercial Strategy, 1887-1939* (Ithaca, NY: Cornell University Press, 1988): chapter 1.

21. Another round of debate regarding the definition and measurement of hegemony took place in the 1980s regarding the question of U.S. decline. See Russett, "The Mysterious Case of Vanishing Hegemony"; Strange, "The Persistent Myth of Lost Hegemony."

22. See William C. Wohlforth, "U.S. Strategy in a Unipolar World," in *America Unrivaled: The Future of the Balance of Power*, ed. G. John Ikenberry (Ithaca, NY: Cornell University Press, 2002): 98–120; William C. Wohlforth, "The Stability of a Unipolar World," *International Security* 24, 1 (Summer 1999): 5–41; Kenneth N. Waltz, *Theory of International Relations* (New York: Random House, 1979).

23. See Barry Posen, "Command of the Commons: The Military Foundations of U.S. Hegemony," *International Security* 28, 1 (Summer 2003): 5–46; Brooks and Wohlforth, *World Out of Balance*, 22: 27–34.

24. Keohane, *After Hegemony*: 35.

25. Charles Kindleberger, *The World in Depression: 1929-1939* (Berkeley: University of California Press, 1973). This type of definition is problematic methodologically because it is somewhat tautological.

26. Lake notes that hegemonic stability theory literature combines two distinct strands: leadership theory, following Kindleberger, and hegemony theory. See Lake, "Leadership, Hegemony, and the International Economy."

27. Layne, "The Unipolar Illusion Revisited": 11.

28. Gilpin, *War and Change in World Politics*: 144.

29. Ikenberry, *After Victory*.

30. Daniel H. Nexon and Thomas Wright, "What's at Stake in the American Empire Debate," *American Political Science Review* 101, 2 (May 2007): 256–257.

31. On subsystems theory, see Leonard Binder, "The Middle East as a Subordinate International System," *World Politics* 10, 3 (April 1958): 408–429; Malcolm Kerr, *The Arab Cold War: Gamal 'Abd al-Nasir and His Rivals, 1958-1970* (New York: Oxford University Press, 1971); Paul Noble, "The Arab System: Pressure, Constraints, and Opportunities," in *The Foreign Policies of Arab States*, eds. Bahgat Korany and Ali E. Hillal Dessouki (Boulder, CO: Westview Press, 1991): 50–60.

32. David A. Lake and Patrick M. Morgan, eds., *Regional Orders: Building Security in a New World* (University Park: The Pennsylvania State University Press, 1997); Barry Buzan and Ole Waever, *Regions and Powers: The Structure of International Security* (Cambridge, UK: Cambridge University Press, 2003). On regional hegemony, see Miriam Prys, "Hegemony, Domination, Detachment: Differences in Regional Powerhood," *International Studies Review* 12, 4 (December 2010): 479–504.

33. Mearsheimer, *The Tragedy of Great Power Politics*.

34. Layne, "The Unipolar Illusion Revisited": 12.

35. Lake, "Leadership, Hegemony, and the International Economy": 467, 469.

36. Waltz, *Theory of International Politics*.

37. Krahmann, "American Hegemony or Global Governance?" 535; Gilpin, *War and Change in World Politics*.

38. On offensive and defensive realism, see Jeffrey W. Taliaferro, "Security Seeking under Anarchy: Defensive Realism Revisited," *International Security* 25, 3 (Winter 2000/01): 128–161.

39. Ikenberry and Kupchan, "Socialization and Hegemonic Power": 283.

40. Ibid.: 286.

41. Ikenberry, *After Victory*: 57.

42. Bruce Cronin, "The Paradox of Hegemony: America's Ambiguous Relationship with the United Nations," *European Journal of International Relations* 7, 1 (2002): 104–105.

43. Robert Kagan, "America's Crisis of Legitimacy," *Foreign Affairs* 83, 2 (March/April 2004): 72.

44. Peter W. Rodman, "The World's Resentment: Anti-Americanism as a Global Phenomenon," *The National Interest* 601 (Summer 2000): 36.

45. Ibid.: 34.

46. Ibid.: 34–36, 38. See also Aaron Friedberg, "The Future of U.S.–China Relations: Is Conflict Inevitable?" *International Security* 30, 2 (Fall 2005): 7–45; Thomas J. Christensen, "Fostering Stability or Creating a Monster? The Rise of China and U.S. Policy toward East Asia," *International Security* 31, 1 (Summer 2006): 81–126.

47. Barry R. Posen, "European Union Security and Defense Policy: Response to Unipolarity," *Security Studies* 15, 2 (2006): 149–186.

48. Waltz, *Theory of International Politics*: 118.

49. Stephen M. Walt, *The Origins of Alliances* (Ithaca, NY: Cornell University Press, 1987): 21.

50. Krahmann, "American Hegemony or Global Governance?": 540.

51. Layne, "The Unipolar Illusion Revisited": 8; Robert A. Pape, "Soft Balancing against the United States," *International Security* 30, 1 (Summer 2005): 7–45; T. V. Paul, "Introduction: The Enduring Axioms of Balance of Power Theory and Their Contemporary Relevance," in *Balance of Power: Theory and Practice in the 21st Century*, eds. T. V. Paul, James J. Wirtz, and Michael Fortman (Stanford, CA: Stanford University Press, 2004); T. V. Paul, "Soft Balancing in the Age of U.S. Primacy," *International Security* 30, 1 (Summer 2005): 46–71. For a critique of soft balancing see Stephen G. Brooks and William C. Wohlforth, "Hard Times for Soft Balancing," *International Security* 30, 1 (Summer 2005): 72–108; Keir A. Lieber and Gerard Alexander,

"Waiting for Balancing: Why the World Is Not Pushing Back," *International Security* 30, 1 (Summer 2005): 109–139; and Pape, "Soft Balancing against the United States."

52. Stephen M. Walt, "Taming American Power," *Foreign Affairs* 84, 5 (September/October 2005): 113.

53. Layne, "The Unipolar Illusion Revisited": 9.

54. Ibid.: 30.

55. Walt, "Taming American Power": 116.

56. Ibid.: 112–115.

57. Ibid.: 115–116.

58. Waltz, *Theory of International Politics*, 126. See also Randall L. Schweller, "Bandwagoning for Profit," *International Security* 19, 1 (Summer 1994): 72–107.

59. Walt, "Taming American Power": 110, 111.

60. Walt, *Taming American Power*: 191–192. See also, Ikenberry, *After Victory*: 62–63.

61. Ikenberry, *After Victory*; Robert O. Keohane and Lisa L. Martin, "The Promise of Institutionalist Theory," *International Security* 20 (1995): 39–51; J. G. March and J. P. Olsen, "The Institutional Dynamics of International Political Orders," *International Organization* 52 (1998): 943–969.

62. Ikenberry, *After Victory*: 51–57, 63; Walt, "Taming American Power": 112–115.

63. Walt, "Taming American Power": 114-115.

64. Efraim Karsh, "International Co-operation and Neutrality," *Journal of Peace Research* 25, 1 (1988): 60.

65. Ibid.: 61.

66. Cooper et al., "Bound to Follow?": 393.

67. Ibid.: 397–998.

68. Ibid.: 408.

69. Ibid.: 405.

70. Andrew Bennett, Joseph Lepgold, and Danny Unger, "Burden-Sharing in the Persian Gulf War," *International Organization* 48, 1 (Winter 1994): 39–75.

71. David Capie, "Between a Hegemon and a Hard Place: The 'War on Terror' and Southeast Asian–US relations," *The Pacific Review* 17, 2 (June 2004): 237.

72. Ibid.: 237- 238.

73. Jurgen Schuster and Herbert Maier, "The Rift: Explaining Europe's Divergent Iraq Policies in the Run-Up of the American-Led War on Iraq," *Foreign Policy Analysis* 2 (2006): 223–244.

74. Galia Press-Barnathan, "Managing the Hegemon: NATO under Unipolarity," *Security Studies* 15, 2 (July 2006): 271–309.

75. Capie, "Between a Hegemon and a Hard Place," 225; Waltz, *Theory of International Politics*.

76. Walt, *Origins of Alliances*; Mohammed Ayoob, "Subaltern Realism: International Relations Theory Meets the Third World," in *International Relations Theory and the Third World*, ed. Stephanie G. Neumann (New York: St. Martin's Press, 1998): 31–49.

77. Brooks and Wohlforth, "Hard Times for Soft Balancing": 88–91.

78. Jervis, "The Compulsive Empire": 84.

GLOBAL HEGEMONS

Part I

2 ROMANIA'S RESISTANCE TO THE USSR

Kristen P. Williams

FOLLOWING THE REMOVAL of Antonin Novotny as leader of Czechoslovakia in January 1968, Alexander Dubcek and other Czechoslovak leaders moved toward political, economic, and social reforms. At the same time, factions within the counterreform movement sought the help of the USSR in an attempt to oust the reformers. The Soviet Union perceived these reforms as a threat to its dominance in the Communist bloc. As Jiri Valenta observes, Dubcek and his regime "did not challenge the basic elements of Soviet national security interests; it did not, for example, recommend revising Czechoslovakia's foreign policy orientation. Czechoslovakia would retain its membership in the Warsaw Pact and COMECON. . . . [but] from the Soviet point of view, the developments in Czechoslovakia were problematic and potentially dangerous."[1] As a result, Warsaw Pact troops from five countries (Bulgaria, East Germany, Hungary, Poland, and the USSR) invaded Czechoslovakia in August 1968.

Not all members of the Warsaw Pact supported the invasion. By refusing to send troops, Romania resisted the hegemon. While Romania neither renounced Communism nor left the Warsaw Pact (as Albania did in 1962), it did seek a more independent foreign policy. This chapter examines Romania's motivations for resisting and will show that domestic politics (framework 3) best explains the balking strategy toward the USSR.

The chapter begins with a discussion of Soviet hegemony in Eastern Europe, particularly the mechanisms for maintaining hegemony. The next section briefly examines the events of the Prague Spring and then discusses Soviet motivations for the invasion. The chapter explores Romania's motivations not to send troops. The chapter concludes with an assessment of the limits of Soviet hegemony, as demonstrated by Romanian opposition to the USSR.

THE SOVIET UNION: HEGEMON IN EASTERN EUROPE

With a leading position in the international system at the end of World War II, the Soviet Union became a global hegemon competing with the United States for dominance. Soviet hegemony primarily focused on Eastern Europe. Given the past experience of Eastern European territory used "as a springboard for an invasion" of the country, "strategic control" of the region was paramount. Thus, in asserting its hegemony over the region, the Soviets would be able to isolate those countries from any Western influence. In addition, according to Alvin Z. Rubinstein, the Soviets sought "to develop a belt of submissive Communist regimes whose leaders governed at Moscow's discretion and depended for their survival on Soviet troops."[2] The elites in Eastern Europe were thus beholden to the USSR for the maintenance of power within their states.[3]

With Stalin's death in 1953, Soviet leaders faced challenges related to the need to preserve Soviet hegemony while also attempting to "decentralize their empire." A related goal was to gain the West's acceptance of Soviet hegemony in Eastern Europe. As a great power, the Soviets also sought to increase their power in the international system but, in so doing, not to endanger their own security as well as their empire. As Rubinstein remarks, "They soon discovered that preserving an empire is more difficult than acquiring one."[4]

Within the USSR, the leadership sought to provide more resources for consumer goods and hence the de-Stalinization program of the mid-1950s (first expressed in Khrushchev's secret speech at the Communist Party of the Soviet Union twentieth congress in February 1956 when he denounced Stalin's crimes).[5] While the de-Stalinization campaign focused on domestic issues, it also had a foreign policy component. The USSR reversed its policy toward Yugoslavia. Josep Broz Tito, the Communist leader of Yugoslavia, had broken with the USSR in 1948, pursuing his own socialist/Communist path, much to the chagrin of the Soviet Union. In the mid-1950s, the USSR and Yugoslavia signed an agreement that ended the Cominform's economic blockade, which had been imposed in 1948. With this reversal in policy, the Soviet leaders also recognized "the principle of 'many roads to socialism.'" Rubinstein asserts that in acknowledging this principle, the Soviets "sought thereby to stem the appeal of Titoism—that is, full independence and equality for all Communist states—and to reconcile loyalty to the Soviet Union with the acceptance of the national autonomy allowed by Moscow."[6]

The problem with the rapprochement policy toward Tito and support for the principle of "many roads to socialism" is that the Eastern European elites were actually weakened by the Soviet policy, as these elites had come to power as a result of the 1948–1949 anti-Titoist purges in their respective states.[7] Nationalist Communists gained power from the Stalinists within these states. They defended and promoted their own state's interests.[8] They were also emboldened by the emergence of anti-Russian and anti-Communist sentiments, which then led to calls for desatellitization and de-Stalinization by leaders and the populations in Poland and Hungary in 1956 specifically. In addition to the proposal for a neutral multiparty system, Hungarian leaders also called for the withdrawal from the Warsaw Pact alliance. For the Soviets, such actions would undermine their hegemony and control of the Eastern European countries as well as their leadership of the world Communist movement. The Soviets responded and deployed troops to Hungary to quell the uprising.[9]

The experiences with Poland and Hungary demonstrated to Soviet leaders the need to maintain control out of concerns that such liberalization would spread to others in the region and threaten its hegemony.[10] Relations with the Eastern European countries were to remain a hierarchical one, dominated by the USSR. The 1957 Moscow Declaration affirmed this position explicitly: "The exchange of opinions revealed *identity* of views of the parties on *all* the questions examined at the meeting and *unanimity* in their assessment of the international situation" (emphasis in original).[11] The Declaration further stated: "The solidarity and close unity of the socialist countries constitute a reliable guarantee of the sovereignty and independence of each."[12]

To maintain hegemony in the region, the USSR looked to two main institutions: the Warsaw Treaty Organization (WTO, or Warsaw Pact) and the Council for Mutual Economic Assistance (Comecon, or CMEA). Established in May 1955, the Warsaw Pact served as an Eastern bloc military alliance for bloc unity and cohesion. The alliance served primarily Soviet political objectives, as "an intrabloc policing function" (only in 1961 were the first joint military exercises conducted).[13] According to Mark Kramer,

The Warsaw Pact provided the Soviet Union with a valuable means of containing the "renationalization" of the East European armed forces which began to accelerate after 1956; the symbolic concession to East European national

feelings embodied in the Pact's formation helped to preclude the erup-
tion of nationalist and anti-Soviet sentiments in most of the East European
countries.[14]

In terms of institutions for economic hegemony, the Soviets used Comecon for the economic integration of the bloc, primarily through a policy of
economic specialization. The Eastern European countries faced difficulties in
adjusting to the new policy of specialization given the autarkic policies imposed during Stalin's reign. Thus, Eastern European leaders opposed the Soviet policy, thereby making this institution problematic for bloc cohesion and
cooperation in the economic sphere. With Brezhnev at the helm, following
Khrushchev's ouster in 1964, the Soviets continued to insist that the countries
specialize (countries in the south would specialize in agricultural production
as well as processing raw materials, while those in the north would specialize
in the production of consumer goods, for example). Yet, again, not all Eastern
European states, such as Romania, which sought to pursue industrialization,
supported the Soviet economic specialization policy.[15]

Overall, in the period 1956–1968, the hegemon's relations and policy toward the followers evolved. The Soviet leaders who followed after Khrushchev's
ouster, Brezhnev and Kosygin, continued on the path of maintaining Soviet
hegemony in the region but made adjustments to ensure the maintenance of
that hegemony. The USSR permitted significant autonomy of the Communist
elites in their domestic affairs as a result of the strength of nationalism in
their respective countries. This autonomy, however, would not be permitted to
threaten "the communist character of the regime or its loyalty to the USSR."
The Soviets also approved of increasing ties, notably cultural and economic
ones, with the West, as long as this did not jeopardize intrabloc relations.[16] The
evolving relationship between the hegemon and its followers would be put to
the test with the reform movement that emerged in Czechoslovakia in 1968.
As Hoffmann claims, "Between 1964 and 1969, the most difficult Soviet decision was the military intervention in Czechoslovakia in 1968."[17]

THE PRAGUE SPRING AND THE INVASION
OF CZECHOSLOVAKIA

At the outset of 1968, Novotny, the first secretary of the Slovak Communist
Party, was ousted from his position at a plenary session of the Czechoslovak
Communist Party's Central Committee and replaced by Dubcek. Accord-

ing to David W. Paul, it was obvious then why he was removed: "Novotny was a living symbol of obsolete dogmatism in a restless society. The nation's economy had been faltering for several years, and economic reforms promised since 1965 had not yet passed beyond the planning stage."[18] Dubcek, on the other hand, while "a loyal party bureaucrat," was also a proponent of liberalizing Czechoslovak society through significant reforms. In this environment, as noted by Rubinstein,

> Democratization flowered. From early February to August 1968, Czechoslovakia experienced a rebirth of political, cultural, and social freedom. The secret police were stripped of their arbitrary powers, and links to the Soviet KGB apparatus were exposed, and criticisms of the past and proposals for the future were aired with a candor and passion that disturbed the oligarchs of Byzantine communism in Moscow.[19]

The perceived challenge to the Czechoslovak Communist Party's rule as a result of these significant reforms carried over as a perception of threat to the stability, both political and military, of the Eastern European bloc, and specifically, the Warsaw Pact. As a result, the Soviets, along with leaders in several of the Eastern European countries, determined that something had to be done to end the reforms in Czechoslovakia.[20]

The Soviets did not decide to invade the country as soon as the reformers took over. The decision was a slow process. At the beginning, Soviet elites seemed supportive of the changed regime.[21] By May there was increasing unease, and thus the Soviets sought "to persuade the Czechoslovak leaders to moderate or postpone their reforms and to restrain the masses' impulses toward independence." The fact that the Soviets had not yet taken a more coercive response only emboldened the Czechoslovak leaders regarding autonomy. The Prague Spring, as it became known, threatened the leaders in other Warsaw Pact countries. As Paul argues, "it is known that the mood of such top priority Soviet allies as Ulbricht [East Germany] and Gomulka [Poland] was bordering on hysteria. And it is quite possible that these allies' influence on specific Soviet Politburo members was strong enough to represent a heavy factor in the decision" to invade.[22]

As a result, Soviet leaders and those of its allies met at several conferences in July and August to discuss the situation in Czechoslovakia. It was at two of these meetings that "the Czechoslovak leaders were given a last chance to reassure their allies of the Prague regime's stability and fidelity; it was an appeal

which Dubcek and his colleagues apparently lost." On August 21, the Prague
Spring ended when the Warsaw Pact countries invaded.[23]

The USSR justified its invasion in a September 26, 1968, article in *Pravda*.
In the so-called Brezhnev Doctrine, the Soviets made it clear that the USSR
alone determined the degree of independence of its followers and that intervention might be necessary to safeguard world socialism. Concerns that the
use of military force might lead to the end of détente with the United States or
to the loss of the backing of Communists in other countries paled in comparison to the perceived threat that such reforms in a satellite state could have on
the primacy of its position in the region.[24]

What were the USSR's and its allies' motivations for invading a member
of their alliance? Rubinstein argues that domestic factors played a strong role
in the Soviet decision. The most important factor was fear of contagion—that
Czechoslovakia's liberalization would spread to the Soviet republics, namely
Ukraine, fomenting nationalism and demands for reform and thus less control by Moscow.[25]

Systemic factors mattered as well. Czechoslovakia's geographic position
demonstrated that "strategic imperatives transcended political risks." The
Soviet military maintained that Czechoslovakia played a significant role in
Soviet strategy in Europe. Moreover, the Soviets looked to Eastern Europe as a
way to gain support in its conflict with China.[26] According to Paul, "the most
important determinant of the Politburo's ability to reach consensus is the external variable, specifically the level of perceived threat to Soviet or Warsaw
Pact security."[27] Soviet leaders perceived Czech actions as an internal threat to
the alliance system. Reforms in Czechoslovakia might spread to demands for
reforms by the populations in East Germany and Poland, thereby challenging
the power and rule of the Communist Party elites in both of those countries,
which, in turn, could threaten the stability of the alliance itself.[28] Thus, both
domestic and international factors mattered.

ROMANIA'S CHALLENGE TO THE HEGEMON:
BALKING STRATEGY

For the Romanian elite, world Communism meant diversity within the movement. As Jowitt notes, the leadership asserted that the diversity of the various
socialist/Communist states meant that the world movement did not require a
center, that is, the USSR.[29] At the same time, Romania did see itself as a member of the Eastern bloc—it did not seek to leave the Soviet sphere but did want

to act independently of it. Movement away from Soviet dominance began in 1958 (for example, Soviet troops were removed from Romanian territory at Romania's request).[30] Gheorghiu-Dej and other elites in power "mounted a successful propaganda campaign against the Soviet economic pressure on Romania" in the period 1962–1965. The Romanian Communist Party (RCP) would be seen "as a champion of Romanian national interests against Moscow's plans for transforming Romania into the agricultural base of the Soviet bloc."[31] In pursuing economic ties with the West and in 1964 rejecting the Soviet call for economic specialization, Romania's independent foreign policy became apparent.[32] Visits to the Soviet Union and China, and the endorsement of Italian Communist leader Palmiro Togliattis's view of world Communism as one with many centers, demonstrate the regime's determination to pursue an autonomous foreign policy.[33] Moreover, while continuing as a member of the Warsaw Pact, it also embraced a military doctrine independent of the USSR.[34]

Even before Ceausescu assumed the leadership position in 1965, the elite argued for noninterference. From 1964 onward, "in every Romanian article on 'socialist internationalism'" the reference to noninterference in domestic politics of socialist/Communist countries was made clear, as demonstrated by the April 1964 statement on party sovereignty and the succession crisis of March–July 1965.[35] As Tismaneanu argues, the April 1964 declaration served as a break with the view of socialist internationalism espoused by the Soviets.[36] The Romanians viewed relations among the socialist states as founded on "the principles of national independence and sovereignty, equal rights, mutual advantage, comradely assistance, noninterference in internal affairs, observance of territorial integrity, [and] the principles of socialist internationalism."[37]

Moreover, Romania maintained economic relations with non-Communist states. These economic relations, therefore, also implied a foreign policy that was more independent than the other Eastern European countries.[38] Additionally, on his accession to power, Ceausescu advocated for the industrialization and modernization of the country. He used Romanian nationalism as a means for enhancing the legitimacy of his rule.[39] A new constitution that "more clearly [served] as part of a continuing break with the Soviet Union" was introduced.[40]

Ceausescu made his views clear in a speech at the Ninth Party Congress, held in July 1965. He stated, "The development and flourishing of each socialist nation, of each socialist state, equal in rights, sovereign and independent, is an essential requirement upon which depend the strengthening of the unity and cohesion of the socialist countries, the growth of their influence upon mankind's advance towards socialism and communism."[41] He argued that Communism's strength rested on the unity and strength of each nationalist Communist state. In doing so, his "redefinition of unity," as Jowitt argues, enabled him to attend to problems at home and the international arena.[42] For example, in December 1965, Romania cosponsored a resolution on East–West relations at the U.N. General Assembly. Known as the "Group of Nine," these states focused on "sovereignty, equality, full participation, and cooperation among European states not between blocs."[43]

Tension between Romania and the USSR continued as evidenced by Ceausescu's absence at a summit meeting of Communist states held in Hungary in mid-July 1967. He did permit the participation of Romanian troops in Warsaw Pact troop maneuvers in Bulgaria. At the same time, much to the chagrin of alliance members, diplomatic ties with West Germany were established. Unlike the other socialist states, Romania did not break diplomatic relations with Israel during the 1967 Arab–Israeli war. As Mary Ellen Fischer observes, this was "a major departure from bloc unity."[44]

In essence, in the period 1965 to 1967, Ceausescu and the Romanian leadership promoted the idea of Romanian nationalism as a way to ensure his regime's legitimacy. In a nod to domestic politics, the regime announced changes in personnel and also reorganized the political and economic spheres. Ceausescu rewarded his supporters with political positions. He promoted policies that "ensured his personal influence over the military and the security forces." At the December 1967 Party conference he was made head of state. Loyalty to the Romanian nation and Party unity were linked.[45]

The elite's view of noninterference, and by extension a challenge to the dominance of the USSR in terms of bloc unity, became ever more obvious with the reforms promoted by the Czechoslovak regime and the concerns of the allies regarding these reforms. Ceausescu declared that the Czechoslovak Communist Party had the "right . . . to decide what was best for its own country."[46]

By the time the decision to invade Czechoslovakia was being discussed by the Warsaw Pact states it was clear that the Romanians would not follow in line. The Soviets did not include Romania in the Dresden meeting held in March 1968 that dealt with Comecon and the WTO.[47] At the time of the meeting, Ceausescu met separately with representatives from Czechoslovakia and Yugoslavia (with which Romania had positive relations). From the Soviet perspective, such meetings might lead to an entente among Czechoslovakia, Romania, and Yugoslavia, which the Soviets would be highly unlikely to support. By April 1968, according to Fischer, "Romanian–Soviet relations were at a postwar low . . . and the bases of inter-Party relations that Romania had carefully established over such a long period of time—sovereignty, equality, and mutual non-interference—were seriously threatened."[48]

In remarking on Ceausescu's trip in May to Yugoslavia the Romanian press noted that these "relations could serve as a proper model for relations among socialist nations."[49] Yet, in the months prior to the invasion, at first Ceausescu did not comment on events in Czechoslovakia. He reiterated his position on equality, noninterference, and sovereignty. His first public statement in support of the Czechoslovak party occurred in mid-July: "The Romanian Communist Party does not share the view of those who are alarmed over what is happening in Czechoslovakia and who consider that there has to be an intervention. . . . We have full confidence in the Communist Party of Czechoslovakia."[50] The allies then appeared to move away from their ultimatum to Czechoslovakia issued earlier in Warsaw (which justified the reasons for a possible invasion). On August 11, Ceausescu responded with a public statement in which he expressed his "satisfaction" with the "acceptable solutions . . . [reached by] patient discussions." While he continued to stress the obligations to the alliance, he also made it clear that Romania would defend itself from an invasion by foreign forces.[51]

In August, Ceausescu visited Czechoslovakia, where he signed a Treaty of Friendship, Cooperation and Mutual Assistance. In doing so, he gave his support for the policy of independence and the Dubcek leadership and regime.[52] When he returned to Romania he followed up with more public pronouncements of support. In a speech on August 20 (a day before the invasion), he expressed his "full satisfaction" with the situation in Czechoslovakia. Noting his impressions of his visit to Czechoslovakia, "We were profoundly impressed. . . . The destinies of the Czechoslovak people are in safe hands, in the hands of the Communist Party. . . . In the Czechoslovak people we have a wonderful friend in the joint struggle for socialism."[53]

On the day of the invasion Ceausescu spoke at a rally in Romania in which he asserted that the invasion was "a great mistake and a grave danger to peace in Europe, to the fate of socialism in the world." He also noted that the invasion was "a shameful moment in the history of the revolutionary movement" and that "there is no justification whatsoever . . . [for] military intervention in the affairs of a fraternal socialist state. . . . The problem of choosing the roads of socialist construction is a problem of the respective Party. . . . Nobody can pose as advisor."[54] In a signal to the Soviets as well as the Romanian public, he also stressed that "the entire Romanian people will not allow anybody to violate the territory of our homeland. . . . Be sure, comrades, be sure, citizens of Romania, that we shall never betray our homeland, we shall never betray the interests of our people."[55]

Ceausescu's political power strengthened following the invasion of Czechoslovakia. He was viewed by the Romanian public, according to Fischer, as "a national hero" for having expressed his criticism of the invasion as an outright violation of that country's territorial sovereignty by alliance troops. His public proclamation that Romania would not permit the occupation of the country by foreign troops and that Romanians were prepared to fight should such an invasion by outside forces occur further increased his power and legitimacy of his rule.[56]

At the same time, it is important to recognize that, while both Romania and Yugoslavia opposed the invasion (and, in fact, Ceausescu and Tito met to discuss the situation), as Adam Ulam remarks, "As time went on, the Soviet leaders must have noted complacently that their action in Czechoslovakia had a desirable educational effect even on the Rumanians." In the period leading up to the invasion, Romania's leaders asserted that the alliance needed to be reformed as a means to make the organization more equal. One Romanian idea was to rotate the supreme command, which traditionally had been held by a Soviet general. After the invasion, "while not yielding any of their autonomy, [Romania] ceased to demand more."[57]

Ceausescu also underscored relations between the hegemon and its follower, deemed friendly in spite of the invasion. In a speech on August 26 he claimed that "Nothing can hinder the good cooperation and friendship between Romania and the Soviet Union. . . . There is no problem that could be a reason for disagreement between our peoples." He also spoke about the other Communist countries of Eastern Europe in positive terms, reiterating that Romania would not abandon its obligations to the WTO "if imperialism attacks a socialist state." In making these remarks he demonstrated Romania's continued alliance commitment to the USSR.[58]

In the year after the invasion, at the Moscow International Conference, an event for the Communist and workers' parties, Ceausescu did not criticize the

Soviet invasion and suppression of the Prague spring.[59] Yet Romania also continued to pursue an independent policy. For example, in 1970 Romania and the USSR signed the Romanian–Soviet Treaty of Friendship, Cooperation, and Mutual Assistance. This treaty, according to William Zimmerman, "stands as vivid testimony to a small power's determination to restrict its commitments to an exclusively regional basis," in this case Europe. Romania viewed the WTO as a European-focused alliance, to counter the NATO member-states. He further argues that the 1970 treaty "constitutes the culmination of a long series of moves designed to disengage Romania from Soviet domination."[60]

Ceausescu continued to reach out to Communist Parties who were critical of what was considered to be "Soviet hegemonist behaviour."[61] As Tismaneau asserts, "his anti-Soviet foreign policy as well as the liberal policies adopted between 1965 and 1971 ensured him a certain level of domestic and international prestige."[62] Fischer also notes that by the early 1970s, though many Romanians became disenchanted with the regime's policies, they "would still point to the events in Czechoslovakia as the major reason for supporting him and the Romanian Communist Party. August 1968 turned any opposition to Ceausescu into betrayal of the Romanian nation."[63] Ceausescu's nationalism in Romanian foreign policy, namely the move toward a more independent foreign policy away from control by the USSR as well as seeking relations with non-Communist states, solidified his power and rule.[64] Romania's balking strategy vis-à-vis the USSR demonstrates that even small, weak states can resist the hegemon.

CONCLUSION: LIMITATIONS OF SOVIET HEGEMONY IN EASTERN EUROPE

Zimmerman notes that global hegemons are world powers; in the case of the Cold War, the Soviet Union was a superpower. As a superpower, it "is deeply involved in the dominant international system, the level of tension in the dominant system greatly affects the behavior of the hegemon within its regional system."[65] Specifically, Soviet hegemony in Eastern Europe remained a significant priority for Soviet leaders from Stalin onward. Military and political influence over those states was solidified by dominance in the Warsaw Pact and as the self-designated leader of the world Communist movement. With the maintenance of troops on Eastern European territory, and the willingness to use force (as demonstrated by the reaction to the uprising in Hungary and the reforms in Czechoslovakia), the Soviets made obvious their unwillingness to allow outright opposition to its hegemony. As Rubinstein states, "Militarily, Moscow [had] a free hand to maintain hegemony over the bloc. The constraints on its use of force [were] internal and bloc-derived."[66] The invasion of Czechoslovakia emphasized the limits of what the Soviets would permit with regard to any significant domestic reforms promoted by the Eastern European countries and the degree of autonomy and independence of their foreign policies.[67]

The Soviet reaction to followers demanding more autonomous foreign and domestic policies demonstrates that, while maintaining hegemony can be quite costly (for example, the threat to détente with the United States, and loss of trade opportunities with the West), the Soviets were more than willing to incur those costs.[68] The states in the Eastern bloc were dependent on Soviet energy and raw materials (Romania imported crude petroleum). In addition, the leaders of these states, "a generation of party-military-secret police cadres," supported the status quo because they benefited from it. While at times they might have appealed to their populations to enhance the legitimacy of their rule, the very survival of their regimes rested on the USSR. They also feared each other, thereby "bind[ing] them to a policy of friendship with the Soviet Union." Poland's leaders worried about a German–Soviet deal that would be disadvantageous to them. In turn, the East Germans feared a deal between the USSR and West Germany. Tension between the various nationalities in the region further enabled the Soviets to argue that their hegemony brought stability and security.[69]

At the same time, this case also demonstrates the limits of Soviet hegemony. As Valerie Bunce claims, "the interaction among domestic, regional, and global factors" explains why the Eastern European states increased their demands on the Soviets and why the Soviets accommodated those demands: "The Soviet Union was forced into the unenviable position of using Soviet resources to prevent economic and political bankruptcy in the bloc."[70] While these regimes were dependent on the Soviet economy for their economic growth as well as on the Soviet military and party patronage, dependence actually provided bargaining leverage for them. She argues that Soviet dominance in the political, military, and economic spheres "opened the Soviets up to the free-rider problem. . . . economic subsidies were far less costly than political and economic reforms."[71]

In the specific case of a follower balking against the hegemon, Romania's decision to oppose the invasion can be explained largely by domestic factors (framework 3). Ceausescu's own personal power and control in the country would be enhanced and legitimized by standing up to the USSR, arguing that Romanian nationalism and national interests superseded that of the USSR's policy vis-à-vis Czechoslovakia (and more generally that socialist states should be able to determine their own policies, both foreign and domestic). The balking strategy was timely for the Romanians as the Soviets were constrained in their response to the Romanian opposition by its conflict with China, for example. Other concerns muted the Soviet counterresponse, a policy that was "cautious and noninterventionary" as Romania's leaders, according to Paul, kept "their 'deviation' under control and their avoidance of provoking the Soviets into a state of alarm."[72]

Even after the invasion, as noted previously, Romania remained within the Eastern bloc. It remained dependent on the USSR for imports (machinery, raw materials, and technology) and markets.[73] As Kramer notes, the Warsaw Pact states consented to Soviet hegemony, including Romania. Romanian leaders' calls for independence and autonomy were muted. The need for Soviet aid to mitigate Romania's economic problems propelled the Romanian leaders to moderate their claims for autonomy.[74] Romania could not, nor would not, balance against the hegemon, but it could engage in behavior that limited the influence of the hegemon, and it did.

NOTES

1. Jiri Valenta, "The Bureaucratic Politics Paradigm and the Soviet Invasion of Czechoslovakia," *Political Science Quarterly* 94, 1 (Spring 1979): 59.

2. Alvin Z. Rubinstein, *Soviet Foreign Policy since World War II: Imperial and Global* (Boston: Little, Brown and Company, 1985): 83; see also Valerie Bunce, "The Empire Strikes Back: The Evolution of the Eastern Bloc from a Soviet Asset to a Soviet Liability," *International Organization* 39, 1 (Winter 1985): 4; Douglas A. MacGregor, "Uncertain Allies? East European Forces in the Warsaw Pact," *Soviet Studies* 38, 2 (April 1986): 228.

3. Bunce, "The Empire Strikes Back": 7.

4. Rubinstein, *Soviet Foreign Policy since World War II*: 83.

5. Ibid.: 84–85.

6. Ibid.: 85.

7. Bunce, "The Empire Strikes Back": 9.

8. Rubinstein, *Soviet Foreign Policy since World War II*: 85.

9. Rubinstein, *Soviet Foreign Policy since World War II*: 87–88; Erik P. Hoffmann, "Soviet Foreign Policy Aims and Accomplishments from Lenin to Brezhnev," *Proceedings of the Academy of Political Science* 36, 4 (1987): 22.

10. Rubinstein, *Soviet Foreign Policy since World War II*: 88; Bunce, "The Empire Strikes Back": 12.

11. As quoted in Kenneth Jowitt, "The Romanian Communist Party and the World Socialist System: A Redefinition of Unity," *World Politics* 23, 1 (October 1970): 39.

12. As quoted in Jowitt, "The Romanian Communist Party": 39.

13. Rubinstein, *Soviet Foreign Policy since World War II*: 102. See also Mark Kramer, "Civil–Military Relations in the Warsaw Pact: The East European Component," *International Affairs* 61, 1 (Winter 1984–1985): 55–56.

14. Kramer, "Civil–Military Relations in the Warsaw Pact": 55.

15. Rubinstein, *Soviet Foreign Policy since World War II*: 104–105; Bunce, "The Empire Strikes Back": 14–15.

16. Rubinstein, *Soviet Foreign Policy since World War II*: 92–93.

17. Hoffmann, "Soviet Foreign Policy Aims": 24.

18. David W. Paul, "Soviet Foreign Policy and the Invasion of Czechoslovakia: A Theory and a Case Study," *International Studies Quarterly* 15, 2 (June 1971): 177–178.

19. Rubinstein, *Soviet Foreign Policy since World War II*: 94; see also Paul, "Soviet Foreign Policy": 178.

20. Paul, "Soviet Foreign Policy": 178–179. For a discussion of the Eastern European elites and their views on the Czechoslovak situation, see Valenta, "The Bureaucratic Politics Paradigm and the Soviet Invasion of Czechoslovakia": 63–64.

21. Paul, "Soviet Foreign Policy": 180–181, 188.

22. Paul, "Soviet Foreign Policy": 197. See also Mark Kramer, "Archival Research in Moscow: Progress and Pitfalls," *Cold War International History Project Bulletin* 3 (Fall 1993), on the recently released archival evidence on the decision to invade.

23. Paul, "Soviet Foreign Policy": 179. See also Rubinstein, *Soviet Foreign Policy since World War II*: 94; on archival evidence regarding Soviet decision making leading up to the invasion see Kieran Williams, "New Sources on Soviet Decision Making during the 1968 Czechoslovak Crisis," *Europe-Asia Studies* 48, 3 (May 1996): 457–470.

24. Rubinstein, *Soviet Foreign Policy since World War II*: 95-96; on the Brezhnev Doctrine, see Adam B. Ulam, *Expansion and Coexistence: Soviet Foreign Policy, 1917-73*, 2nd edition (New York: Praeger Publishers, 1974): 745.

25. Rubinstein, *Soviet Foreign Policy since World War II*: 96. See also George Gross, "Communism Divided: Some Considerations for American Policy," *Russian Review* 28, 3 (July 1969): 268; Jiri Valenta, "The Explosive Soviet Periphery," *Foreign Policy* 51 (Summer 1983): 87.

26. Rubinstein, *Soviet Foreign Policy since World War II*: 97, 99.

27. Paul, "Soviet Foreign Policy": 169.

28. Paul, "Soviet Foreign Policy": 175, 199–200; on Soviet motivations, see also Karen Dawisha, "Soviet Security and the Role of the Military: The 1968 Czechoslovak Crisis," *British Journal of Political Science* 10 (1980): 341–363.

29. Jowitt, "The Romanian Communist Party": 42–43.

30. Barry Hughes and Thomas Volgy, "Distance in Foreign Policy Behavior: A Comparative Study of Eastern Europe," *Midwest Journal of Political Science* 14, 3 (August 1970): 491; Gross, "Communism Divided": 269; MacGregor, "Uncertain Allies?": 229.

31. Vladimir Tismaneanu, "Personal Power and Political Crisis in Romania," *Government and Opposition* 24, 2 (1989): 179.

32. Ronald H. Linden, "Socialist Patrimonialism and the Global Economy: The Case of Romania," *International Organization* 40, 2 (Spring 1986): 356. For a discussion on the April 1964 "declaration of independence," see Daniel N. Nelson, "Organs of the State in Romania," *The International and Comparative Law Quarterly* 25, 3 (July 1976): 651–664.

33. Tismaneanu, "Personal Power and Political Crisis in Romania": 179–180.

34. Kramer, "Civil–Military Relations in the Warsaw Pact": 46.

35. Jowitt, "The Romanian Communist Party": 45, 50.

36. Tismaneanu, "Personal Power and Political Crisis in Romania": 180.

37. As quoted in Jowitt, "The Romanian Communist Party": 38.

38. Linden, "Socialist Patrimonialism and the Global Economy": 347. See also Hughes and Volgy, "Distance in Foreign Policy Behavior."

39. Linden, "Socialist Patrimonialism and the Global Economy": 354.

40. Nelson, "Organs of the State in Romania": 654.

41. As quoted in Jowitt, "The Romanian Communist Party": 43.

42. Ibid.: 43.

43. Jeanne Kirk Laux, "Small States and Inter-European Relations: An Analysis of the Group of Nine," *Journal of Peace Research* 9, 2 (1972): 153-154.

44. Mary Ellen Fischer, *Nicolae Ceausescu: A Study in Political Leadership* (Boulder, CO: Lynne Rienner Publishers, 1989): 98.

45. Ibid.: 108–109, 119.

46. Ibid.: 120.

47. Jowitt, "The Romanian Communist Party": 54; Fischer, *Nicolae Ceausescu*: 121.

48. Fischer, *Nicolae Ceausescu*: 122.

49. Jowitt, "The Romanian Communist Party": 57.

50. As quoted in Fischer, *Nicolae Ceausescu*: 142.

51. As quoted in Fischer, *Nicolae Ceausescu*: 142.

52. Fischer, *Nicolae Ceausescu*: 142–143.

53. As quoted in Fischer, *Nicolae Ceausescu*: 143.

54. As quoted in Fischer, *Nicolae Ceausescu*: 143.

55. As quoted in Fischer, *Nicolae Ceausescu*: 144. See also Christopher D. Jones, "Soviet Hegemony in Eastern Europe: The Dynamics of Political Autonomy and Military Intervention," *World Politics* 29, 2 (January 1977): 237.

56. Fischer, *Nicolae Ceausescu*: 141; Jones, "Soviet Hegemony in Eastern Europe": 237.

57. Ulam, *Expansion and Coexistence*: 745.

58. As quoted in Fischer, *Nicolae Ceausescu*: 144.

59. Tismaneanu, "Personal Power and Political Crisis in Romania": 184.

60. William Zimmerman, "Hierarchical Regional Systems and the Politics of System Boundaries," *International Organization* 26, 1 (Winter 1972): 29.

61. Tismaneanu, "Personal Power and Political Crisis in Romania": 184.

62. Vladimir Tismaneanu, "The Revival of Politics in Romania," *Proceedings of the Academy of Political Science* 38, 1 (1991): 86.

63. Fischer, *Nicolae Ceausescu*: 145.

64. Ibid.: 258.

65. Zimmerman, "Hierarchical Regional Systems": 21-22.

66. Rubinstein, *Soviet Foreign Policy since World War II*: 107.

67. F. Stephen Larrabee, "Instability and Change in Eastern Europe," *International Security* 6, 3 (Winter 1981/82): 57.

68. Rubinstein, *Soviet Foreign Policy since World War II*: 108. On the costs to the Soviets for their invasion of Czechoslovakia, including the possible loss of Western credits and "the not inconsiderable burden of underwriting the Czech economy to save it from a complete and politically dangerous collapse," see Ulam, *Expansion and Coexistence*: 747.

69. Rubinstein, *Soviet Foreign Policy since World War II*: 107–108.

70. Bunce, "The Empire Strikes Back": 28.

71. Ibid.: 32–33.

72. Paul, "Soviet Foreign Policy": 169. On more about why the Soviets may not have responded so harshly to the Romanian policy, see also MacGregor, "Uncertain Allies?": 232.

73. Bunce, "The Empire Strikes Back": 42; Gross, "Communism Divided": 274; Kramer, "Civil–Military Relations in the Warsaw Pact": 56.

74. Kramer, "Civil–Military Relations in the Warsaw Pact": 56.

3 CUBA, ANGOLA, AND THE SOVIET UNION

Jennifer Kibbe

ON NOVEMBER 4, 1975, Cuba decided to send 650 elite troops to Angola to help its revolutionary ally, the Popular Movement for the Liberation of Angola (Movimento Popular de Libertação de Angola, MPLA), one of three factions fighting for control in the soon-to-be independent country. Seen through the Cold War lens dominant at the time, Cuba's move was interpreted as having been executed at the behest of Moscow.[1] According to a 1978 account of U.S. policy making, "Most U.S. officials, including the Secretary of State, and a host of journalists argued that the Cubans went to Angola to pay off their approximately five and one-half billion dollar 'IOU' to the Soviet Union for military and economic assistance extended since 1960."[2] Over time, however, it has become increasingly clear that Cuba's decision was made independently of the USSR and, in some respects, in contravention of the latter's wishes.[3]

Why would Cuba, which by the mid-1970s was increasingly dependent on the Soviet Union, risk such an autonomous step?[4] Cuba's actions were the result of systemic, neorealist constraints and opportunities combined with domestic level imperatives (explanatory frameworks 1 and 3). Intervening in Angola presented a chance to fulfill its deeply felt "internationalist" obligation to help a revolutionary ally at a time when international conditions were such that it ran little risk of a punitive response from either superpower. Both the United States and the USSR were preoccupied with détente, and having finally left Vietnam in April 1975, the United States was unlikely to embark on any new foreign ventures so soon. Cuba's response to Angola's civil war presents a useful case study of how its relationship with the Soviet hegemon was far more complex than is normally assumed. This chapter discusses the principles underlying Cuban foreign policy and then examines the history of its involvement in Africa before 1975, both of which provide the background necessary for understanding its actions in Angola. The third section explains how Cuba intervened in Angola; finally, the chapter concludes with a discussion of Cuba's motivations and objectives.

CUBAN FOREIGN POLICY

For the first three decades after its revolution, Cuba's foreign policy was driven by two central goals. The first was fundamentally pragmatic: to ensure the survival of revolutionary rule on the island through close relations with the USSR and a broad network of diplomacy designed to break U.S.-imposed isolation and to gain influence. Only slightly less important, though, was the ideological drive to promote national liberation movements and defend existing progressive governments in the developing world, what Cuba termed "internationalism." It felt a strong sense of "solidarity with all oppressed peoples of the world" and a moral responsibility to help other movements and governments facing conditions similar to those faced in Cuba, both before and after the revolution.[5] A sense of this notion of responsibility is captured in a passage of the Second Declaration of Havana, read by Fidel Castro on February 4, 1962, in response to the Organization of American States' (OAS's) decision to suspend Cuba: "It is the duty of every revolutionary to make the revolution. In America and the world, it is known that the revolution will be victorious, but it is improper revolutionary behavior to sit at one's doorstep waiting for the corpse of imperialism to pass by."[6] Castro's doorstep metaphor also served to highlight the distinction between the Cuban approach and many Soviet-oriented Communist Parties that argued that revolutionaries ought to wait for favorable "objective conditions" before trying to assume power.[7] Castro was even more explicit in January 1966 in his closing speech at the Havana Tricontinental Conference to support revolutions in Africa, Asia, and Latin America: "The imperialists are everywhere in the world. And for Cuban revolutionaries the battleground against imperialism encompasses the whole world. . . . And so we say and proclaim that the revolutionary movement in every corner of the world can count on Cuban combat fighters."[8]

For Castro and those in his ruling elite, there was another aspect to their sense of "internationalist duty" as well. They felt a particular responsibility as a representative of the Third World. The Soviets and East Europeans were white and, compared to the Third World, rich, while the Chinese were unable to adapt to Latin American and African culture. Cuba, on the other hand, "was nonwhite, poor, threatened by a powerful enemy, and culturally Latin American and African. It was, therefore, a special hybrid: a socialist country with a Third World sensitivity in a world where [according to Castro] . . . the major fault line was not between socialist and capitalist states but between developed and underdeveloped countries."[9]

Cuban leaders were clear, however, that internationalism served their overarching pragmatic goal as well as a means of revolutionary self-defense. The more contact they could make with revolutionary movements and governments around the world, the more they could undermine U.S. attempts to isolate the island (and the less dependent they would be on the Soviet Union).[10] In addition to defusing U.S. aggressiveness, Cuba's internationalism served its primary goal of preserving the revolution at home in another way as well. Internationalism was seen as a crucial tool for the "creation of the socialist consciousness and ethos that would underpin the new social order," as the "revolutionary leadership sought to neutralize and negate capitalist values."[11]

One final element of Cuba's foreign policy that provides important context for understanding its moves in Angola in 1975 is its complex relationship with its Soviet patron during the 1962–1975 period. Although aware of its obvious dependence on the USSR for economic and military support in the face of U.S. hostility, Cuba was by no means always a compliant client and was willing to speak and act independently. Its leaders bristled at the way the Soviets settled the 1962 missile crisis, particularly resenting the fact that they had removed their missiles without even consulting Castro.[12] The next six years were a time of increasing frustration. First, Cuba felt that the Soviets were not paying enough attention to the island's fears of another attack by the United States. In October 1964, a senior Cuban official went to Moscow for help because "we were convinced that the United States was planning to attack Cuba; this was what I had come to tell him, but Khrushchev said it wasn't so. . . . The tone was bitter. Khrushchev spent almost all the time talking about the Chinese. He was fixated on them."[13]

Even after Khrushchev's ouster, the Cubans did not feel entirely secure that Moscow would come to their defense. Castro voiced these doubts quite explicitly in a 1968 conversation with high-ranking East German officials: "You are members of the Warsaw Pact, so you have a guarantee against imperialist aggression. You have a lot of Soviet divisions nearby which are ready to fight on your side. This is not the case in Cuba."[14]

The two states were also increasingly at odds over Latin America, with Cuba pushing to export the revolution via armed struggle and the USSR advocating more peaceful means, for fear of antagonizing the United States. Finally, Cuba was fundamentally disappointed with what it saw as the weak Soviet response to the flexing of U.S. muscle as Washington intervened with 20,000 troops in the Dominican Republic in April 1965 and began to escalate the Vietnam War. Havana saw Moscow's response to an attack on a Soviet ally as overwhelmingly weak in both cases, which only served to raise further questions about the Soviets' commitment to defend Cuba.[15]

Thus, from 1962 to 1968, the Cuban–Soviet relationship was quite rocky, with Cuba continually balking at Soviet directives and trying to assert its independence in foreign policy. Cuba used its radical foreign policy to try to create a third force within the socialist camp, as a way of forging allies against U.S. aggression and lessening its dependence on the Soviets.[16] Matters came to a head in 1968 when the Cuban Central Committee denounced a "microfaction" in its midst, whose members had opposed Cuba's domestic and international policies and had been communicating with the Soviet and East European governments and Communist Parties.[17] The members of the microfaction were expelled from the party and imprisoned. The Soviets, who had already cut back on oil exports to Cuba, suspended all military shipments and technical assistance.

These sanctions, on top of the already existing U.S. and Chinese ones, soon proved too much for the Cuban economy to bear.[18] In August 1968, in responding to the Soviet invasion of Czechoslovakia (see Chapter 2 for more on the "Prague Spring"), rather than standing up for a small state being bullied by a superpower as expected, Castro conceded that Cuba "accept[ed] the bitter necessity that required sending those troops into Czechoslovakia."[19] Thus, Cuba had shown the USSR that the latter could count on it for support in a crisis and, in exchange, called for a renewed Soviet commitment to support and defend it. Thus, while initially pursuing a balking strategy, Soviet pressure led Cuba to change to a bandwagoning strategy.

As a result, the Cuban–Soviet relationship was far calmer during 1968–1975 and more recognizable as one between a client and a hegemon. Cuba's recognition of its ongoing need for Soviet assistance led it to restrain its criticism of Moscow's foreign policy and to reshape its domestic institutions more in line with the Soviet model.[20] One of the most tangible symbols of Cuba's new acceptance of the Soviets' preeminent position came at the Fourth Conference of Non-Aligned Nations in Algiers in 1973, when Castro denounced the "theory of two imperialisms" (those of the United States and the USSR) that was prevalent at the conference and defended the Soviet Union as a natural ally of the Third World.[21]

Nonetheless, Cuba's fundamental commitment to internationalism during this period continued. It moved away from supporting guerrilla movements toward focusing on those movements already in power or that could succeed in taking power in the short term.[22] The early 1970s also saw Cuba paying heightened attention to cultivating its image as a leader of the Third World, a key part of which was being seen as the vanguard and defender of progressive African states.[23] Soviet interest in Africa had flagged since the mid-1960s, allowing Cuba a certain amount of room to advocate armed struggle without complicating its relationship with Moscow.[24] The Non-Aligned Movement offered Cuba the chance to expand its influence in an arena that was, by definition, not dominated by either of the superpowers and thus to increase its leverage with both (although its dependence on the USSR did hamper its Third World appeal to a certain degree).[25]

CUBA'S HISTORY IN AFRICA

Cuba's involvement in Africa began with its aid to the National Liberation Front of Algeria (FLN) in 1961, thus long predating sending troops to Angola in 1975. Cuba's role in Algeria was rooted in a widespread identification with the Algerian people, which started before 1959 as the two states' revolutions developed along similar paths. Moreover, in risking tangible interests, including its relationship with French President Charles de Gaulle and an important contract with Morocco, Cuba's Algerian policy epitomized the idealistic strain of its foreign policy. As historian Piero Gleijeses argues, "If Cuba's foreign policy was based solely on realpolitik, Cuba would not have helped Algeria."[26] Cuba went on to aid the new Algerian government once it gained independence.

Cuba's next major foray in Africa came in 1965 when Cuba sent an armed column led by Che Guevara to Zaire to help rebels fighting against the corrupt, pro-American Joseph Mobutu. Another column was sent to the Congo to help protect the revolutionary government from invasion by Zaire and any incipient military coups, as well as to help the Angolan MPLA, based in Brazzaville at that time.[27] Although the Zairian government successfully repressed the rebellion with the help of 1,000 white mercenaries sent by the United States,[28] and although the Congolese revolution turned out to be a disappointing "verbal revolution,"[29] the episodes signaled an important step in the evolution of Cuba's foreign policy, as it began to focus its policy of internationalism on Africa. By the mid-1960s, Cuban leaders felt that Africa was ripe for revolution. This assessment was strengthened by defeats suffered by guerrilla movements in Argentina, Peru, and Venezuela, and by Salvador Allende's defeat in the 1964 Chilean election. Cuba was also increasingly frustrated with Latin Americans' growing support for America's attempts to isolate Cuba, particularly in light of the OAS's vote to impose sanctions on Cuba for sending weapons to Venezuelan guerrillas.[30] Moreover, given Africa's geographic distance from the United States and the fact that in most places the Cubans were helping forces fight colonial governments, the risks were far less than with their efforts to spread revolution in Latin America.[31] Africa's attraction as the focus of Cuba's internationalism was further enhanced by the latter's strongly felt Afro-Cuban historical and cultural legacy. Finally, Cuba's expanding contacts in Africa were a way to nurture political support among developing states at the United Nations, to increase its status in the Third World, and to increase its leverage in the socialist world.[32]

Although Cuba's Africa-centric strategy fell short in Zaire and the Congo, it achieved greater success in Guinea-Bissau. Gleijeses shows that the roots of Cuba's relationship with the country were independent of Moscow and grew instead from Che's trip to Africa in 1964–1965 and Cuba's own interest in sub-Saharan Africa.[33] Cuba began giving food, medicine, and arms to the rebels in their fight against the Portuguese in 1965 and military advisers in 1966, continuing aid through independence in 1974. In the early 1970s, as Soviet interest in Africa continued to fade, Cuba developed relations with an array of other African states, including sending military missions to Sierra Leone, Equatorial Guinea, Somalia, Algeria, and Mozambique.[34]

CIVIL WAR IN ANGOLA

By the time of Cuba's decision to send troops to Angola in 1975, then, it already had a long history of assisting guerrilla movements in Africa. Its initial contact with the MPLA, in fact, was in early 1965, during Che's trip to Africa. Cuba was deeply interested in helping the fight against Portuguese colonialism and chose the MPLA over its two rival groups, the National Front for the Liberation of Angola (Frente Nacional de Libertação de Angola, FNLA) and the National Union for the Total Independence of Angola (União Nacional para la Independência Total de Angola, UNITA) because the MPLA was not only the oldest liberation movement in Angola but was also the most staunchly anti-imperialist and prosocialist.[35] At that time, the Angolan movement was headquartered in Brazzaville in the Congo, and the Cubans sent assistance and military instructors to help them move forces into Angola. Cuban hopes for the MPLA proved too optimistic, though, and they became increasingly critical of the Angolans' military performance, which served only to breed resentment between the two. Thus, after 1967, their relationship cooled considerably. The Soviets, meanwhile, cut off aid to the MPLA in 1963–1964, reduced it again in 1972–1973, and stopped it completely during 1974.[36]

The key trigger event for the Angolan civil war was the overthrow of the Marcello Caetano dictatorship in Portugal in 1974. Beset by ongoing instability at home, the new Portuguese government moved quickly toward decolonization, recognizing Guinea-Bissau's independence in September 1974 and doing the same for Mozambique in June 1975. The difference in Angola was that the three movements fighting for independence had never been able to unify, making the process of handing over power far more difficult. By late 1974, the MPLA was in the weakest position of the three, partly because its leader, Agostinho Neto, had only recently been able to consolidate power over rival factions[37] and partly because, although the USSR had resumed aid in October, most of the heavy weaponry would not arrive until May 1975 at the earliest. Meanwhile, the FNLA began receiving aid from China in 1973 and then the United States in 1974, while South Africa initially backed one of the non-Neto MPLA factions in 1974 and then switched to supporting UNITA.[38] Consequently, the MPLA reached out to Cuba once again, first requesting renewed aid in July 1974. Although Havana said yes, nothing happened. When Neto made an urgent request in October for five military officers to organize his troops, Castro originally said yes and then reconsidered. In light of Cuba's overoptimism and the resulting African disappointments of the 1960s, he opted instead to send a two-person research team to assess the situation.[39]

Portugal's attempt to resolve the Angolan problem was the Alvor Accords, which it signed with the three rebel groups in January 1975. Under the terms of the Accords, a Portuguese high commissioner would govern the country until independence, set for November 11, 1975. He would be assisted by a transitional government consisting of representatives from each of the three rebel groups. Elections for a Constituent Assembly, which would elect the first president, were to be held by October 31, 1975.[40]

The Accords began to fray almost immediately, as armed fighting broke out among the three groups. With each group having at least one external sponsor fueling the situation, and with none of the outside powers having a stake in Alvor, all three parties' priority was controlling territory, not sharing power. In addition, once the political situation in Portugal worsened with an unsuccessful rightist countercoup in March 1975, Lisbon refocused its attention at home and lost all interest in shepherding Angola through a peaceful decolonization process. One final element that sealed the country's descent into civil war was the new Portuguese government's none-too-subtle preference for the MPLA. With the FNLA and UNITA convinced that the high commissioner and the transitional government were biased against them, they lost any incentive to make Alvor work and concentrated all their efforts on expanding their areas of control. Much of the fighting in the first six months of 1975 was between the militarily stronger FNLA and the more politically popular MPLA for control of the capital of Luanda. After several rounds of fighting followed by unsuccessful cease-fires, the MPLA expelled the FNLA from the capital for good in early July.

By mid-August, Portugal conceded the reality that the transitional government was a government in name only, most of the ministers having fled the capital. The high commissioner dissolved the government and assumed its responsibilities himself, although most of the vacant positions were filled by MPLA members. On August 29, Lisbon formally annulled the Alvor Accords but, to most observers' surprise, offered no other mechanism for the transition to independence in their place, while simultaneously reaffirming that independence would be granted on November 11. Furthermore, the high commissioner announced that the withdrawal of Portuguese troops would begin in mid-September.[41] To no one's surprise, the ensuing seven weeks saw a desperate struggle among the three groups for control of Luanda on independence day.

The two Cubans who had been sent to determine the MPLA's viability in early 1975 submitted a positive report at the end of March, but Cuba still did not respond. Neto repeated his request for military instructors in May, now asking for just under 100, as well as weapons, clothing, and food for recruits. The MPLA was desperate for instructors for its new recruits, especially after the Soviets had refused to provide their own (although they had been providing weaponry since March).[42] Cuba finally responded in late June when an official met with Neto at Mozambique's independence celebration. The eventual response, which reached the MPLA in late July, consisted of $100,000 (for transporting weapons the MPLA had stockpiled in Tanzania), 480 instructors (nearly five times what was requested), and weapons, food, and clothing for the recruits.

On August 15, Castro sent a message to Leonid Brezhnev advocating the increased need for support for the MPLA, including the introduction of Cuban special troops. Specifically, Castro asked for Soviet transport assistance and the use of Soviet staff officers, both in Havana and Luanda, to help with planning the military operations. He emphasized the political strength of the MPLA as well as "the threat which foreign assistance to the FNLA/UNITA alliance posed to socialism and independence in Angola."[43] Despite their overall policy of supporting the MPLA, the Soviets disapproved of the Cuban plan. The Soviets objected to the use of Soviet transport planes and officers in Angola before independence, concerned that such a move would damage the policy of détente with the United States, as well as offend many African countries. At the time, Brezhnev was focused on the strategic arms limitation talks (SALT II) with the United States and the upcoming February 1976 Congress of the (Soviet) Communist Party. As Director of Central Intelligence Richard Colby told the U.S. National Security Council in July 1975, "[Brezhnev] knows it is his last Congress—they occur every five years—and he doubtless sees it as the occasion for securing his place in Soviet history. . . . [He] wants to go before the Congress proclaiming the success of détente."[44]

The Soviets had had military advisors helping the MPLA in Brazzaville, but once the group moved its headquarters to Angola in August, the Soviets refused to accompany them there.[45] Moscow also felt the Cubans were underestimating the degree to which even a solely Cuban intervention could undermine détente, given that the United States would assume they were acting as Soviet proxies anyway. Furthermore, Moscow was not convinced that the MPLA's situation warranted a military intervention. The Soviet General Staff opposed any participation in the Cuban operation, and even the KGB warned against the effects of direct Soviet intervention on U.S.–Soviet relations. As a result, Brezhnev rejected Castro's requests.[46]

Further evidence of the Soviets' displeasure with Cuba's policy is found in the fact that, when they found out that Cuba had gone ahead with the plan to send the 480 military instructors, they tried to stop it. Georgi Kornienko, head of the American department of the Soviet Foreign Ministry in 1975, later recalled in an interview that the Soviets found out when their ambassador in Conakry, Guinea relayed that the Cuban ambassador had just told him that Cuban planes would be refueling there on their way to Angola. It was reported to Foreign Minister Andrei Gromyko, who knew nothing about it and reported it to the Politburo "suggest[ing] that we stop Castro. It took some hours to write the report, to get the decision, and to send the message to Castro. By this time the planes were in the air."[47]

Cuban military instructors filtered into Angola over the next two months, but their impact was almost immediately overtaken by events on the ground. Throughout September, the FNLA pushed toward Luanda from the north, with the help of Zairian forces. The pressing threat from the north served to distract the MPLA from UNITA's, and more importantly, South Africa's, moves in the south. South Africa had actually moved thirty miles into Angola to occupy the Calueque hydroelectric installation in August 1975, claiming it merely wanted to protect the electricity supply going to South West Africa (Namibia). Soon thereafter, however, South Africa established its first training camp for UNITA within Angola. As UNITA met increased resistance from the MPLA in early October, Pretoria decided to invade in mid-October, apparently with Washington's encouragement.[48]

After Operation Savannah began on October 14, the invasion force moved rapidly through MPLA-held southern Angola. On November 2 and 3, the MPLA tried to halt the South Africans' advance at the town of Catengue. The MPLA and the Cuban instructors fighting with them were no match for the South Africans and quickly withdrew. Catengue, and the shock of being pushed back, proved to be a pivotal point in Cuba's decision making. With only eight days left before independence, unable to stop the South Africans, and with the FNLA still pressing from the north, the head of the Cuban military mission sent an urgent message stressing the need for Cuban troops. Although Castro hoped to be able to hold off until after independence, Catengue changed his mind. According to senior Cuban official Jorge Risquet, "It was then that we understood that the South Africans had invaded"[49] and that there was a very real risk that South Africa could reach Luanda before November 11. On November 4, Castro decided to send a 652-troop battalion of elite Special Forces to help the MPLA. According to Gleijeses, "The decision was made hurriedly and under pressure, with the feeling that time was running out. It was taken by Fidel Castro without consultation with the political bureau, probably after speaking with his closest advisers, particularly his brother Raúl."[50]

Despite the widespread assumption at the time that Cuba's action was merely that of a Soviet puppet, the majority of scholars have now concluded that Cuba acted independently. As Castro described it at a conference in 1992, "That was a decision of ours. The only thing that came from the Soviet Union was worries. They conveyed them to us in 1975, but it was an absolutely free and sovereign decision by our country."[51] His statement is corroborated by several Soviet sources. Arkady Shevchenko, who was an adviser to Foreign Minister Gromyko from 1970 to 1973 and then served as undersecretary-general of the United Nations before defecting in 1978, wrote that in 1976 acting Foreign Minister Vasily Kuznetsov asked him to join a group reviewing Soviet policy in Africa. Shevchenko asked Kuznetsov, "'How did we persuade the Cubans to provide their contingent?' . . . Kuznetsov laughed . . . [and] told me that the idea for the large-scale military operation had originated in Havana, not Moscow."[52] Similarly, Anatoly Dobrynin, the Soviet ambassador to the United States at the time, wrote in his memoirs that the Cubans sent their troops "on their own initiative and without consulting us."[53] Even Henry Kissinger, one of the foremost proponents of the "Cuba as proxy" characterization, conceded in his memoirs that it wasn't true: "At the time, we thought he [Castro] was operating as a Soviet surrogate. We could not imagine that he would act so provocatively so far from home unless he was pressured by Moscow to repay the Soviet Union for its military and economic support. Evidence now available suggests that the opposite was the case."[54]

While Cuba's decision did not run directly counter to Soviet interests, given that it was about sending troops to support a Marxist-Leninist movement that the Soviets were aiding as well, Cuban policy nonetheless constitutes a clear case of a secondary state balking at the hegemon's wishes. Moscow had been explicit about not wanting Soviet or Cuban troops in Angola before independence, and yet Cuba went ahead anyway. The fact that Cuba initially asked for help in transporting Cuban troops indicates that its goal was not to subvert Soviet wishes. And when Moscow said no in August 1975, Cuba did not proceed right away. When South Africa's invasion and the approaching date of independence increased the urgency of the situation, however, Cuba did not hesitate and did not give the Soviets a chance to stall or say no.

EXPLAINING CUBA'S POLICY

Cuba's decision is best explained by a combination of the domestic-level (framework 3) and external factors (framework 1). At the domestic level, ideology played the most prominent role in its decision making. Not only did it have a long-standing policy of internationalism and revolutionary solidarity, but it had had a continuous relationship with the MPLA since 1965, based largely on the latter's Marxist-Leninist orientation and its commitment to armed struggle.[55] Another domestic factor that worked in tandem with Cuba's ideology was its sense of historical obligation to Africa, something the Cubans emphasized by naming the intervention Operation Carlota after the African slave woman who led a revolt against slavery in Cuba on November 5, 1843.[56] These two factors comprised the Cubans' own explanation of their actions. In a speech in March 1976, Castro maintained that: "We Cubans have helped our Angolan brothers, first because it is a revolutionary principle, because we are internationalists. Second, because our people are an Afro-American people . . . and [because] today our people are revolutionary, free, internationalist, capable of fulfilling their revolutionary duties."[57] Furthermore, South Africa's invasion enabled Cuba to combine these factors and characterize its own intervention as defending the socialist black Africans against the white South African invaders operating in collusion with the imperialist Americans.

But ideology and historical legacy alone are not enough to account completely for Cuba's actions. Cuba's foreign policy had always combined ideology with a certain amount of pragmatic realpolitik, pushing internationalism and armed struggle as long as they did not endanger the primary goal of preserving the revolution at home. In practice, that had meant weighing its actions in terms of their potential effect on either superpower, each of which loomed large in Cuba's foreign policy calculations, albeit in different ways. Angola represented a relatively low-risk opportunity for Havana to pursue its internationalist drive as well as to act on its decade-old policy of fighting back against its major threat, the United States, in its theater of choice, Africa. Not only was the United States known to be supporting the FNLA-UNITA forces—helping the MPLA win could be seen as directly defying the United States—but, while there was some risk that Cuban intervention would trigger further U.S. support, Washington's Vietnam hangover meant there was little chance of incurring a direct U.S. response.[58] Moreover, the risk of even just increased U.S. support for the FNLA-UNITA forces was diminishing by the day in late

1975 as a Congressional committee[59] conducted ongoing hearings into covert operations (including the assassination attempts against Castro). Anyone paying any attention at all to U.S. domestic politics could tell there was very little appetite in Congress for continuing the covert program in Angola and, in fact, the Senate passed the Clark Amendment ending the program in December (which then became law in 1976).[60]

Other international factors that also played a role in the decision included the fact that, because supporting the MPLA wasn't directly against the Soviets' interests, the risk of Moscow penalizing Cuba in any significant way was minimal. Angola thus offered Cuba a chance to strengthen its position as a leader of the Third World both by defending an ally against invasion by the U.S.-assisted South Africans and by demonstrating its autonomy from the USSR.[61]

Thus, a full explanation of the Cuban decision to send troops to Angola in November 1975 requires both the domestic level and neorealist frameworks. In balking at the hegemon's wishes not to send troops to Angola before independence, Cuba's actions were clearly driven by its deeply ingrained internationalist ideology and its own historical and cultural roots. These were internal characteristics of the state itself that helped determine its policy choice. These domestic-level factors, however, cannot quite explain the entirety of Havana's decision. Its foreign policy history clearly shows that, had there been a higher risk of negative ramifications from either the United States or the USSR, Cuba probably would not have sent its troops, at least not without checking with Moscow first. Thus, Cuba's ideological and historical motivations cannot be separated from its longstanding primary foreign policy goal, the neorealist drive for survival.

NOTES

1. See, for example, Roger Morris, "Proxy War in Angola: Pathology of a Blunder," *The New Republic* 174 (January 31, 1976): 19–23; Kim Willenson, "Angola: The Russians Have Come," *Newsweek* (December 1, 1975): 56.

2. Gerald J. Bender, "Kissinger in Angola: Anatomy of Failure," in *American Policy in Southern Africa*, ed. Rene Lemarchand (Washington, DC: University Press of America, 1978): 95.

3. The assumption that the Cubans were merely Soviet proxies still lingers, however. See, for example, Roger E. Kanet, "The Superpower Quest for Empire: The Cold War and Soviet Support for 'Wars of National Liberation,'" *Cold War History* 6 (2006): 337.

4. Carmelo Mesa-Lago, "Cuban Foreign Policy in Africa: A General Framework," in *Cuba in Africa*, ed. Carmelo Mesa-Lago and June S. Belkin (Pittsburgh: Center for Latin American Studies, University of Pittsburgh, 1981): 3.

5. Richard L. Harris, "Cuban Internationalism, Che Guevara, and the Survival of Cuba's Socialist Regime," *Latin American Perspectives* 36 (2009): 30.

6. Quoted in Jorge L. Dominguez, *To Make a World Safe for Revolution: Cuba's Foreign Policy* (Cambridge, MA: Harvard University Press, 1989): 116.

7. Dominguez, *To Make a World Safe for Revolution*: 116.

8. Ibid.

9. Piero Gleijeses, *Conflicting Missions: Havana, Washington, and Africa, 1959–1976* (Chapel Hill: University of North Carolina Press, 2002): 377.

10. Nelson P. Valdés, "Revolutionary Solidarity in Angola," in *Cuba in the World*, ed. Cole Blasier and Carmelo Mesa-Lago (Pittsburgh: University of Pittsburgh Press, 1979): 88.

11. Isaac Saney, "Homeland of Humanity: Internationalism within the Cuban Revolution," *Latin American Perspectives* 36 (January 2009): 113.

12. Antoni Kapcia, *Cuba in Revolution: A History since the Fifties* (London: Reaktion Books, 2008): 33.

13. Jorge Risquet, quoted in Gleijeses, *Conflicting Missions*: 94–95.

14. Quoted in Gleijeses, *Conflicting Missions*: 95.

15. Dominguez, *To Make a World Safe for Revolution*: 70.

16. William M. LeoGrande, "Cuban–Soviet Relations and Cuban Policy in Africa," in *Cuba in Africa*, ed. Carmelo Mesa-Lago and June S. Belkin (Pittsburgh: Center for Latin American Studies, University of Pittsburgh, 1981): 17.

17. W. Raymond Duncan, *The Soviet Union and Cuba: Interests and Influence* (New York: Praeger, 1975): 73; Dominguez, *To Make a World Safe for Revolution*: 72–74.

18. Dominguez, *To Make a World Safe for Revolution*, 76; Duncan, *The Soviet Union and Cuba*: 74–75.

19. Quoted in Dominguez, *To Make a World Safe for Revolution*: 76.

20. Duncan, *The Soviet Union and Cuba*: 77–78.

21. Kapcia, *Cuba in Revolution*: 124; Dominguez, *To Make a World Safe for Revolution*: 104–105; Duncan, *The Soviet Union and Cuba*: 127.

22. Valdés, "Revolutionary Solidarity in Angola": 89.

23. Duncan, *The Soviet Union and Cuba*: 127; Valdés, "Revolutionary Solidarity in Angola": 111.

24. Duncan, *The Soviet Union and Cuba*: 124.

25. Dominguez, *To Make a World Safe for Revolution*: 219–222.

26. Gleijeses, *Conflicting Missions*: 54.

27. Gleijeses, *Conflicting Missions*: 161; Valdés, "Revolutionary Solidarity in Angola": 92.

28. Gleijeses, *Conflicting Missions*: 60–159.

29. Ibid.: 163.

30. Olga Nazario and Juan Benemelis, "Cuba's Relations with Africa: An Overview," in *Cuban Internationalism in Sub-Saharan Africa*, ed. Sergio Díaz-Briquets (Pittsburgh: Duquesne University Press, 1989): 15.

31. Gleijeses, *Conflicting Missions*: 93.

32. Ibid.: 98.

33. Ibid.: 185–213.

34. Duncan, *The Soviet Union and Cuba*: 125.

35. William M. LeoGrande, *Cuba's Policy in Africa, 1959–1980* (Berkeley: Institute of International Studies, University of California, 1980): 13.

36. Duncan, *The Soviet Union and Cuba*: 128; LeoGrande, *Cuba's Policy in Africa*: 15.

37. Odd Arne Westad, *The Global Cold War: Third World Interventions and the Making of Our Times* (New York: Cambridge University Press, 2005): 222.

38. Edward George, *The Cuban Intervention in Angola, 1965–1991* (New York: Frank Cass, 2005): 53–54.

39. Gleijeses, *Conflicting Missions*: 244–245.

40. George, *The Cuban Intervention in Angola*: 49–56.

41. Ibid.: 58–60.

42. Ibid.: 63.

43. Westad, *The Global Cold War*: 232.

44. Quoted in Gleijeses, *Conflicting Missions*: 260.

45. George, *The Cuban Intervention in Angola*: 65.

46. Westad, *The Global Cold War*: 233.

47. Quoted in Westad, *The Global Cold War*: 439n63.

48. George, *The Cuban Intervention in Angola*: 68–71.

49. Quoted in Gleijeses, *Conflicting Missions*: 305.

50. Gleijeses, *Conflicting Missions*: 305.

51. Quoted in Laurence Chang and Peter Kornbluh, *The Cuban Missile Crisis, 1962* (New York: New Press, 1992): 334.

52. Cited in Gleijeses, *Conflicting Missions*: 307.

53. Cited in Gleijeses, *Conflicting Missions*: 307.

54. Henry Kissinger, *Years of Renewal* (New York: Simon & Schuster, 1999): 816.

55. Saney, "Homeland of Humanity"; Gleijeses, *Conflicting Missions*: 377; George, *The Cuban Intervention in Angola*: 274; Dominguez, *To Make a World Safe for Revolution*: 132.

56. Saney, "Homeland of Humanity": 115.

57. Quoted in Valdes, "Revolutionary Solidarity in Angola": 109.

58. Dominguez, *To Make a World Safe for Revolution*: 132.

59. U.S. Senate Select Committee to Study Governmental Operations with Respect to Intelligence Activities, better known as the Church Committee.

60. Gregory F. Treverton, *Covert Action: The Limits of Intervention in the Postwar World* (New York: Basic Books, 1987): 158–159.

61. Dominguez, *To Make a World Safe for Revolution*: 132.

4 IRELAND'S SINGULAR STANCE
Pursuing Neutrality as a Means to Resist the
Hegemon

Neal G. Jesse

THE REPUBLIC OF IRELAND has pursued neutrality since World War II.[1] Shielded by the bulk of the British mainland, Ireland's geographic isolation provided it with a perfect place to hide from the last century of European conflict. In addition, the lack of any true capability to project power beyond its shores, and perhaps the inability to protect its shores from external threat, makes a foreign policy choice of belligerence unobtainable. With the exception of its historic, hegemonic neighbor, Britain, Ireland has no enemies and no international intrigues.

However, a number of authors have painted Irish neutrality as much more complex. Irish neutrality wraps itself in its historical relations with Britain, the continuing separation of Northern Ireland, notions of independence and sovereignty, party politics, and the continuance of myths in Irish public opinion. Trevor Salmon labels Irish neutrality "unprincipled non-belligerency" and with "a certain consideration" toward its neighbor Britain.[2] Patrick Keatinge labels the unique Irish neutrality a "Singular Stance." He contends that most international observers underestimate the contributions of domestic factors to the establishment and maintenance of Irish neutrality.[3]

Ireland's singular stance contains the core element of nonparticipation in military alliances while also promoting activity in international peacekeeping operations, particularly under the auspices of the United Nations. Moreover, Irish unarmed neutrality sets it apart from its contemporary counterparts, such as Finland, Sweden, Switzerland, and Austria. Given these factors, I show that realist theory underestimates the contributions of domestic factors to the establishment and maintenance of Irish neutrality.

In this chapter, I compare Ireland's response to hegemony based on the frameworks in Chapter 1. The unique form of Irish neutrality can best be examined as driven by domestic-level factors and employing an institutionalist strategy. Specifically, Ireland's twentieth-century struggle for self-determination set into motion the domestic pressures for neutrality. On the global stage, Ireland pursues neutrality through international institutions, a strategy more consistent with the second framework.

A BRIEF HISTORY OF IRISH NEUTRALITY

Formally, Irish neutrality as policy begins with World War II.[4] However, Keatinge argues that Irish neutrality as a "political value" began with the Anglo-Irish Treaty of 1921.[5] Kennedy and Skelly argue that "the history of Ireland since 1916 is, in many respects, the history of Irish foreign policy."[6] This treaty clove the island of Ireland into two separate parts (based on the Government of Ireland Act of 1920): the six northern counties to remain in the United Kingdom and the twenty-six counties in the south to be a self-governing free state or dominion of Britain. The treaty also stipulated that certain naval facilities in the South would remain under British control. Article 7 of the Anglo-Irish Treaty obliged Ireland to "supplement these facilities at Britain's request" during warfare or international tension.[7] Ireland thus found itself in the favorable position of being in a "British naval exclusion zone," protected from European powers by British naval might.[8]

Under the umbrella of an international order conditioned by the nascent League of Nations, Ireland pursued the simultaneous strands of cooperation with British forces and a stated ambition of remaining neutral in foreign affairs.[9] Moreover, the pursuit of Irish neutrality is often associated with Eamonn de Valera, founder of the anti-Treaty party Fianna Fail, head of government until 1937, *taoiseach* (prime minister) of parliament and later president of the republic. In this light, neutrality fit de Valera's pursuit of a fully independent Irish state and consequently full sovereignty from Britain.[10] He also used neutrality to intensify "action against the IRA."[11]

Of consequence is that the Irish Free State came into existence as a member of the British Commonwealth. Ireland possessed internal autonomy, but like all Commonwealth states it was not free to pursue an independent foreign policy from that of the United Kingdom.[12] British embassies represented

Irish interests in most foreign countries, although starting in 1923 the Dublin government insisted on establishing its own legations in a few places, such as the United States and Canada. Ireland possessed limited resources and an economy dependent on trade with Britain. Establishing a foreign policy would prove to be difficult. Therefore, Irish neutrality during this period was at best ambiguous. Keatinge points to debates in parliament as evidence of an internal lack of consensus on neutrality. In addition, Ireland appeared to betray neutrality with acceptance of its obligations to impose economic sanctions on Italy following Italy's invasion of Ethiopia in 1935. Thus, while de Valera publicly stated on occasion that Ireland was pursuing neutrality, it is not clear that it actually did so.[13]

It is clear that the foundation of neutrality as a political value derives from the Irish desire to be independent of Britain. Keatinge illustrates the "anti-British" sentiment that fostered the deployment of neutrality, particularly through reference to de Valera's statements about possible British aggression against Ireland. In other words, the more that Ireland could divorce its foreign policy from British foreign policy, the more Ireland appeared to have true independence and sovereignty.[14] It appears here that Irish resistance to British hegemony took on a unique pattern. Unable to engage British power and authority directly, the Irish established their foreign policy, and pattern as a nonfollower, as a means of showing their resentment of British hegemony. Ireland may have been a free state, but it was also a "postcolonial" British state.[15] Its economic and political systems were a by-product of the long British occupation. Moreover, economic and political relations with Britain were not only paramount but asymmetrical in power. This early neutrality was a covert resistance to this asymmetry.

Ireland would take a great step toward both true independence and sovereignty with the 1938 constitution. Aside from granting Ireland true independence from Britain, the 1938 agreement between de Valera and the British government led to Britain relinquishing its defense rights under the 1921 treaty. Keatinge suggests that neutrality moved from just a political value to a true state policy at this time.[16] Both de Valera and his political opponents saw neutrality in the same three ways: as a way to avoid a European war, as a way to avoid civil war between the new republic and Northern Ireland, and as a "litmus test of sovereignty."[17] Fisk suggests that for once "symbol and reality were one," as sovereignty and independence overlapped with neutrality as a defense.[18]

Irish neutrality meant staying out of the growing division in Europe; it did not mean that Ireland was impartial. In 1938 de Valera was willing to strike a naval agreement with Britain if, in return, it would settle the partition issue.[19] From 1939, de Valera's neutrality policy tried to walk a fine line. It sought to maximize Irish independence but also realized the strategic importance of Ireland to British defense. This required Ireland to remain benevolent toward Britain, including military cooperation in case of a German invasion after the fall of France in June 1940. However, the Irish insistence on maintaining diplomatic relations with Germany irritated the Allies (especially the United States and Britain) right up to the end.[20] As an example, while de Valera was evenhanded in his relations with Hitler's Germany, the Irish chargé d'affaires in Germany from 1933 to 1938, Charles Bewley, became a fascist sympathizer and Hitler admirer before de Valera recalled him from Berlin.[21]

The consequences of Irish neutrality in World War II were fourfold. First, Ireland emerged unscathed relative to the rest of Europe. One author notes that "apart from isolated German bombings, and an occasional explosion caused by drifting mines, independent Ireland suffered not at all."[22] Second, neutrality contributed to international diplomatic isolation of Ireland after the war. This culminated in Ireland's failure to gain U.N. membership until 1955, due to vetoes cast by the USSR.[23] Third, it widened the divide between the North and the South. The Germans bombed Northern Ireland mercilessly; consequently, its inhabitants suffered, unlike their comrades to the south, with rare exceptions. Fourth, the success of neutrality created a popular attachment to it and "fostered enduring illusions about the moral basis of staying out of other people's wars."[24] Keatinge goes so far as to say, "to the nationalist justification for neutrality was added an appeal to universal moral principles . . . by 1945 the basis for a national tradition of neutrality, both as a value and as a policy, had been laid; an orthodoxy, if not a dogma, had been established."[25]

After the war, Irish foreign policy contained four key features: neutrality, continuing preoccupation with partition, emigration, and few close relations with states other than Britain and the United States.[26] Of these four, neutrality was the central policy. Doherty suggests that the basic principle behind Irish neutrality after the war was the avoidance of any military alliance. He posits that "Irish neutrality is not so much principled neutrality as unprincipled non-belligerency."[27] This is because Irish security did not need Irish neutrality, as NATO insured the former.[28] Thus, Ireland did not maintain a credible defense force, something that distinguished it from the other European neu-

trals in postwar Europe. Keatinge posits that this pattern of neutrality continued until 1961 when Irish involvement with emerging European integration
began to drive Irish foreign policy.[29]

Here again is a rather unique Irish response to the change in hegemony
from Britain to the United States. No longer would Britain provide the overarching defense of Ireland, but rather the military/defense alliance sponsored
by the new hegemonic power, the United States, would provide coverage for
Ireland. Of course, Irish foreign policy makers, especially the secretary of the
Department of External Affairs, Frederick Boland, worried about "unwar-
ranted interference" by the now dominant United States and its impact on the
recovery of Western Europe.[30]

In 1961, the Irish government's economic foreign policy began to stress ties
to the European Economic Community (EEC), mainly due to the economic
advantages inherent in such a relationship. A debate began in Ireland about
whether linking itself to the increased political integration of Europe might
interfere with its policy of neutrality. The debate between *Taoiseach* Sean Le-
mass and the opposition led Ireland to a "reappraisal of neutrality" in the face
of the "realities and responsibilities of EEC membership."[31] Ireland did not
become a member of the EEC until 1973, and by that year political cooperation within the EEC was not seen as a threat to neutrality. The main Irish argument was that European Political Cooperation tolerated differing national
positions. Moreover, defense and security policy cooperation in Europe occurred chiefly through NATO, of which Ireland was not a member. Therefore,
Ireland could continue its traditional policy of neutrality.

By the late 1990s, most of the other European neutrals (but not Switzerland)
had also joined the EU, and the Irish position no longer looked so "singular." If
Irish neutrality in the 1980s had no clear doctrine, it remained so in the 1990s.[32]
Irish neutrality even adapted to inclusion in the European security order, including its participation in NATO's PfP (Partnership for Peace) since December 1999; observer status in the Western European Union (WEU), a loose-knit
defense organization; and support for the EU and its crisis-management role in
European politics.[33] Thus, Irish neutrality seems to exist more in label than in
practice. Yet, the core remains: nonparticipation in military alliances.

The "White Paper on Foreign Policy" continues to list, in accordance
with Article 29.1 of the Irish Constitution, that one of the central elements
of Irish security policy is "a policy of military neutrality, embodied by nonparticipation in military alliances."[34] The White Paper continues that the

policy of neutrality is based on public opinion, specifically that "the majority of the Irish people have cherished Ireland's military neutrality, and recognize the positive values that inspire it, in peace-time as well as war."[35] Furthermore, it sets neutrality as a central aspect of all foreign policy, stating that "the values that underlie Ireland's policy of neutrality have therefore informed almost every aspect of our foreign policy."[36]

Irish foreign policy seems to be generated from a set of values more than from a realist perspective of balance of power or geostrategic considerations. In particular, the reasons given for Irish neutrality did not change when the international order changed from a bipolar Cold War to a multipolar (or if one prefers, unipolar) system after 1991. Sweden, Finland, and Austria have all rejected neutrality in favor of nonalignment with partiality toward the EU.

NEUTRALITY AND NATIONAL SELF-DETERMINATION

As I have argued elsewhere, neutrality can be seen as a logical extension of a state's right to self-determination.[37] The sovereign has the *rightful* power of the state to enforce its authority.[38] Neutrality is thus a means by which a state can assert its sovereignty vis-à-vis the international order. This does not mean that observers all appreciate a state's neutral stance, especially a hegemonic power that would prefer the small state pursue a bandwagoning strategy instead. During World War II, Winston Churchill criticized Ireland's neutrality as did the head of the British Foreign Office, Sir Alexander Cadogan. During the Cold War, U.S. Secretary of State John Foster Dulles called neutrality "an immoral and short-sighted conception."[39]

Because foreign policy is a national choice, a policy of neutrality embeds nationalism and self-determination, that is, the desire of the nation to exert its separate cultural identity, independent statehood, and sovereignty against a hostile international environment.[40] Consequently, if neutrality is an extension of nationalism, then the neutral state not only chooses to pursue neutrality but also chooses how to define its neutrality and how to conduct its neutrality in accord with its definition of self-determination and sovereignty.[41]

HEGEMONY AND IRISH NEUTRALITY

Irish neutrality policy began during the time of a declining hegemon, Britain, and continued during the rise of another hegemon, the United States. In the former case, Irish neutrality is more of a resistance to a long history of British hegemony and a rejection of the British international order. Of course, such behavior fits the realist notions of hegemony that predict that "under condi-tions of declining hegemony there will be a weakening of regimes" and the beginning of resistance to the hegemon and its wishes.[42] On the other hand, one realist argues that the weakening of hegemony should have led to more collaboration and a sharing of the burden by smaller states to provide collec-tive goods in the international system.[43] Ireland clearly did not do this during World War II, staying out of the conflict and avoiding its "share" of providing the collective good of world democracy.

Irish neutrality in the face of a rising hegemon, in other words the United States after World War II, also belies realist theories of hegemony. As the United States was establishing many international regimes, Ireland decided to remain neutral and not participate (that is, neither bandwagon nor free-ride), foregoing a number of collective goods in the process. The issues of sover-eignty and noncommitment to military alliances kept Ireland out of a number of international organizations, limiting and isolating Irish foreign policy and even its economy. Such behavior makes little sense from a realist perspective that emphasizes the desire to free-ride.

THE THREE FRAMEWORKS AND THE IRISH CHOICE
OF NEUTRALITY

The Irish version of neutrality is different from that of its European counter-parts in two aspects. First, Ireland has not in the past nor does it now employ a credible defense of its territory. Second, Ireland has not historically been im-partial. During World War II and the Cold War, Ireland was clearly pro-West. On the first point, Keatinge puts Irish neutrality into comparative perspective. He compares Irish neutrality to that of four other European neutrals: Austria, Finland, Sweden, and Switzerland. Unlike the Irish neutrality of the twen-tieth century, Swiss and Swedish neutrality dates back to the sixteenth and nineteenth centuries, respectively, while Austrian and Finnish neutrality be-gan during the Cold War. The first two are "historical" neutrals who adopted neutrality during an international order based on empires. Neutrality for the Swiss and Swedes appears to be driven by realist concerns and a long tradition of armed neutrality. The second two adopted neutrality during the Cold War in response to their geographical proximity to the Eastern bloc. Both main-tain a fairly sizeable proportion of their population in arms as a credible cost to invasion and occupation.[44] The Cold War neutrality of Austria and Finland appears rational and realist, fitting easily into the first framework.[45]

The Irish case is not so obviously realist. Ireland maintains a minimal defense force. The Irish government spends less than 1.5 percent of its gross national product (GNP) on defense.[46] Its defense expenditure per capita has typically been the lowest of all five neutral nations and remains so today. In 2008, Ireland spent 1.081 million Euros on defense, roughly 0.6 percent of the Irish GDP.[47] Ireland has almost no military capacity with which to carry out foreign policy. The Permanent Defence Force (PDF) maintains a full complement of 9,933 personnel and the Reserve Defence Force of 6,644 personnel.[48]

Thus, Keatinge calls Ireland a "disarmed neutrality."[49] Likewise, Gilland calls Irish policy a "military neutrality."[50] Irish singularity is partially a product of its amazing lack of any credible defense, while geographical and strategic reasoning contributes to the ability of Ireland to pursue this policy. NATO implicitly guarantees the security of Ireland. Further, during the Cold War, when the other neutrals occupied a space between the two competing blocs, Ireland was safely tucked away behind Britain.

Ireland is not quite so singular in its lack of impartiality (that is, its partiality). One author even suggests that it is doubtful that Ireland has ever "aimed at projecting an image of impartial neutrality."[51] As stated earlier, Ireland was not impartial during World War II. Despite its anti-British sentiment and its diplomatic relations with Germany and Japan, Ireland coordinated its intelligence and defense policies with Britain. Moreover, all of the five Cold War neutrals are pro-Western. Therefore, Ireland's diplomatic relations with the West do not set it apart from the others. Furthermore, all but Switzerland are now in the EU. What is unique is the degree to which Irish trade historically has relied on the West and specifically on NATO members.[52] This is a bit singular because the other neutrals have a much more balanced pattern of trade. In particular, Austria and Finland maintained a good level of trade with the Eastern bloc countries during the Cold War.

Irish neutrality is not very clear, but there is a singular principle to which it has always adhered: the exclusion of involvement in any military alliance.[53] This has typically meant not assisting Britain in its conflicts and confrontations and not allowing others to use Ireland against Britain and its interests— neither balancing nor bandwagoning. Therefore, it is this lack of follower behavior that must be explained by factors other than standard realist theories. The weakness of realist theories is supported by a comprehensive study of Irish neutrality during World War II by Conor O'Loughlin in which he concludes that realist theories "cannot wholly account for Irish Foreign Policy."[54]

IRISH NEUTRALITY: SOVEREIGNTY, AUTONOMY, AND
INTERNATIONAL INSTITUTIONS

Abandoning the first framework as insufficient, I now explore the other two frameworks: liberal institutionalism and domestic sources. From the discussion of Ireland's history, one can argue that Ireland bases its peculiar, and unique, definition of neutrality on issues of independence and sovereignty. Importantly, both Irish leader de Valera and his opponents saw neutrality in World War II as the "litmus test of sovereignty."[55] O'Halpin argues that neutrality was one of the keystones of the independence argument and a pragmatic policy by which de Valera could keep Ireland united.[56] Thus, there appears to be a strong indication that domestic factors play a key role in policy choice. Yet, I cannot yet rule out liberal institutionalism because Ireland also promoted its image of independence through intergovernmental organizations, particularly its participation in the British Commonwealth and the League of Nations.[57] Ireland also pursues the promotion of human rights and international human rights standards, seeks to limit or defeat international terrorism, is fairly active in disarmament, and is involved in arms-control negotiations.

Ireland's acceptance of neutrality as a means by which to assert its independence and sovereignty carried over into the 1938 Irish Constitution. Article 29.3 states, "Ireland accepts the generally recognized principles of international law as its rule of conduct in its relations with other States." Eventual membership in the United Nations, the EEC, and the PfP continue Ireland's presence in intergovernmental organizations. Thus, lacking a credible defense, Ireland pursues diplomatic relations as a way to assert itself. Karsh calls this approach the "positive" strategy. Small neutral states use "total reliance on diplomatic skill . . . with the goal of exploiting every possible chink in the belligerents' armour to advance the preservation of the state's independence and sovereignty."[58]

If Irish neutrality is truly singular, it also makes sense to look for internal sources. As Tonra concludes, "The context from which Irish foreign policy choices were made was the internal environment of economic, political, cultural and military influences."[59] There are three separate domestic factors that contribute to Ireland's choice of neutrality and its continuation of that policy: public opinion, party politics, and interest groups.

Public opinion in Ireland about neutrality began during World War II. The government shielded the public from information about the war, and consequently information about the implementation of the Irish neutrality policy, through strict censorship laws. Among the public, Irish neutrality was based on the moral principle of staying out of other people's wars. Keatinge claims that as the decades moved on neutrality became more than just a policy, it became a "traditional symbol and national myth."[60] Gilland reports that public support of neutrality policy remains high and that "anywhere between 55 and 69 percent of respondents want to retain it [neutrality]."[61]

But does the public know what neutrality entails? Forty-eight and forty-six percent of respondents, respectively, replied that it meant either "no involvement in wars" or "no military alliances."[62] When the survey asks about specific events, the public's interpretation of neutrality becomes less clear. A 1992 poll shows that regarding the U.S.-led war against Iraq in 1991, 35 percent thought that Ireland should "align with the US/allies to resolve [the] crisis" and another 29 percent said that "Ireland should NOT be neutral in the Gulf."[63] Thus, a segment of the Irish public is willing to abandon neutrality under some circumstances.

Karen Devine explicitly tests the relationship between "hostile relations with Britain, the continuing separation of Northern Ireland, and notions of independence and sovereignty as drivers of Irish neutrality."[64] Her analysis determines that only independence and patriotism are significant predictors of public support for neutrality.[65] Interestingly, her measure of "efficacy," on in other words, the realist gain that neutrality could bring Ireland in foreign affairs, is not a significant predictor of public opinion.[66]

On whether membership and continued integration in the EU will conflict with neutrality, the public appears to have no clear view.[67] Yet, it is interesting to note that a 1996 poll showed that 57 percent of the respondents "believe that Ireland should come to the aid of another [EU] Member State if attacked."[68] In contradiction, a 2001 poll following the Treaty of Nice found that 72 percent of the respondents favored continuing the policy of neutrality.[69] Lyons also reports a poll taken after the events of September 11, 2001. Sixty-three percent of Irish voters "felt that allowing the US air force landing and refueling facilities at Irish airports was a sufficient contribution to the 'war against terrorism.'"[70] Consequently, while it appears that EU membership might be slowly changing the public's impression of neutrality and its usefulness, it is still too early to make any serious prediction as to the trajectory of the public's view on continued neutrality.

Second, the nature of party politics and political institutions supported the instigation and supports the continuation of neutrality. The initial impulse toward neutrality came from the anti-British sentiment following the Anglo-Irish Treaty. At this time Ireland needed only a small military force necessary to subdue internal threats and adopted a policy of military neutrality regarding the external international system. The Irish Civil War of 1922–1923 did not create a divide between the two factions regarding support for neutrality.[71] The party system, despite its division during the Civil War, was quite stable. By 1933, the two halves of the pro- versus antitreaty debate consolidated their positions in Fine Gael and Fianna Fail, respectively. These two parties dominated politics and "impeded the emergence of clearer class-based politics that might have been expected to challenge established socio-economic orthodoxies" or even the current foreign policies.[72] The two main parties "were not engines of policy-making or particularly of interest aggregation . . . they were simply mechanisms of election mobilization."[73] Thus, the party system presented few challenges to the executive.

Moreover, the executive had firm control over the making of foreign policy: "Parliamentary powers were theoretically strong over a very narrow range of foreign policy activity, but these were circumscribed by administrative and political constraints."[74] During this period, the Dáil could declare war, execute emergency powers, vote on international agreements, and approve money bills related to foreign policy, but it could do little otherwise.[75]

Postwar politics changed the Irish policy landscape very little. The Department of External Affairs was restructured to take into account economic-based interests in foreign policy.[76] "By the late 1970s there was a widespread consensus amongst the three main parties . . . that neutrality was perhaps negotiable in the distant future, but that it was not at present a live issue."[77] Consensus between the two main parties emerged even as recently as December 1999. Both Fianna Fail and Fine Gael supported Irish entry into PfP, and the interpretation that Irish involvement in PfP peacekeeping did not violate the principle of neutrality.[78] Gilland argues that "the meaning of neutrality has evolved among policy makers" and that "in the post-[cold] war era a new set of activities, previously ruled out, has emerged as complementary to neutrality."[79] She asserts that policy makers from both large parties hold neutrality in a "quasi-constitutional" status and that, while the parties are willing to debate the issue of neutrality in the public domain, they never question the overall policy of neutrality.[80]

The third domestic factor is the role interest groups play. Keatinge suggests that "in Irish political culture neutrality . . . appears as a manifestation of sovereignty and independence . . . [and] this characterization might apply to many of the active supporters of neutrality outside the arena of party politics."[81] He points to the presence of the Irish sovereignty movement as well as the peace movement that started in the 1980s as examples. Gilland supports this position, asserting that groups such as the Peace and Neutrality Alliance (PANA) campaign for Ireland to retain neutrality. Interest groups have organized around the EU debate (that is, whether Ireland should accept further integration into the EU), but they have not directly challenged neutrality.[82]

CONCLUSION: DOMESTIC SOURCES AND AN INSTITUTIONALIST STRATEGY AS A RESPONSE TO HEGEMONY

For these reasons, I find it clear that domestic factors (explanatory framework 3) favor neutrality. In no instance do the domestic sources consider the balance of power in the international environment to be a key to a neutrality policy. In fact, it appears that "preoccupation with external military pressures is . . . almost wholly absent from Irish politics."[83] The lack of any credible threat to Ireland certainly sets the parameters under which the Irish government and population must act. Given this, domestic forces drive the nature of the most malleable and inexpensive policy of neutrality. The use of international institutions to bolster claims to sovereignty is a complementary strategy aimed at maintaining the same goal: autonomy from the hegemon.

Instead of realist theories providing a persuasive argument for continued Irish neutrality, domestic factors give us a better understanding. Preoccupation with its sovereignty, a gift from its early-twentieth-century independence movement, leads Ireland to adopt a policy of unarmed neutrality. Moreover, the Irish idea of neutrality has changed as the nation progressed from escaping British dependence to asserting its independence to managing European interdependence.[84] This "singular stance" paints Ireland as unique among the European neutrals. Public opinion, party politics, political institutions, leaders, and interest groups all contribute to maintaining Irish neutrality, even as Ireland integrates its economy, military, and society with the European Union.

NOTES

Portions of this chapter are drawn from the following two articles: Neal G. Jesse, "Contemporary Irish Neutrality: Still a Singular Stance," *New Hibernia Review/Iris Éireannach Nua* 11 (2007): 74–95; and Neal G. Jesse, "Choosing to Go It Alone: Irish Neutrality in Theoretical and Comparative Perspective," *International Political Science Review* 27 (2006): 7–28.

1. See Efraim Karsh, *Neutrality and Small States* (New York: Routledge, 1988) and Patrick Keatinge, *A Singular Stance: Irish Neutrality in the 1980s* (Dublin: Institute of Public Administration, 1984) for the distinctions among *neutrality, neutralization,* and *nonalignment.*

2. Trevor C. Salmon, *Unneutral Ireland: An Ambivalent and Unique Security Policy* (Oxford, UK: Clarendon Press, 1989).

3. Keatinge, *A Singular Stance*: 84.

4. The idea of Irish neutrality predates Irish independence. The Irish Neutrality League and its President, James Connolly, espoused neutrality during World War I. Ronan Fanning, "*Raison d'Etat* and the Evolution of Irish Foreign Policy," in *Irish Foreign Policy, 1919–66: From Independence to Internationalism,* ed. M. Kennedy and J. M. Skelly (Dublin: Four Courts Press, 2000): 312.

5. Keatinge, *A Singular Stance*; Patrick Keatinge, *A Place among the Nations: Issues of Irish Foreign Policy* (Dublin: Institute of Public Administration, 1978).

6. Michael Kennedy and Joseph Morrison Skelly, "The Study of Irish Foreign Policy from Independence to Internationalism," in *Irish Foreign Policy, 1919–66: From Independence to Internationalism,* ed. M. Kennedy and J. M. Skelly (Dublin: Four Courts Press, 2000): 13.

7. Keatinge, *A Singular Stance*: 13.

8. Gerard Keown, "Taking the World Stage: Creating an Irish Foreign Policy in the 1920s," in *Irish Foreign Policy, 1919–66: From Independence to Internationalism,* ed. M. Kennedy and J. M. Skelly (Dublin: Four Courts Press, 2000): 32.

9. Eunan O'Halpin, *Defending Ireland: The Irish State and Its Enemies since 1922* (Oxford, UK: Oxford University Press, 1999); Eunan O'Halpin, "Irish Neutrality in the Second World War," in *European Neutrals and Non-Belligerents during the Second World War,* ed. Neville Wylie (Cambridge, UK: Cambridge University Press, 2002): 283–303.

10. Roisin Doherty, *Ireland, Neutrality and European Security Integration* (Burlington, VT: Ashgate, 2002).

11. Salmon, *Unneutral Ireland*: 133.

12. Keown, "Taking the World Stage:" 26.

13. Keatinge, *A Singular Stance*: 15.

14. Keown, "Taking the World Stage": 28.

15. Stephen Howe, *Ireland and Empire: Colonial Legacies in Irish History and Culture* (Oxford, UK: Oxford University Press, 2000).

16. Keatinge, *A Singular Stance*: 16–17.

17. See O'Halpin, *Defending Ireland*; O'Halpin "Irish Neutrality in the Second World War"; and Doherty, *Ireland, Neutrality and European Security Integration.*

18. Robert Fisk, *In Time of War: Ireland, Ulster and the Price of Neutrality, 1939–1945* (Dublin: Gill & MacMillan, 1983): 552.

19. Salmon, *Unneutral Ireland*: 97.

20. Of particular note was de Valera's extension of his condolences to a German minister on the death of Hitler in May of 1945. This action met international ridicule. Mervyn O'Driscoll, "Inter-War Irish-German Diplomacy: Continuity, Ambiguity and Appeasement in Irish Foreign Policy," in *Irish Foreign Policy, 1919–66: From Independence to Internationalism*, ed. M. Kennedy and J. M. Skelly (Dublin: Four Courts Press, 2000): 74–95.

21. O'Driscoll, "Inter-War Irish-German Diplomacy": 75–87.

22. O'Halpin, *Defending Ireland*: 254.

23. See O'Halpin, *Defending Ireland*; "Irish Neutrality in the Second World War"; and Doherty, *Ireland, Neutrality and European Security Integration*.

24. O'Halpin, *Defending Ireland*: 254.

25. Keatinge, *A Singular Stance*: 20.

26. Bernadette Whelan, "Integration or Isolation? Ireland and the Invitation to Join the Marshall Plan," in *Irish Foreign Policy, 1919–66: From Independence to Internationalism*, ed. M. Kennedy and J. M. Skelly (Dublin: Four Courts Press, 2000): 214.

27. Doherty, *Ireland, Neutrality and European Security Integration*: 17.

28. There is evidence that the coalition government was willing to join NATO in exchange for a united Ireland. Troy Davis, *Dublin's American Policy: Irish-American Diplomatic Relations, 1945–1952* (Washington, DC: Catholic University of American Press, 1998).

29. Keatinge, *A Singular Stance*: 24.

30. Till Geiger, "The Enthusiastic Response of a Reluctant Supporter: Ireland and the Committee for European Economic Cooperation in the Summer of 1947," in *Irish Foreign Policy, 1919–66: From Independence to Internationalism*, ed. M. Kennedy and J. M. Skelly (Dublin: Four Courts Press, 2000): 238.

31. Dermot Keogh, "Irish Neutrality and the First Application for Membership of the EEC, 1961–3," in *Irish Foreign Policy, 1919–66: From Independence to Internationalism*, ed. M. Kennedy and J. M. Skelly (Dublin: Four Courts Press, 2000): 266.

32. Karin Gilland, "Ireland: Neutrality and the International Use of Force," in *Public Opinion and the International Use of Force*, ed. Philip Everts and Pierangelo Isernia (New York: Routledge, 2001): 141–162.

33. Doherty, *Ireland, Neutrality and European Security Integration*: 235–236.

34. Department of Foreign Affairs, available at http://foreignaffairs.gov.ie.

35. Ibid.

36. Ibid.

37. Jesse, "Choosing to Go It Alone": 12–13.

38. Graham, *Ethics and International Relations*: 11–13.

39. Neville Wylie, "Switzerland: A Neutral of Distinction?" in *European Neutrals and Non-Belligerents during the Second World War*, ed. Neville Wylie (Cambridge, UK: Cambridge University Press, 2002): 1–2.

40. Keatinge, *A Singular Stance*: 7.

41. Wylie, "Switzerland": 2–3.

42. Stephen D. Krasner, "State Power and the Structure of International Trade," *World Politics* 28 (1976): 317–347.

43. Arthur A. Stein, "Coordination and Collaboration: Regimes in an Anarchic World," in *International Regimes*, ed. Stephen D. Krasner (Ithaca, NY: Cornell University Press, 1983).

44. Keatinge, *A Singular Stance*: 42.

45. Keatinge, *A Singular Stance*: 33–56.

46. Ben Tonra, *The Europeanisation of National Foreign Policy: Dutch, Danish and Irish Foreign Policy in the European Union* (Aldershot, UK: Ashgate, 2001): 118.

47. Stockholm International Peace Research Institute (SIPRI); available at www .sipri.org/.

48. Department of Defence, "Defence Forces Annual Report (DFAR)" (2009); available at www.defence.ie.

49. Keatinge, *A Singular Stance*: 72–74.

50. Gilland, "Ireland": 141.

51. Karsh, *Neutrality and Small States*: 169.

52. Keatinge, *A Singular Stance*: 46–47.

53. Doherty, *Ireland, Neutrality and European Security Integration*: 16.

54. Conor O'Loughlin, "Irish Foreign Policy during World War II: A Test for Realist Theories of Foreign Policy," *Irish Studies in International Affairs* 19 (2008): 117.

55. O'Halpin, *Defending Ireland*: 290.

56. Ibid.: 302.

57. Keatinge, *A Singular Stance*: 75.

58. Karsh, *Neutrality and Small States*: 69.

59. Tonra, *The Europeanisation of National Foreign Policy*: 123.

60. Keatinge, *A Singular Stance*: 100.

61. Gilland, "Ireland": 149.

62. Ibid.: 150–151.

63. Ibid.: 152.

64. Karen Devine, "Stretching the IR Theoretical Spectrum on Irish Neutrality: A Critical Social Constructivist Framework," *International Political Science Review* 29 (2008): 474.

65. Devine, "Stretching the IR Theoretical Spectrum on Irish Neutrality": 480.

66. Ibid.

67. Gilland, "Ireland": 152–154.

68. Doherty, *Ireland, Neutrality and European Security Integration*: 223.

69. Pat Lyons, "Public Opinion in the Republic of Ireland—2001," *Irish Political Studies, Data Yearbook 2002*, supplement 17 (2003): 4–16.

70. Lyongs, "Public Opinion in the Republic of Ireland—2001": 9.

71. O'Halpin, "Irish Neutrality in the Second World War": 283.

72. Tonra, *The Europeanisation of National Foreign Policy*: 114.

73. Ibid.

74. Ibid.: 118.

75. Ibid.: 118–119.

76. Michael Kennedy and Joseph Morrison Skelly, "The Study of Irish Foreign Policy from Independence to Internationalism," in *Irish Foreign Policy, 1919–66: From Independence to Internationalism*, ed. M. Kennedy and J. M. Skelly (Dublin: Four Courts Press, 2000): 23.

77. Keatinge, *A Singular Stance: Irish Neutrality in the 1980s*: 102.

78. Fianna Fail actually changed position on this issue. It had originally been against Irish involvement. Doherty, *Ireland, Neutrality and European Security Integration*: 220–221.

79. Gilland, "Ireland: Neutrality and the International Use of Force": 157.

80. Ibid.: 158.

81. Keatinge, *A Singular Stance*: 108–109.

82. Tonra, *The Europeanisation of National Foreign Policy*.

83. Keatinge, *A Singular Stance*: 57.

84. Fanning, "*Raison d'Etat* and the Evolution of Irish Foreign Policy": 310.

5 POWER DISPARITIES AND STRATEGIC TRADE

Domestic Consequence of U.S.–Jordan Trade
Concessions

Steven E. Lobell

A GLOBAL OR REGIONAL HEGEMON can use trade arrangements as a deliberate
policy to transform states into followers and supporters, instead of challengers. Rather than treating the secondary or tertiary state as a unitary actor,
global and regional hegemons can encourage shifts in the domestic balance of
power among competing state and societal actors.[1] I focus on the use of trade
agreements and commercial concessions, rather than political concessions.
The intent is that the domestic beneficiaries in follower states will favor accommodating and bandwagoning with the hegemon and its policies without
having to use coercive force. However, rather than acquiescing, the internal
losers and victims threatened by the hegemon's policies often balk against it.
Domestic politics (explanatory framework 3) best explains the differing responses to the hegemon.

In the case of Jordan, through the creation of Qualified Industrial Zones
(1996), the U.S.–Jordan Free Trade Agreement (2001), and International Monetary Fund (IMF) and World Bank programs, the United States deliberately
set out to strengthen outward-oriented state and societal leaders. The intent
was to strengthen the Crown and to increase the size of the internationalists'
win-set in order to assist the Palace in its domestic and international realignment toward the West, commercial liberalization, political democratization
(renewal of Parliament), and normalization of relations with Israel, as well
as to balance domestic opposition. One real danger of this policy was that it
ignited nationalists, anti-Americanism, and Islamists to push the government
to pursue balking against the United States (and Israel).

INDUCING SHIFTS TO THE DOMESTIC BALANCE
OF POWER

Diverse authors highlight the ability of a global or regional hegemon to use trade concessions and inducements to alter the incentive structure in another state in order to change its foreign and domestic policy; unilateral changes in the hegemon's commercial policies can trigger changes in states abroad. For Rawi Abdelal and Jonathan Kirshner, the foreign economic policy of a great power can affect another state's domestic political competition.[2] In asymmetrical power relationships, the more powerful state makes economic sacrifices to alter the domestic political interests in other societies to enhance internal support for international agreements. This is possible because different domestic actors in the target state have competing positions of what is in their state's best interest. The outcome, according to Abdelal and Kirshner, is that the smaller state's policies will "converge towards that of the larger" power.[3]

For Scott James and David Lake, an economic hegemon can use its market power, and specifically changes in its own domestic or foreign trade policy, to influence indirectly the trade practices of other states. First, by unilaterally lowering tariffs on its own products, factors, or sectors, the hegemon can alter the societal incentives abroad. Second, these opportunities will lead to a shift in the domestic balance of political power among inward and outward firms, sectors, and factors and thereby favor the other country's free trade bloc. Finally, the newly empowered actors will mobilize to lobby the government for trade liberalization at home and abroad. For the hegemon, this is an "invisible hand" strategy. As they assert, "Once set in motion . . . the process is automatic and hidden from view by the veil of market forces."[4]

A number of authors emphasize the use of trade concessions and inducements to target specific groups with the intent of boosting their power and position to reorient a secondary state's domestic and foreign policy. According to William Long and Scott Kastner, the domestic targets are internationalist economic interests who gain from international trade.[5] For Lars Skålnes, states in need of allies and supporters will offer favorable discriminatory foreign economic policies to the target country. Foreign beneficiaries will have a vested stake in closer military and economic relations with the initiating country.[6] Similarly, for Paul Papayoanou, economic interdependence generates domestic economic interests that affect a leader's capacity to mobilize resources.[7] The more extensive the commercial and financial ties between states, the easier it is for political leaders to mobilize domestic support for an ally, and the more credible the counterbalancing alliance in the view of potential challengers.

Foreign Policy Executive

A hegemon can use economic statecraft both at home and abroad, and in particular trade agreements and concessions, to enable a favorable foreign policy coalition in other states or disable an unfavorable coalition by driving a wedge between state leaders and societal elites. In opening up the black box of the state, I distinguish the foreign policy executive (FPE) from other government leaders.[8] The FPE comprises the head of the government and the ministers and officials responsible for making foreign and security policy. The FPE occupy critical positions in an administration and are the "authoritative foreign policymaker."[9] In addition to the president or prime minister, the FPE include elected politicians, bureaucratic chiefs, and tenured officials. These individuals, as Thomas Christensen notes, "are more likely than average citizens to be concerned with the long-term security of the nation."[10] They also possess private information and a monopoly on intelligence about foreign countries. In focusing on the FPE I do not distinguish among political systems, though there is no doubt that they offer different political access.

Internationalists and Nationalists

Within the state, I distinguish between two broad and log-rolled societal coalitions: *internationalists* and *nationalists*. Unlike the FPE, economic elites are primarily concerned about maximizing their firm's, factor's, or sector's income and relative wealth rather than maximizing the state's national security. The internationalist coalition is defined as the internationally competitive sectors plus their outward-oriented supporters. These supporters have overseas investments or interests, benefit from international economic exposure, or have strong international ties. Supporters favor a grand strategy that entails heightened involvement in the international system, and they prosper from greater economic, political, and military engagement in the international system.[11] Supporters require coordinating and collaborating with other governments and business cohorts on matters of international commerce, finance, and security policy. Constituents include fiscal conservatives, export-oriented industries, large banking and financial services, liquid asset holders, skilled labor, and finance–oriented government bureaucracies.[12]

The nationalist coalition is defined as the noninternationally competitive sectors and domestic-oriented supporters.[13] They have few foreign assets,

sales, and links, and they compete with foreign imports. Nationalists will contest calls for greater international engagement because it undermines their
constituents' domestic power and position. Nationalists oppose the costs and
risks of internationalism and favor limiting foreign involvement by restricting
military spending to defense of the homeland, curbing foreign aid, and rejecting overseas commitments and foreign entanglements.[14] Supporters include
parochial and confessionalist groups, inefficient industry and agriculture,
import-substituting manufacturing, labor-intensive industry, public sector
managers and workers, and state-owned enterprises.

The advantage of disaggregating the state rather than treating it as a unitary actor is that it is possible to identify state and societal leaders who will
acquiesce and bandwagon with the hegemon's policies and those who will
oppose and adopt strategies of balking against it. Concessions and inducements or a hard-line stance by the hegemon can: (1) strengthen the hand of
moderates/internationalists (or hardliners/nationalists) at the helm of the
government, who are engaged in power struggles with hardliners/national-
ists (or moderates/internationalists) for leadership; and (2) increase the size
of the moderates/internationalists' or hardliners/nationalists' domestic win-
set or domestic base of support. A follower's large domestic win-set/base of
support is important to assist the leadership in implementing their desired
foreign (and domestic) policy agenda.[15]

Some of the commercial strategies that a hegemon can use to boost the
power and improve the position of the internationalists within the follower
state include increasing trade, economic growth abroad, and export opportunities; helping to make previously noninternationally competitive sectors
in the target state more internationally competitive; benefiting domestic sectors that use foreign inputs intensively, thereby making them more efficient in
the home market (and abroad too); weakening domestic firms that produce
the input and firms that compete with users of the imported input; and uniting both nationalist and internationalist sectors in favor of a foreign policy of
market-sharing schemes in third markets and managed international trade
over the alternative of foreign expansion and a closed autarchic system. A
hard-line policy can have the opposite impact and can empower the nationalists.

There are several dangers from concessions that can lead states to balk
against the hegemon. First, if the hegemon adopts an accommodative foreign policy with the intent of enhancing the more moderate elements in the

target power, foreign state leaders might interpret a softer stance as a sign of weakness and concessions and thereby prompt them to adopt a harder stance. Second, even if the hegemon can strengthen moderate elements they might not have access to state leaders or be able to influence the policies of state leaders. Worse, the moderates might be viewed with suspicion and persecuted as fifth-column agents by the hard-liners. Third, engaging the state in trade agreements with the intent of enhancing moderate societal elements will concomitantly strengthen the economic (and military) power of a challenger.

Finally, attempts to strengthen moderates might rally hard-liners to balk against the moderate opposition and the hegemon. As discussed in the Introduction, balking entails ignoring or refusing the hegemon's demands. Hard-line nationalists might seize on foreign engagement as an opportunity to weaken and stifle the opposing moderate internationalist bloc.

JORDAN: THE DOMESTIC DISTRIBUTIONAL CONSEQUENCES OF QIZS AND THE FTA

In the 1980s, Jordan faced many economic difficulties, including the dwindling of Arab and Gulf aid transfers and foreign remittances (due to changes in the regional oil economy, the 1979 Iranian revolution, and the 1980 Iraqi invasion of Iran). The result was that it suffered from a severe and destabilizing national debt crisis (twice its GDP), devaluation of the dinar, rising inflation, and growing unemployment.

In 1988, to restore its economy, the Jordanian government entered into a structural adjustment agreement with the IMF to restructure its debt payment schedule. In return for IMF austerity program and World Bank loans, Jordan agreed to economic reforms, cuts in government spending and subsidies, reductions in tariffs and nontariff barriers, and tax increases to boost government revenues. In 1989, the cut in subsidies on basic commodities to government and public sector workers led to rapid price increases of bread and dairy products and sparked "bread riots" by the king's trans-Jordanian constituency. (In 1996, bread riots again erupted among trans-Jordanians in southern cities when the government announced another round of cuts in subsidies following IMF austerity plans.)

Following the Iraqi invasion of Kuwait in August 1990, the U.N. Security Council passed resolution 661, which imposed economic trade sanctions against Iraq (Jordan's most important export destination). U.N. trade sanctions harmed Jordan's economy due to the loss of trade and markets; the decline of aid, grants, and low-interest loans; and the reduction in Jordan's transit trade in agriculture and industry. Jordan looked to other avenues for economic growth.

In 1991, during the First Gulf War, which followed Iraq's invasion of Kuwait, Jordan sided with Iraq, its longtime ally, against the U.S.-led coalition forces. While never a challenger, the United States subsequently used trade agreements, rather than political concessions alone, to strengthen the Crown and the internationalist bloc in Jordan to assist the Palace in its strategic realignment toward the West, commercial liberalization (IMF and World Bank structural adjustment program), political democratization (renewal of Parliament), normalization of relations with Israel, and to balance against domestic primary threats.[16] One danger of this policy is that it elicited the domestic opposition to push the Palace and domestic moderates to balk against the United States (and Israel) by igniting a nationalist, anti-U.S., and Islamist reaction.

In 1996, two years after the Jordan–Israel peace treaty, the United States established Qualified Industrial Zones (QIZs).[17] For Jordanian goods to enter the United States duty free (the relationship was nonreciprocal), two conditions were essential: The product had to be produced in a QIZ that by definition encompassed portions of territory of both Jordan and Israel, and at least 8 percent of the appraised value of any product had to come from Israeli sources.[18]

In 1999, with King Abdullah II's ascension to the throne, the United States and the King took steps to link further Jordan to the global economy. In 2001, superseding the QIZs, the U.S.–Jordan Free Trade Agreement was signed into law, granting Jordan unfettered access to the world's largest economy. Exports to the United States rose from around $16 million in 1998 to $670 million in 2003, with a total of around $3 billion in annual exports. The QIZs remain economically significant because full tariff elimination will not take place until 2012. One significant change is that the FTA removed provisions requiring Israeli contribution in the final product.

BANDWAGONING AND ACCOMMODATION: THE INTERNATIONALIST BLOC

The IMF and World Bank structural adjustment programs, the QIZs, and the FTA encouraged the acceleration of economic liberalization in Jordan. The outward-oriented sectors of the Jordanian business community supported and benefited from these moves, favoring fewer price controls, especially re-duced government control over commodity prices, and thereby pushing for bandwagoning with the United States (and even Israel). By the late 1990s, the business community pushed for additional reforms including privati-zation, reduced state intervention, deregulation, and bureaucratic reform of public enterprises. After King Abdullah II's ascension, he accelerated the pace of reforms. In October 2002, Abdullah II launched an effort to mobilize the country under the slogan "Jordan First."[19] Under this program, domestic socioeconomic development, economic industrialization, modernization, and political reform would take precedence over regional and foreign issues.

With U.S. financial and political support, Jordan moved to invigorate the private sector, further enlarging the domestic base of support necessary for further reforms. Policies included enacting a series of laws to strengthen the private sector, adopting Western economic norms, introducing capital to areas normally monopolized by the state, and privatizating public sectors enterprises in telecommunications, transport, and government-owned indus-try. Private sector elites recognized the importance of foreign investment for Jordan's economic development and a favorable investment climate. These outward-oriented supporters favored better economic, political, and even cul-tural relations with Israel and reached out to outward-oriented societal and government elites within Israel.[20] Internationalists supported further reduc-ing and amending laws that banned trade with Israel and the sale of land to Israel or Israelis.

These liberalization measures boosted the "new actors" in Jordan.[21] The king's pro-Western supporters include military personnel, top bureaucrats and cabinet appointees, private sector elites and Palestinian businessmen close to the palace, and a Westernized "Palace" elite. They benefited as a result of their ties with companies in the United States and Europe, government spending on defense contracts, and capital-intensive projects. The predomi-nantly trans-Jordanian army also shared the King's pro-Western orientation. The leadership in the army received its training in the West, in particular in the United States and Britain.

One tangible outcome is the emergence of a Palestinian business elite, which is young and foreign educated and willing to engage in joint ventures with foreign partners, including Israeli companies.[22] While trans-Jordanians control the public sector, Palestinians (of East Jordan background) and Palestinian-owned companies dominate the private sector, especially key areas of banking and commerce.[23] Due to their close ties to the Palace they are able to defy opposition from the professional associations (see the following discussion) and support the QIZs, normalization with Israel, and the FTA with the United States. While support by the king for the private sector will increase the Palestinians' political influence in Jordan, thus far they have been slow to convert their economic gains into political power.[24]

SIDE PAYMENTS AND BANDWAGONING: TRADITIONAL SUPPORTERS

Southern and rural trans-Jordanians, the Palace's historic constituency, are the swing voting bloc in Jordan. Trans-Jordanians make up an overwhelming proportion of state employees, the bureaucracy is under their control, and they manage a majority of state-owned companies. No surprise, there exists a revolving door between public companies and government officials. Trans-Jordanians dominate public sector jobs, including education, agriculture, transportation, and public works. Finally, trans-Jordanians serve as the backbone of the armed forces, the police, intelligence, and the security system.

As state and public sector employees, trans-Jordanians are harmed by the FTA and by IMF and World Bank structural adjustment programs and could have allied with the hard-liners in balking against the United States. These programs translated into the elimination of subsidies, reductions in social services, and the layoff of public employees. The result was riots in 1989 and 1996 by the trans-Jordanians. Privatization and the shrinking of the state at the expense of the public sector further weakened the trans-Jordanians through unemployment, poverty, and the loss of public services. Concomitantly, trans-Jordanians recognized that these programs risk altering the distribution of societal power by boosting the Palestinians who rule the outward-oriented private sector.[25] Trans-Jordanians also fear that demographic shifts will favor the Palestinian community and thereby undermine the power of the East Bank tribal elite.

The king used economic and political "side payments" to compensate his traditional supporters for their losses and to encourage them to continue to support the Palace rather than oppose it. For instance, following Jordan's peace treaty with Israel, salaries for schoolteachers were increased (the largest group of state employees), and the military and security services were modernized with American financial assistance.[26] Initiated in 2002 (along with the Jordan First campaign), King Abdullah II's Socio-Economic Transformation

Plan (SETP) seeks to create jobs, reduce poverty, and improve the overall standard of living. The majority of the government spending targets rural areas dominated by the trans-Jordanians, while the business community benefits from privatization. The United States has directly and indirectly (through World Bank loans) funded the SETP.

The king also revived national elections in the Lower House and municipal councils, which favor trans-Jordanian loyalists or clans over party candidates, and thereby enhanced his supporters. The 1986, 1993, and 2001 election law reforms reversed the redistribution of political power. In 1993, the government changed the electoral laws to a "one person, one vote" system, thereby weakening the Islamists in the lower house of Parliament (and more broadly ideological based representatives).[27] Under the old system, individuals could vote for both clan members and ideological candidates, helping the Islamic, leftist, and pan-Arab candidates.[28] The new laws restricted citizens to one vote. As the palace predicted, voters supported members of their regional clan or tribe instead of ideological and religious candidates. The outcome was two-fold. First, leftist parties, religious, Palestinians, and Islamists candidates were undermined in their ability to win seats in the Parliament.[29] Second, rural areas dominated by trans-Jordanians and tribally based and independent candidates were overrepresented. In 2001, Abdullah added new seats and districts to the Lower House. This policy further favored southern tribally based and independent candidates (over more densely populated and Palestinian areas), and smaller trans-Jordanian clans and tribes to win greater representation.[30]

The benefit for the Crown is that through legislation the trans-Jordanian representatives control the distribution of economic rewards to loyal patrons and constituencies. As Scott Greenwood notes, following the 1993 election reforms, "The Palace could now rely on the Lower House to play a pivotal role in the distribution of patronage to its key Transjordanian constituency."[31] By devolving legislation to the Parliament and away from the Palace, the king is insulated from discontent with IMF and World Bank austerity programs; the East Bank tribes and clans use their control over Parliament to protect their local constituency.[32]

BALKING: ECONOMIC NATIONALIST BLOC

The economic nationalist bloc opposed the outward-oriented policies of the internationalist coalition and balked against the United States. Nationalists called for the cancellation of government and IMF-mandated economic austerity packages, opposed further liberalization of Jordan's economy, and rejected improved relations with the United States and especially normalization of relations with Israel. Opposing "normal" relations with Israel is the lightening rod for the opposition to broader Jordanian integration into the global economy. For instance, in 1996, a broad and log-rolled coalition of Islamists, centrists, and leftists united to oppose an Israeli trade and industrial fair to be hosted in Amman.[33] Unable to block the peace treaty, antinormalizers campaigned against full relations with Israel, and more broadly against the king and the internationalists' worldview and agenda. For antinormalization members, the QIZs and the FTA are exogenous threats to their domestic power and position.

Antinormalization members represent groups that are harmed politically, economically, socially, or culturally by an outward-oriented foreign policy. These include Islamists and especially the Muslim Brotherhood and its political party, the Islamic Action Front (IAF), ultranationalists, trade union syndicates, leftist parties and pan-Arabists (who fear being distanced from the Arab world), and trade and professional associations.[34] Opposition figures, especially Islamists, regularly won elections in professional associations, university student councils, and other civil society institutions.[35] Civil servants and workers in state-sector industries, who are also active in the professional associations, are also threatened by the QIZs, the FTA, and the IMF, World Bank, and World Trade Organization policies.

The Islamic Muslim Brotherhood and the IAF oppose both the IMF-mandated austerity plans and the normalization of relations with Israel. Another source of support for the antiglobalizers and antinormalizers comes from the professional associations, which function like guilds because membership in them is compulsory. Under threat of being marginalized to allow for the king's outward-oriented policies, Danishai Kornbluth notes that "the professional associations embarked on a stormy struggle to save their powerful role in the new emerging political system."[36] In the 1950s, the government passed legislation that required membership in the relevant association as a condition for most professionals to work in their field. The intent was to block pro-Nasserists who were threatening the regime and to allow government officials to determine what forms of political activity would be legitimate and what behaviors were proscribed. Islamists began to court the associations in the mid-1970s. By the mid-1990s they had won control of the presidency and the boards of the largest and most influential associations.

Antiglobalizers and antinormalizers have used a number of tactics to balk against and resist the United States, Israel, and the internationalist camp within Jordan. In Parliament, Islamist representatives demanded that Jordan recall its ambassador from Israel and freeze all aspects of normalization. Antinormalizers have targeted Jordanian professionals by blacklisting and expelling them from the guild—especially threatening because membership is necessary to practice a profession. The names of companies and individual normalizers, called the "List of Shame," are available on the Internet, and boycotts are publicly urged against those who work with Israel or Israelis in any context.[37]

Myth making and emotion play an important role in drumming up support for the antinormalizers, especially the threat of Israeli regional economic and political hegemony (in addition to its military hegemony). The opposition plays on the fears of Western and Zionist influence overwhelming the Arab world. They profess that Israel's economic integration in the region is a bridgehead for cosmopolitan culture at the expense of traditional Arab identity.[38] Other hyped fears include that, given Israel's economic and financial advantages, Israel's economic gains in any future regional economic integration would be far greater than those of its Arab neighbors.[39] These relative gains would allow Israel to attain political primacy in the Middle East and increased clout over the Arab world.

BANDWAGONING AND BALKING

The U.S. intent in creating QIZs and signing the U.S.–Jordan FTA was to alter indirectly the societal distribution of power and thereby strengthen the regime's support. By boosting the outward-leaning business elites and weakening the inward-oriented opposition (especially the Islamic Brotherhood and the IAF), the United States sought to assist the Palace in its domestic and international accommodation toward the West, commercial liberalization, political democratization, and normalization of relations with Israel and to counterbalance domestic primary threats.

There are many tangible results from the use of QIZs and the FTA for the United States. Since 2001, these include Jordan's active support for the "War on Terror," sharing of intelligence, training Palestinian police officers in Jordan under Lieutenant General Keith W. Dayton, allowing the United States to station troops for search and rescue missions in Jordan, and permitting U.S. warplanes to use Jordanian airspace.[40] Jordan was the only Arab country to send troops to assist in humanitarian efforts in Afghanistan. Jordanian troops also guard supply routes in Afghanistan, and experts participate in demining operations.[41] As in its role in Afghanistan, Jordan has dispatched medical and humanitarian specialists to Iraq. Jordan has also helped to train Iraqi police officers.

There are a number of shortcomings in the use of the QIZs and the FTA for Jordan. First, the expected economic dividends in creating a "New Middle East Market" have not materialized.[42] Unemployment remains high, population growth is rapid, and poverty and income disparity is growing.[43] There were popular expectations of tourism (a new source of foreign exchange), trade, foreign investment and international funding, and American (and British) debt relief and bilateral and multilateral aid on the scale of the 1978 Camp David Accords—which failed to materialize in significant amounts.[44] The 1993 Oslo Accords and the 1994 Israel–Jordan Peace Treaty also created some popular images of a BENELUX-style economic entity consisting of Israel, Jordan, and the Palestinian Authority.[45] Finally, proponents suggested that Jordan would be the Arab gateway between Israel and the Arab world.[46] Some of those who had expected the peace treaty with Israel to yield such a peace dividend have subsequently joined the ranks of the opposition. Even the QIZs, which have brought jobs to Jordan, have been exploited by Asian companies as a backdoor opportunity to gain quota and tariff-free access to the U.S. garment and textile market.[47] Many of these companies are not concerned with further developing local industries or a labor force that will remain competitive beyond the near term.

Second, the FTA and QIZs heightened intercommunal tensions between the trans-Jordanian–dominated public sector and the Palestinian-dominated private sector—both constituencies of the Crown. The Crown's balancing act includes sheltering the trans-Jordanian public sector while advancing the business community's worldview. Trans-Jordanians are swing voters who are not committed to liberalization or normalization. While the local business community has supported privatization, it is opposed by trans-Jordanians who favor subsidies, state intervention, and control over commodity prices. Thus far, trans-Jordanians have been compensated with side payments and elections. The government also suspended privatization of state industry for fear that the main buyers would be Palestinians. Trans-Jordanians will continue to fear that Palestinians will convert their economic power into political influence and thereby alter the nature of the regime.[48] The Palestinians, though, remain underrepresented in cabinet, parliament, and ministry positions.[49]

Third, in pursuing a balking strategy, nationalist leaders effectively argued that economic liberalization and normalization with Israel led the regime to retreat from political openness and thereby pushed some would-be internationalist supporters into the nationalists' camp.[50] The government increased press censorship by amending the press law, passed election law reform to cut the Islamist presence in parliament, limited permissions to hold rallies, confiscated passports to silence opposition, blocked antiliberalization and antinormalization rallies, and arrested and harassed opposition leaders and editors.[51]

CONCLUSION

In this chapter I use explanatory framework 3 to examine U.S.–Jordanian relations during and after the Cold War. I argue that the United States, as a global hegemon, used a "divide and conquer" strategy, namely one aimed at dividing the domestic power base of another state through trade agreements and concessions; while there was an existing domestic cleavage, the United States needed to facilitate strengthening the internationalist bloc. By strengthening the Palace and the outward-leaning internationalist bloc, the United States sought to assist the Crown in its domestic and international repositioning toward the West, including commercial liberalization, political democratization, normalization of relations with Israel, and the balancing of domestic opposition. Thus, within Jordan, the outward-oriented internationalist bloc favored bandwagoning and accommodating the United States (and the West).

One danger from the use of trade agreements and concessions is that they can backfire and result in balking behavior; to keep their power and position from eroding, hard-line nationalists will push their constituency to oppose the United States and domestic moderates (and one reason why the United States could not support some of the nationalist coalition).[52] This outcome is especially likely if the conditions are perceived to benefit the United States or Israel over Arab firms, investors, or citizens.[53] As this chapter shows, the economic nationalist bloc opposed these outward-oriented policies and favored balking. Specifically, they rejected government and IMF-mandated economic austerity packages, opposed further liberalization of Jordan's economy, and rebuffed improved relations with the United States and especially normalization of relations with Israel.

NOTES

Some of the material in this chapter was presented at "The Role of Business in Conflict and Peace," *Lauder School of Government, Diplomacy and Strategy*, IDC, Herzliya, Israel (June 6, 2010) and appeared in "The Second Face of American Security: The U.S.–Jordan Free Trade Agreement as Security Policy," *Comparative Strategy* 27, 1 (2008): 1–13.

1. David A. Baldwin, *Economic Statecraft* (Princeton, NJ: Princeton University Press, 1985): 41–42.

2. Rawi Abdelal and Jonathan Kirshner, "Strategy, Economic Relations, and the Definition of National Interest," *Security Studies* 9, 1–2 (1999–2000): 119–156.

3. Ibid.: 120.

4. Scott James and David A. Lake, "The Second Face of Hegemony: Britain's Repeal of the Corn Laws and the American Walker Tariff of 1846," *International Organization* 43, 1 (1989): 8.

5. William J. Long, *Economic Incentives and Bilateral Cooperation* (Ann Arbor: University of Michigan Press, 1996); Scott L. Kastner, "Does Economic Integration across the Taiwan Strait Make Military Conflict Less Likely?" *Journal of East Asian Studies* 6, 3 (2006): 319–346. Also, see Paul A. Papayoanou and Scott L. Kastner, "Sleeping with the (Potential) Enemy: Assessing the U.S. Policy of Engagement with China," *Security Studies* 9, 1 (1999): 157–187.

6. Lars S. Skalnes, *Politics, Markets, and Grand Strategy: Foreign Economic Policies as Strategic Instruments* (Ann Arbor: The University of Michigan Press, 2000).

7. Paul A. Papayoanou, *Power Ties: Economic Interdependence, Balancing, and War* (Ann Arbor: University of Michigan Press, 1999).

8. David A. Lake, *Power, Protection, and Free Trade: International Sources of U.S. Commercial Strategy* (Ithaca, NY: Cornell University Press, 1988); Norrin Ripsman, *Peacemaking by Democracies: Domestic Structure, Executive Autonomy and Peacemaking after Two World Wars* (University Park: Penn State University Press, 2002); and Steven E. Lobell, Norrin M. Ripsman, and Jeffrey W. Taliaferro, eds., *Neoclassical Realism, the State, and Foreign Policy* (Cambridge, UK: Cambridge University Press, 2009). Also see Thomas J. Christensen, *Useful Adversaries: Grand Strategy, Domestic Mobilization, and Sino-American Conflict, 1947–1958* (Princeton, NJ: Princeton University Press, 1996).

9. Lake, *Power, Protection and Free Trade*: 37.

10. Christensen, *Useful Adversaries*: 18.

11. Benjamin O. Fordham, *Building the Cold War Consensus: The Political Economy of U.S. National Security Policy, 1949–51* (Ann Arbor: University of Michigan Press, 1998): 3; Etel Solingen, *Regional Orders at Century's Dawn: Global and Domestic Influences on Grand Strategy* (Princeton, NJ: Princeton University Press, 1998): 26–29.

12. Solingen, *Regional Orders*.

13. Herman Lebovics, "'Agrarians' versus 'Industrializers' Social Conservative Resistance to Industrialism and Capitalism in Late Nineteenth Century Germany," *International Review of Social History* 12, 1 (1967): 12, 31–65.

14. Fordham, *Building the Cold War Consensus*: 3–4.

15. Jack Snyder, "International Leverage on Soviet Domestic Change," *World Politics* 42, 1 (1989): 2.

16. Scott Greenwood, "Jordan's 'New Bargain': The Political Economy of Regime Security," *Middle East Journal* 57 (Spring 2003): 248–267.

17. Robert J. Bookmiller, "Abdullah's Jordan: America's Anxious Ally," *Alternatives* 2 (Summer 2003): 177.

18. Marc Lynch, *State Interests and Public Spheres: The International Politics of Jordan's Identity* (New York: Columbia University Press, 1999).

19. Marc Lynch, "No Jordon Option," *Middle East Report Online*, June 21 (2004).

20. Avraham Sela, "Politics, Identity and Peacemaking: The Arab Discourse on Peace with Israel in the 1990s," *Israel Studies* 10 (2005): 48.

21. Oliver Wils, "Competition or Oligarchy? The Jordanian Business Elite in Historical Perspective," in *Management and International Business Issues in Jordan*, eds. Hamed El-Said and Kip Becker (New York: Haworth Press, 2001).

22. Markus E. Bouillon, "The Failure of Big Business: On the Socio-Economic Reality of the Middle East Peace Process," *Mediterranean Politics* 9 (Spring 2004): 3, 9.

23. Yitzhak Reiter, "The Palestinian-Transjordanian Rift: Economic Might and Political Power in Jordan," *Middle East Journal* 58 (Winter 2004): 1–28.

24. Ibid.

25. Glenn E. Robinson, "Defensive Democratization in Jordan," *International Journal of Middle East Studies* 30 (August 1998): 387–410.

26. Ibid.: 405.

27. Danishai Kornbluth, "Jordan and the Anti-Normalization Campaign, 1994–2001," *Terrorism and Political Violence* 14 (Autumn 2002): 83.

28. Robinson, "Defensive Democratization in Jordan."

29. Greenwood, "Jordan's New Bargain": 257–259.

30. Ibid.: 264.

31. Ibid.: 257.

32. Ibid.: 263.

33. Kornbluth, "Jordan and the Anti-Normalization Campaign."

34. Robinson, "Defensive Democratization in Jordan."

35. Lynch, *State Interests*.

36. Kornbluth, "Jordan and the Anti-Normalization Campaign": 103–104.

37. Paul L. Scham and Russell E. Lucas, "'Normalization' and 'Anti-Normalization' in Jordan: The Public Debate," *Middle East Review of International Affairs* 5 (September 2001): 141–164.

38. Kornbluth, "Jordan and the Anti-Normalization Campaign": 84; Scham and Lucas, "'Normalization' and 'Anti-Normalization'": 149.

39. Sela, "Politics, Identity and Peacemaking": 46.

40. Greenwood, "Jordan's 'New Bargain'": 264–265.

41. Robert J. Bookmiller, "Abdullah's Jordan: America's Anxious Ally," *Alternatives* 2 (2003): 178–179.

42. Lynch, *State Interests.*

43. Pete W. Moore, "The Newest Jordan: Free Trade, Peace and an Ace in the Hole," *Middle East Report Online*, June 26, 2003.

44. Russell E. Lucas, "Jordan: The Death of Normalization with Israel," *The Middle East Journal* 58 (Winter 2004): 108.

45. Sela, "Politics, Identity and Peacemaking."

46. Scham and Lucas, "Normalization and Anti-Normalization."

47. David Makovsky, "Peace Pays Off for Jordan," *Los Angeles Times*, January 31, 2003.

48. Robinson, "Defensive Democratization": 391–392.

49. Reiter, "The Palestinian–Transjordanian Rift": 74.

50. Laurie A. Brand, "The Effects of the Peace Process on Political Liberalization in Jordan," *Journal of Palestine Studies* 28 (Winter 1999): 52–67; Lucas, "Jordan": 102–105.

51. Lynch, *State Interests.*

52. Fred H. Lawson, *Why Syria Goes to War: Thirty Years of Confrontation* (Ithaca, NY: Cornell University Press, 1996).

53. Pete W. Moore and Andrew Schrank, "Commerce and Conflict: The U.S. Effort to Counter Terrorism with Trade May Backfire," *Middle East Policy* 10 (Fall 2003): 112–120; Robert Looney, "U.S. Middle East Economic Policy: Are Trade-Based Initiatives an Effective Tool in the War on Terrorism?" *Strategic Insights* 4 (January 2005).

6 COMPLY OR DEFY?

Following the Hegemon to Market

Maria Sampanis

THIS CHAPTER EXAMINES followers and hegemons in the realm of trade. The nature of the follower strategy, accommodating or opposing, may be understood along two facets: hegemonic power (strength) and the number of followers (lateralism). Reiterating the neorealist trajectory, the hegemon is at the center of the trading realm. The stronger the hegemon (that is, the closer to its peak period), the more consistently states choose to follow. The expectations for states to follow are at a high because the gains from following offer great potential. Further, the cost of resistance is too great: for example, market exclusion. Followers that support the creation of multilateral institutions likely would bandwagon, where following is the norm within the hegemonic system when economic benefits may be realized. The number of followers may be an influence because, as more potential followers do follow, there may be a perceived cost in being the one left out. For example, there was bandwagoning with the inception of institutions such as the General Agreement on Tariffs and Trade (GATT). Specialized treatment that is exclusive to club members, such as most-favored-nation status, served as a lure for membership and accommodation. These institutions, however, eventually can serve to bind the hegemon's behavior. With binding, followers continue to follow, but the rules from the institutions the hegemon created restrict or even direct the hegemon's behavior.

States may choose to oppose by balancing. This strategy suggests coordination among states that seek to oppose the hegemon. Multilateral opposition to the hegemon perhaps could manifest at the outset, with balancing against the creation of institutions that the hegemon seeks. It is more probable that the opposition appears later, at a time when a small group within the institution can buttress hegemonic initiatives. Opposition is likely to take the form of soft balancing. The strategy is opposition, but the challenge is within the rules established by the hegemonic power.

As hegemonic strength wanes, so does the consistency in following. The cost of defiance or opposition is reduced, especially because secondary states may offer a consumer market that is comparably lucrative. Multilateral settings once dominated by the hegemon eventually provide an arena where followers may "just say no." If this story holds, then in the multilateral context, followers pursued bandwagoning, binding, and soft balancing (moving from a strategy of accommodation to one of opposition). This chapter explores the multilateral aspect by examining the last three negotiation rounds of the GATT and the first of the World Trade Organization (WTO).

Bilaterally, the story differs. Followers may have accommodated all along, but the hegemon did not need to woo followers one by one. The multilateral institutional environment sufficed, particularly because accommodation was the norm. Bilateral arrangements were extra deals to reward or curry favor. As hegemonic influence wanes, there are more instances of bilateral accommodation. For this, free trade areas, bilateral investment treaties, and trade and investment framework agreements serve as examples of bilateral accommodation. As multilateral progress stalls—as it has—there will be more of these bilateral examples of accommodation. Those states who wish to follow the weakened hegemon will do so bilaterally.

The following is a discussion on the significance of multilateral and bilateral cases and how that distinction has mattered in the post–World War II period. The expectation is that strategies of opposition are more likely to be observed in a multilateral trade environment coupled with hegemonic decline, where comfort in numbers renders it easier to oppose the hegemon. This chapter argues that bilaterally followers have a greater motivation to support the hegemon because the concessions evoked from the hegemon may exceed a group benefit and be of particular interest to the follower. In multilateral settings, within an institutional context, more states will pursue opposition, but those who do wish to follow will do so bilaterally.

A HEGEMON FROM PEAK TO DESCENT

Since the inception of the GATT in 1947, there has been an institutional core to the trade regime. The fact that the International Trade Organization (ITO) never came to be is due to U.S. opposition—an opposition determined by domestic forces. The GATT incorporated many of the ITO's provisions, minus those perceived as challenging sovereignty, and came into effect as a "temporary" fix.

Like other institutions, the GATT evolved through usage. In its initial years, the United States essentially dictated agenda and outcomes, especially at the key negotiation sessions known as rounds. (The United States also requested and obtained the most waivers, such as significant exemptions in the agricultural sector.[1]) During the last three of these rounds, one each in the 1960s, 1970s, and the 1980s, the United States. gradually controlled less. There was more opposition and less accommodation in the multilateral environment, as demonstrated in the following discussion.

The Kennedy Round lasted from 1963 until 1967. The main focus was on industrial products. Tariff reduction averaging 35 percent was one of the main results from the session. Deferred to a later time were agriculture and the whole issue of obstacles to trade other than tariffs—NTBs (nontariff barriers). The example of the Kennedy Round is an indicator that while the hegemon is still at its peak, it determines goals in trade issue areas and other states bandwagon. The United States treated the other industrialized states with priority, even preference, and the lesser-developed economies did not fare as well. Tariffs on sensitive products such as steel or textiles were not reduced as much as tariffs on raw materials.[2] This rendered the negotiations palatable domestically in the United States and the secondary states. The third framework suggests that public opinion and interest groups within the secondary states prompted accommodation.

This same feature, greater reductions on tariffs of raw materials, led the less developed countries (LDCs) to export more raw materials because they could not afford the technology and additional needs for manufacturing. As a consequence, many of the tertiary states selected strategies of opposition. In 1964, the Group of 77 evolved out of the U.N. Conference on Trade and Development (UNCTAD). Now numbering 130 members, the organization pledged to coordinate the economic interests of its members. This attempt at soft balancing drew attention to the elite focus of the general multilateral settings.

More glaringly, in 1974, the LDCs proposed a New International Economic Order (NIEO). The frustration after the Kennedy Round led those left out to suggest an overhaul, effectively dumping the economic structure established after World War II and replacing the old with new institutions. This agenda would favor the not fully developed economies. At the base of the proposal was the need to sustain dialogue with the developed countries, which did not share the view that the overhaul was necessary. Framework 2 suggests that the motivation of states may be to use the institutions created by the hegemon to coerce a behavioral change. Both the Group of 77 and the call for the NIEO came out of the United Nations, UNCTAD specifically. The hegemon was bound to the institutions; even if the strategy were binding, the gains were minimal for these tertiary states. Deserting the Bretton Woods arrangement and demanding a whole new order was a strategy in opposition to the hegemon and the world it created. The formation of coalitions, those larger numbers, enabled the soft balancing strategy in opposition to hegemonic leadership, but the hegemon still dominated most sectors in the international economy.

As much as the Kennedy Round had been an elitist club, the Tokyo Round (1973–1979) demonstrated that diversity had arrived in membership. The European Community (EC) demonstrated that a bloc could challenge hegemonic leadership at the GATT.[3] By the 1970s, the EC with a newly powerful economic Japan created a three-player game. The tremendous gap between the United States and its nearest competitors had diminished. European and Japanese domestic industrial interests successfully directed their trade representatives to secure industrial benefits; one area of success was in civil aircraft trade with improvement both on NTBs and reduction of tariffs. This was a sector of interest primarily to secondary followers. The EC and Japan used binding as a strategy to extract compromises from the United States. There was incredible progress on NTBs, but this and other progress reflected EC and Japanese priorities as much if not more than U.S. preferences. Even if the five new codes on NTBs were hailed as progress, the interpretation proved contentious.[4] During the Tokyo Round, interpretations varied on how to measure injury from another's subsidies before countervailing duties could be instituted. One of the codes addressed technical barriers to trade, but the language was vague and left clarification on country-of-origin labeling and phytosanitary restrictions until a later round of talks.[5] As an example of the ambiguity, the EC implemented restrictions on which hormones could be used on beef products. This hormone ban effectively barred U.S. products, and the code was used as a legal citation in the subsequent U.S. complaint. Similarly, when Japan blocked U.S. construction firms from competing for the huge project to build Kansai airport, the United States cited the code on government procurement in its complaint. The secondary states had altered what had been a hegemonically controlled environment to one where the hegemon could be bound and controlled in return, filing complaints through its institutional channels when it did not get its way.

Hegemonic decline was in effect, and the secondary states were now viable competitors. The United States was able neither to dictate the agenda nor to control the proceedings. Every point seemingly was negotiated, and the Tokyo Round was one of compromise. Increasingly, as the EC and Japan competed in sectors once controlled by U.S. companies—automotive, electronic, aeronautic, steel—subsidies came to be the new norm. The secondary states of the EC and Japan pursued opposition through binding, relying on the institutional environment to elicit concessions. The motivation for such a strategy may be drawn most clearly from explanatory framework number 2, which anticipates followers relying on institutional arenas. Additionally, the domestic factors within the EC and Japan, for example in the automotive and aircraft industries, preferred binding rather than outright balancing since it would lead to improved U.S. market access. How else can one explain voluntary export restraints?

By the 1980s, the rise of Japan and the consolidation through enlargements and economic growth of the EC restructured the game at the Uruguay Round (1986–1993). The United States no longer dominated the agenda, no longer controlled the direction of the talks. After decades of serving as the world's leading agricultural exporter, the world's food basket, the United States felt competition in agriculture and wanted to liberalize that sector. Japan and the EC agreed in principle, but interpretations and definitions were far apart. This meant that the hegemon and some secondary states were not in alignment; it was not clear that these states would follow at all. However, a grouping of secondary and tertiary states allied with the hegemon. This Cairns Group advocated addressing NTBs in agriculture, agricultural trade liberalization, improving the dispute settlement procedure under the GATT, and cultivating markets in new sectors, such as the burgeoning electronic subsectors. The Cairns Group represents support for hegemonic leadership and can be understood as a strategy of bonding. These secondary and tertiary states became strategic partners with the hegemon on the common goal of agricultural trade liberalization.

Cairns Group members included several of the world's premier agricultural exporters—Argentina, Australia, Brazil, Canada, and the United States. These states also had considerable export promotion programs that could be viewed as subsidies. Nonetheless, European support levels were higher. French farmers protested any reduction in government support programs, since French and EU support programs helped guide France to rank among the world's top food producers. EU pursuit of an opposition strategy was complicated by Germany. Its manufacturing sectors feared ramifications and pushed for an accommodation strategy.

A similar split manifested in Japan. Industries, such as the automotive, heavily dependent on exports, pressured Japan to accommodate in order to preserve access to the U.S. market. Japanese agricultural interests, however, carried incredible influence, and the sector was notoriously protected. Japan argued food security and cultural preservation as justification against liberalizing agricultural trade, especially rice. Amazingly, only one-third of its rice producers were full-time farmers.[6] Kobe beef producers argued that Japanese intestines could not digest U.S. beef. With such pressure, Japan pursued a strategy of opposition against the United States in 1979, in 1984, and again in 1988, over beef and citrus quotas. Eventually, however, the Japanese Ministry for International Trade (MITI) complied with international demands and opened the Japanese domestic market to rice, beef, and citrus. MITI's principal motivation was to ensure continued access to foreign markets for Japanese exports in lucrative sectors such as automobiles and electronics. Japan ultimately accommodated, not due singly to hegemonic pressure but to the combined risk of losing market access to the developed and developing markets of the agricultural producers—the Cairns Group.

This split within secondary states and particularly within the EC bloc reflects the influence that domestic interests may play (explanatory framework 3). Ultimately, the split results in partial accommodation and partial opposition. Secondary and tertiary states supported the creation of the WTO, but these same states opposed the hegemon on other points. Liberalization in sectors such as agriculture remains elusive. Domestic pressures, such as on rice production in Japan or in Europe with the argument of "rurification" to maintain the green belt, stall further accommodation. The opposition strategy during the Uruguay Round was soft balancing, the followers who pursued the opposition were both secondary and tertiary states, but not all GATT members of those categories.

In November 2001, ministers inaugurated what was to be a round of multilateral talks. The Doha Development Agenda, named after the city in which the ministerial declaration was made, boldly listed an agenda addressing agriculture, services, and the challenges facing many tertiary states in the implementation of GATT/WTO rules. These potential followers had much greater involvement from the start than they had with the last round, Uruguay.

Two years later in September 2003, another ministerial meeting, this time in Cancun, Mexico, had the task of determining how to proceed and get the talks back on track. The meeting was unsuccessful. Even the agricultural negotiations could not advance past deep fissures on support for production of commodities such as cotton. No progress was realized on agriculture or any of the "Singapore Issues" until the following July in Geneva. Then, the General Council issued a series of decisions to move the talks forward.

Still, not much moved forward. In December 2005, a ministerial meeting in Hong Kong had the task of determining the progress since the Geneva July Package, eighteen months earlier. There was not much to report. All along, the main task for negotiators was to render the agenda more precise to draft language that could be approved by the members. In Hong Kong, the ministers managed to refine negotiation goals, boosting optimism about progress. Perhaps most importantly, the deadline was extended through 2006 from the original Doha-determined January 1, 2005. Nonetheless, the General Council voted to suspend the Doha Round at the end of July in 2006.

In every year since the end of 2006, there has been talk of restarting the trade rounds again. Then-U.S. Trade Representative Susan Schwab pitched to other trade ministers at the World Economic Forum in 2007 that the future can bring increased trade but that increased trade starts with reductions in tariffs and other barriers in agriculture, manufactured goods, and services.[7] In December 2009, the pitch was the same; the response was "political energy."[8] Andrés Velasco, the chair of the conference and Chile's finance minister, discussed the recognition that the round needs to be concluded. He continued, "There was strong convergence on the importance of trade and the Doha Round . . . and particular attention should be paid to issues of importance to developing countries."[9]

The hegemon–tertiary divide in multilateral trade negotiations experienced some amelioration during the Uruguay Round. This rapprochement is neither consistent nor certain. In some areas, many of the tertiary states share interests. In other sectors, however, they formed their own coalitions, such as the African Group and the Least-Developed Countries Group. A major goal of the Doha Agenda is to enable developing countries to participate more fully and gainfully in the international marketplace. Specific negotiation objectives ranged from continued efforts to liberalize agriculture to gradually eliminating quotas on tertiary exports of textiles and clothing. Additionally, developing countries still face hurdles both in the competitive environment of trade and in domestic adjustments as part of the implementation of WTO rules. The session on agricultural negotiations commenced with some of the same players still trying to liberalize agricultural trade: Canada and Australia pitched domestic support, the United States emphasized market access, and Korea, Argentina, and Uruguay focused on the new technical formula for determining the extent of support in the sector.[10] The followers here are again a mix of secondary and tertiary states, as in the Uruguay Round. At least with agricultural liberalization, bonding continues with support for hegemonic leadership.

EVIDENCE OF HEGEMONIC WANE: THE INCREASE IN BILATERAL TRADE AGREEMENTS

As hegemony wanes, followers may shift their strategies to seek extra gains from accommodating the hegemon. Bilateral trade agreements are the natural mechanism by which followers can lock in greater gains for themselves vis-à-vis other followers of the same hegemon. Followers may accommodate bilaterally with the negotiation of bilateral investment treaties, trade and investment framework agreements, and of course free trade areas. There has been an increase in the number of such arrangements as multilateral economic efforts stall.

Bilateral investment treaties (BITs) are designed to protect U.S. investors. Before the beginning rapprochement of North–South trade relations in the 1980s, restrictions in many potential trade partner states made hegemonic investment difficult, to say the least. Risk was high; expropriation was common. Company investors were required to comply with a series of conditions, including local content and labor formulas. There was no real recourse for dispute settlement, and frequently the investment was lost. As these tertiary states began to relax investment restrictions, more investment capital flowed from the hegemon and secondary states, but there remained obstacles. Without guarantees, investment risk remained high.

Multilaterally, opposition strategies included soft balancing with calls for a revamping of the institutions. Today, working within the institutions may stall, but many of these tertiary states pursue BITs as means of luring investment and development. BITs are treaties subject to U.S. Senate ratification like other treaties. The United States has entered into thirty-nine of these agreements that are already in force, with seven more negotiated. The gains for the United States are clear: improved climate for U.S. investment interests. But what is the advantage for the followers? The agreements are reciprocal, which means that these same guarantees are available to investment interest from within the partners. An incentive is inferred: foreign direct investment. All are emerging or developing economies, some in transition.

Trade and investment framework agreements (TIFAs) frequently serve as precursors to more integrated arrangements, such as free-trade agreements. For example, a 1995 TIFA with Morocco paved the course for the eventual U.S.–Morocco Free Trade Agreement; Bahrain and Jordan (as discussed in Chapter 5) experienced similar progression. TIFAs address specific area obstacles to improve the environment for bilateral trade, including resolving outstanding disputes. Standard provisions of the agreement include the creation of a council to address and ameliorate obstacles to trade and investment between the two states. In a specific case, Mauritius and the United States created a TIFA to promote and expand bilateral trade. The council created by the TIFA meets to assess implementation and demonstrate to business that the dialogue continues. TIFAs also facilitate and promote private sector participation by consulting with business to identify problems and challenges that should be addressed. This directly involves domestic interests, consulted by the council overseeing the bilateral trade. Essentially, "TIFAs are an important rung on the ladder to an FTA."[11]

For Mauritius, an advantage is an improved climate in trade; the same may be said for the United States. The United States exports machinery, precious stones in the form of jewelry, and plastics. Mauritius exports apparel and precious stones, such as diamonds. An additional incentive for the United States is to improve its position in Africa. As Deputy USTR Karan Bhatia stated, "I'm pleased . . . to stimulate our relationship with key African trading partners."[12] For Mauritius, an additional incentive may be some of the agenda items discussed by the TIFA council: deeper bilateral relationship, WTO cooperation, and implementation of the African Growth and Opportunity Act.[13] As with the BITs, most of the followers are emerging or developing economies, some in transition.

Bilateral free-trade agreements (FTA) have launched regional FTAs, most famously the Canadian agreement that served as the springboard for the North American Free Trade Agreement (NAFTA). FTAs with Chile and Singapore went into effect on January 1, 2004. One year later, a FTA with Australia went into effect, followed by a FTA with Central America and the Dominican Republic (CAFTA). The benefit from these arrangements is mutual, with sizeable gains in the agriculture and manufacturing sectors. In the first year with Chile and Singapore, U.S. exports to those markets increased by $4 billion, and exports reached nearly that figure in just the first quarter with the deal with Australia. These increases are more apparent in terms of shares: U.S. exports to Chile increased by 33.5 percent that first year, with high-end machinery exports experiencing gains of 33 percent and vehicles and parts by 36 percent. U.S. manufacturer Caterpillar doubled its exports to Chile in one year.[14] The benefit for Chile also is measurable. Its exports to the United States have increased overall, abetted by a U.S. tariff elimination on 95 percent of Chilean exports into the U.S. market. Agricultural products have a complementarity due to different growing seasons between the northern and southern hemispheres. Consequently, both agricultural sectors have realized gains. In the first quarter of 2009, Chile's export picture to the United States was among its most diverse. About half was processed goods, based on natural resources, 39.6 percent natural resources, and 10.4 percent industrial products—valuing $1.17 billion for that quarter alone.[15]

Similarly, U.S. gains in exports to Singapore measured an 18.4 percent, or $19.6 billion from 2003. With Australia, many of the most startling increases were in agricultural products, such as pork exports, which increased by 885 percent. Overall agricultural increases were about 20 percent. Though these figures demonstrate gains for the United States, the greatest advantage may be the adjustments in the U.S. trade balance: Each of these cases is a trade surplus for the United States and improved the overall U.S. trade deficit.[16] From the follower perspective, the gains are U.S. market access. Overall, U.S. imports from Singapore have increased by 4.9 percent since 2003, the year before the FTA, valuing $15.9 billion in 2008.[17] For Australia, the increase in exports to the United States since from pre-FTA (2004) is 40.3 percent.[18]

Interestingly, the FTAs with Singapore and Australia are so well received in those states that both are on board for another link with the hegemon. In September 2008, the United States expressed its interest in the Pacific Strategic Economic Partnership agreement. This would be a high-standard FTA among Singapore, Chile, New Zealand, and Brunei Darussalam. Shortly after the U.S. decision to join the negotiations, Australia, Peru, and Vietnam indicated their interest in participating as well. Secondary and tertiary states are pursuing these agreements with the hegemon.[19]

CAFTA was signed on August 2, 2005, and linked the United States with six partners, though implementation will be staggered as each of the six meets its domestic goals requisite for the agreement. El Salvador and the United States entered into the FTA on March 1, 2006; with Honduras and Nicaragua on April 1, 2006; and Guatemala on July 1, 2006. The region offers a larger U.S. export market than Russia, India, and Indonesia combined. For the followers, most exports into the U.S. market already entered duty free under the Caribbean Basin Initiative (CBI) or other preferential programs.[20] The motivation, therefore, is unclear, other than some overall improvement and better positioning for the bigger goal of a Free Trade of the Americas.

The examples explored in the preceding paragraphs are but a handful of the potential case studies, but a trend emerges: the United States continues its pursuit of vertical arrangements, and a by-product of this "sequential bilateralism" could be to infuse the U.S. bargaining position with greater clout at multilateral negotiations.

POSSIBLE FOLLOWER MOTIVATIONS

It would be intuitive to simplify this section as surmising that the primary motivation for the followers is self-interest. There must be some gain, some incentive, for the followers to enter into the arrangements examined in the previous section. But also of consideration is that following the United States may be a *strategy of nonsupport* of another actor. For example, in agriculture, in spite of the programs and supports enjoyed by some sectors within the U.S. industry, the United States in the aggregate remains export oriented. Thus, its interest aligns with other agricultural producers who are also export oriented. This shared view enabled the formation of the Cairns Group in the 1980s to stand as a bloc against the subsidization and protection levels of the EU and Japan. This coalition celebrated its twenty-fifth anniversary in September 2010. Typically, one may anticipate a short duration for coalitions based on negotiation strategy, but this one exceeded those expectations. The Cairns Group continues its efforts to liberalize agricultural trade, though admittedly its targets run the gamut from big to small.

Today, many of those states following the United States into a series of bilateral arrangements share a commitment to agricultural trade liberalization, for example, and thus may *share strategy*. With progress stalled at the multilateral talks, it could be a shared strategy to create a domino effect, one deal at a time.

Other partners may offer some similar advantages, but the followers entering bilateral—and eventual regional—arrangements with the United States do so for a reason. Domestic motivations likely vary across cases, but it is expected that one pattern may emerge: The arrangements with the United States offer improvement for several sectors. This improvement typically includes U.S. market access, with reciprocity and cooperation in related areas, rendering this tactic a *shared benefit strategy*. The inference is that linking with the U.S. economy remains most desirable. If this is so, then the limitations on hegemony may not be realized in an arena such as trade where there are still fruitful gains—far outweighing costs—to be made from direct association and commitment with the hegemon, albeit a declining one.

One suggested trend is that the United States pursues its goals BIT by BIT, if you will, in the pursuit of establishing footholds in potential markets of tomorrow. For those following, incentives include the obvious access to the U.S. market and U.S. investment—historically a double-edged sword. There are likely additional gains, perhaps not immediately realized. For the small, usually considered weak and irrelevant, there is the opportunity to play among the big. The increased attention and support expressed by the United States toward tertiary states over the last three GATT rounds is an indicator of this shift in focus. This shifted attention continues; for the small, the lure may be the opportunity finally to get into the game.

CONCLUSION

Why do followers follow? Material power distribution matters. At the time of peak U.S. hegemonic influence, a period when the distribution of economic power was concentrated in the hegemon, there was bandwagoning. This accommodation enabled the creation of the GATT and provided the hegemon autonomy and leverage. As that influence waned, there was soft balancing within the multilateral context as challengers grew in economic influence. Soft balancing manifested by the 1970s in a larger-numbered grouping calling for more equitable treatment of tertiary states, particularly in response to exclusion by an inner elite of the more dominant states. The opposition also manifested later in a challenge by secondary states within the institutional arena. From the Kennedy Round of the 1960s, these states became more involved in goal setting; by the 1970s and the Tokyo Round, they were in a position to challenge the hegemon. This change parallels a shift in the material power distribution as the preeminence of the hegemon wanes and the hegemon faces real opposition. Here, the story becomes more interesting as hegemonic behavior becomes more overt.

Institutions matter too. There was binding during the 1970s and the Tokyo Round. Keeping the United States playing by the institutional rules was the binding strategy, the opposition tendencies beginning to emerge. To the extent that domestic politics determine trade policy, the EC and Japan presented mixed strategies—accommodation and opposition—as export interests competed with protectionist ones. Soft balancing, a strategy of opposition, was a tactic employed by some secondary and tertiary states in the Uruguay and Doha Rounds. The U.S. commitment to both of these negotiation sessions has been stalwart, but progress in both examples was tedious. One by-product has been an increase in bilateral and smaller grouping progress.

This observation supports the assumption that hegemonic power and commitment buttress institutional strength. Further investigation may revisit the familiar trajectory of whether institutions can survive without the hegemonic power that created them. It is not yet clear whether the trigger is the hegemon's declining ability to influence the institution as a whole or the institution's declining viability. What is argued here is that, from the perspective of the followers, it is of greater benefit to seek bilateral options with the hegemon. Long-term commitment to an institution may be challenged as economic competition becomes the new security frontier. Thus, the expectation is for greater frequency of opportunistic side deals.

Domestic interests can also direct trade policy. Export-oriented sectors, like the automotive in Japan and Germany, will pressure their governments to cede on other sectors such as agriculture, as occurred during the Uruguay Round. Increasingly, the avenue is not in the multilateral institutional sessions, but separately—though under the multilateral, institutional umbrella. Perhaps reflecting greater international exposure, domestic interests may wield greater influence in domestic policy making.

As multilateral progress stalls, those who want to pursue the deal will follow bilaterally. The listing of the numerous followers is indicative that, for many tertiary states, accommodation is the preferred course in trade. Essentially, as a hegemon declines—as the United States has—accommodation by followers in multilateral contexts becomes less likely. There is much diversity in interest, and many states are now in a position to affect the setting of goals as the gap by which the hegemon once dominated has decreased. As already mentioned with the first framework, the material power has been redistributed. Inversely, over the same period, where follower opposition increases multilaterally, it decreases bilaterally. Thus, accommodation by follower states increases bilaterally where potential followers may enjoy greater success in garnering particular goals in negotiation sessions with reduced numbers. The frameworks help to explain this, as follower motivation is more likely to be met with personalized incentives in bilateral deals. A hegemon in decline is still a hegemon after all.

NOTES

An earlier form of this chapter was presented at the annual meeting of the International Studies Association, February 28–March 3, 2007, Chicago, Illinois. I would like to thank Nancy Lapp for her helpful comments on this version.

1. For example, in 1955, citing Section 22 of U.S. trade laws, the United States successfully requested a waiver for its dairy quotas.

2. John Evans, *The Kennedy Round in American Trade Policy; The Twilight of the GATT?* (Cambridge, MA: Harvard University Press, 1971): 284; Gilbert Winham, *International Trade and the Tokyo Round Negotiation* (Princeton, NJ: Princeton University Press, 1986): 67; Maria Sampanis, *Preserving Power through Coalitions: Comparing the Grand Strategy of Britain and the United States* (Westport, CT: Praeger Publishers, 2003): 97.

3. Joseph Grieco, *Cooperation among Nations* (Ithaca, NY: Cornell University Press, 1990); Winham, *International Trade.* See also Sampanis, *Preserving Power.*

4. The NTB codes included Customs Valuation, Technical Barriers to Trade, Government Procurement, Import Licensing, and Anti-Dumping Practices.

5. Phytosanitary restrictions include, for example, dirt residue on cut flowers or treatments on agricultural products during production or preparation for shipment.

6 For the distinct views on the rice issue, see, for example, "The Politics of Rice," California Council for International Trade (CCIT), xii (Winter 1988): 4–7. The section is comprised of three articles: Bill Huffman, "Justice Denied for US Rice Producers," CCIT, xii (Winter 1988): 4, 6, 7; Maria Sampanis, "Will Japan Ever Buy California Rice?" CCIT, xii (Winter 1988): 5–6; and Tatsuro Katsuyama, "Japanese Agriculture and Rice," CCIT, xii (Winter 1988): 4–6.

7. Office of USTR, "Schwab to Press for Doha Progress at World Economic Forum," Press Release, January 24, 2007; available at www.ustr.gov/Document_Library/ Press_Releases/2007/January/Schwab_to_Press_for_Doha_Progress_at_World_ Economic_Forum.html.

8. World Trade Organization, WTO 2009 news items. December 2, 2009, "Day 3: Ministers show "political energy" for ending Doha Round"; available at www.wto.org/english/news_e/news09_e/mn09a_02dec09_e.htm.

9. Ibid.

10. World Trade Organization, "Farm Talks Start 2010 Quietly but More Substance Lies Ahead"; available at www.wto.org/english/news_e/news10_e/agng_21jan10_e.htm.

11 USTR Robert B. Zoellick, "Global Trade and the Middle East," remarks prepared for delivery to the World Economic Forum, Dead Sea, Jordan, June 23, 2003; available at www.ustr.gov/Document_Library/USTR_Speeches/2003/Global_Trade_the_Middle_East.html.

12. Deputy USTR Karan Bhatia, via digital video conference, in USTR Press Release, "United States and Mauritius Conclude Meeting to Strengthen Trade and Investment Relations," February 6, 2007; available at www.ustr.gov/Document_Library/Press_Releases/2007/February/United_States_Mauritius_Conclude_Meeting_to_Strengthen_Trade_Investment_Relations.html.

13 The African Growth and Opportunity Act (AGOA) is part of the Trade and Development Act of 2000 and designed to encourage, through real incentives, African countries to liberalize.

14. Office of the USTR, CAFTA Facts: Free Trade Agreements Are Working for America, CAFTA Policy Brief, May 26, 2005; available at www.ustr.gov/assets/Document_Library/Fact_Sheets/2005/asset_upload_file204_7872.pdf.

15. Office of the USTR, "The US–Chile Free Trade Agreement: An Early Record of Success," April 22, 2009; available at www.ustr.gov/about-us/press-office/fact-sheets/archives/2004/june/-us-chile-free-trade-agreement-early-record-suc.

16. Office of the USTR, CAFTA Facts: "Free Trade Agreements Are Working for America," CAFTA Policy Brief, May 26, 2005; available at www.ustr.gov/assets/Document_Library/Fact_Sheets/2005/asset_upload_file204_7872.pdf.

17. USTR, "Singapore," December 14, 2009; available at www.ustr.gov/countries-regions/southeast-asia-pacific/singapore.

18. USTR, "Australia, December 14, 2009; available at www.ustr.gov/countries-regions/southeast-asia-pacific/australia.

19. USTR, "Free Trade Agreements, Australia," April 24, 2009; available at www.ustr.gov/trade-agreements/free-trade-agreements/australian-fta.

20. Office the USTR, "CAFTA Briefing Book"; available at www.ustr.gov/Trade_Agreements/Bilateral/CAFTA/Briefing_Book/Section_Index.html.

7 WESTERN EUROPE, NATO, AND THE UNITED STATES
Leash Slipping, Not Leash Cutting

Galia Press-Barnathan

THIS CHAPTER ADDRESSES the dilemmas confronting, and the strategies adopted by, America's European allies in NATO in the aftermath of the end of the Cold War. Whereas NATO was created in the bipolar world of the Cold War, after the breakdown of the USSR the European partners found themselves in an alliance/security institution with the world's hegemon.

Western Europe has adopted a strategy closest to Layne's leash slipping, that is, a strategy aimed at building up their military capabilities to maximize their ability to conduct an independent foreign policy (explanatory framework 1).[1] At the same time, the European goal is not "leash cutting." They have also adopted a strategy aimed at binding the United States closer to European security (explanatory framework 2). This chapter suggests that there is an inherent tension in advancing these goals. Strategies enhancing autonomy can be interpreted as possible balancing acts, thus upsetting the hegemon or conversely convincing the hegemon it is no longer needed. This may then be counterproductive if one wants the hegemon's continued security involvement in regional security affairs. The unique institutional setting of NATO allows Western European states to try to advance both strategies and to minimize this built-in tension between them. The only way for small states to achieve these goals is via regional cooperation. Only such cooperation can allow them to develop significant security capabilities that would allow them both to deal independently, if necessary, with regional security threats and to offer meaningful burden sharing to the hegemon by creating some form of a division of labor with it.

Reviewing the European capacity to operate collectively in the security realm reveals a significant enhancement of regional cooperation capabilities since the early 1990s.[2] I argue that the most important underlying factor leading to these changes was the systemic shift to unipolarity. As described in Chapter 1, hegemony has several dimensions: material, motivational, and relational. The argument here is that the *material* change in global power distribution (the shift to "unipolarity") has led to changes in the dynamics of the *relations* between the United States and its European allies. These changes stem in part from changes (or at least perceived changes) in the U.S. *motivation* to lead anytime, anyplace. The systemic shift led to a greater divergence and fluctuation in allied threat perceptions. Shift in material capabilities has also led to a greater impact of domestic factors on the shaping of national threat perceptions and national policies, compared to the bipolar era (explanatory framework 3). This, in turn, helps to explain part of the divergence of European and American threat perceptions. The strategies chosen by the Europeans were meant to offer them the best possible tools to deal over time with such fluctuations in threat perceptions.

In what follows I first briefly establish my basic observation that European states have invested in regional security cooperation capabilities. Then I explain in greater detail the impact of the shift to unipolarity on European allies and the logic behind the strategies they have chosen to pursue vis-à-vis the United States. I then demonstrate how this logic has played out since 1991. Finally, I briefly explore the arguments regarding the relative importance of regional and domestic factors in shaping the European response to U.S. hegemony, as well as the possible impact of normative factors.

THE POST–COLD WAR BUILDUP OF EUROPEAN SECURITY COOPERATION: ACHIEVEMENTS AND LIMITATIONS

Since the early 1990s we have witnessed an increased effort within Europe to invest in security cooperation. Throughout the Cold War era, the elaborate regional cooperation on the economic front has not been paralleled by such cooperation on the military-security front, with a few exceptions. In 1992, the new Maastricht Treaty also created, for the first time, a European security institution, as it revived the old Western European Union (WEU). It created the concept of a Common Foreign and Security Policy (CFSP), and the Amsterdam Treaty (1997) created the post of the high representative of the CFSP. In the Helsinki summit (1999) it was agreed to create a European Rapid Reaction Force (RRF) of 60,000 soldiers. The vague notion of a European Security and Defense Policy (ESDP) gradually gained at least an institutional life, with the establishment of the EU Military Committee, an EU military staff, meetings of defense ministers, Political and Security Committee, and politico-military structures in the Council Secretariat. This political-military structure was formally approved at the Nice Summit in 2000.[3] Earlier, in 1995 the European pillar within NATO was enhanced with the creation of the Combined Joint Task Force (CJTF) concept, which enabled independent European military action without the United States, using NATO assets. This formula of "separable but not separate" forces in many ways epitomized the optimal European strategy. In 2003, however, the EU states agreed to construct a military planning capability independent of NATO. Since then the EU has been involved in several independent military missions in Macedonia, Bosnia, and Congo, as well as police or rule-of-law missions in these places and also in Iraq (2005) and Georgia (2004). European security cooperation increased also in the related fields of joint arms production and coordinated use of economic sanctions.[4]

Compared to developments in these fields during the Cold War, these are quite remarkable. However, at the same time, they are more limited than it may appear, and several scholars and practitioners are skeptical with regard to their overall military impact. The concept of a 60,000 troop RRF of 1999 gave way by the time of the Headline Goal 2010 to the concept of battle groups, that is, units of 1,500 troops, which is less ambitious than the large rapid-reaction force, and the EU has been reluctant to deploy these battle groups, even while declaring that they were already fully operational in January 2007. Funds for defense spending remain very scarce in Europe, where military spending in 2005 was decreasing rather than increasing, and of the large number of active service personnel (2 million) of the twenty-seven member states, only 30 percent could actually operate outside Europe due to either legal restrictions or inadequate training. The elaborate institutional structure surrounding the ESDP has also remained strictly intergovernmental, thus limiting the ability to conduct serious joint operations of the EU force.[5] Furthermore, beyond the institutional structure that can facilitate joint action, there is great skepticism about the political will of European states to threaten and, if necessary, to undertake military action. Current European rhetoric only mentions "crisis management" and "conflict prevention," rather than "power projection." There is no indication that these motivations are likely to change dramatically.[6]

The difficulty of characterizing this overall European response in part reflects the lack of consensus among Europe's main actors themselves about what it is that Europe should do vis-à-vis the United States. But even more so, it reflects a European strategy aimed at combining creatively several strategic responses to U.S. hegemony. The options facing Europe are unique due to the preexistence of a strong multilateral alliance with the United States, already institutionalized during the Cold War. The developments in European security capabilities since the early 1990s aimed at enhancing independent European capabilities and the European pillar within NATO. This combination allowed the Europeans to avoid difficult costly choices between alternative strategies and helped to mitigate negative U.S. reactions. As events in Kosovo proved to the Europeans, there is still no real alternative to U.S. military power, so reliance on the United States is still necessary, especially in dealing with larger potential threats like Russia. Furthermore, NATO still allows the Europeans to pass the buck to the United States whenever feasible. The preexisting institutional arrangements also mitigate future potential threats from the United States itself, while enjoying the benefits of being aligned with the strongest state in the system. Translating this into the various types of responses to hegemony, we find binding the hegemon, bandwagoning with the hegemon when attractive (though it is a bit awkward to bandwagon with an actor you are already in an alliance with), and at the same time leash slipping (increasing autonomy without risking the breakdown of the preexisting alliance, "the leash").

But, more concretely, what is the meaning of the increased efforts of building regional security cooperation? By developing enhanced regional security capabilities, the Europeans are able to achieve several interrelated goals. They are able to prepare for a possible U.S. retreat from Europe, which would force them to deal independently with regional security threats. In the aftermath of Kosovo, many Europeans have wondered whether the United States would actually get militarily involved in any future crisis of that sort. Such concerns have increased following the "War on Terror" and the apparent shift in American focus from Europe to Asia and the Middle East. They are also able to increase the potential value of European burden sharing with the United States. The EU collectively can offer a more significant contribution than any single European state, even the large ones. One good example of this can be found in the operations of the International Security Assistance Force (ISAF) in Afghanistan. While the United States has sent over 45,000 troops to the force,

Europe has sent a little over 33,000 troops, that is, about 40 percent of the force. In recent years the United States has grown more and more dependent on NATO cooperation to sustain its operations in Afghanistan.[7] Such significant burden sharing, in turn, can serve two goals. First, it can reduce the risk that the United States will retreat from Europe or from NATO because European contributions are important, even in a unipolar system. Second, it can also increase the ability of the EU to exert greater influence on U.S. policies, at least within the alliance. This is a common approach in Europe today.

Can systemic material factors, the changing international power distribution, as well as regional power distribution, explain those strategies? Are domestic factors crucial here? Is the European behavior normatively driven? And finally, to what extent is the European reaction dependent on preexisting institutional arrangements within Europe and across the Atlantic? I suggest that, while this is obviously a multifaceted process, and while clearly there are differences in the reactions of specific European states, the underlying logic driving greater regional cooperation is the systemic change to unipolarity.

UNIPOLARITY, STRATEGIC UNCERTAINTY, AND DIVERGING THREAT PERCEPTIONS

Any significant systemic change is likely to increase the level of strategic uncertainty for all actors in the system and especially for smaller ones. Under bipolarity there was a relatively low level of uncertainty. Small allies could rely on the strong security commitment of their allied superpower. While superpowers' and secondary powers' interests and threat perceptions were never the same, there was still an underlying convergence and a stable set of expectations, given the dynamics of bipolar systems.[8] When scholars discussed U.S. hegemony in Western Europe during the Cold War, they pointed to these stable regional expectations regarding U.S. motivation to lead the Western camp. The shift to unipolarity (that is, U.S. relative power becoming preponderant not only on a regional but also on a global level) created a greater likelihood for divergence in threat perceptions between the hegemon and its secondary allies. Such divergence could come in several forms: Regional partners may attach greater importance to threats emanating from their region that are less strategically important for the hegemon. Conversely, the hegemon may attach a higher value to certain global threats that are of limited interest to regional partners. Under unipolarity there is greater potential for divergence on the various elements comprising an actor's threat perception (à la Walt). Differences in geostrategic concerns are likely to become accentuated. Secondary regional states are more likely to focus on regional proximate threats, whereas a hegemonic power is likely to have global interests. Finally, because there is no longer one overwhelming and unifying external threat (in the form of the USSR) uniting allies within the U.S. "pole," systemic constraints and signals are likely to be less decisive, and consequently domestic pressures and ideological differences can play a greater role in shaping alliance dynamics.[9] In other words, the strengthening of the material dimension of U.S. hegemony (the unipolar structure of the international system) created challenges for its relational dimensions.

When looking at post–Cold War Europe we can see this growing divergence. Europeans are more concerned over ethnic factionalism, migratory pressures, terrorism, transnational criminal activities, and environmental threats, and they are geographically focused on threats emanating from the European periphery.[10] Americans are focused on the global war on terror and in general on more traditional security threats (Iran, China). There is also a clear divergence with regard to the best means to deal with various threats, as the debate before the war in Iraq and the ongoing dialogue regarding Iran demonstrate. This divergence is evident when comparing U.S. and European national security documents.[11]

THE CHALLENGE OF MANAGING DIVERGENT THREAT PERCEPTIONS

Under unipolarity one of the biggest challenges for the European allies is the need to design a strategy able to deal with the hegemon under very different scenarios. The different possible threat divergence scenarios described in the preceding discussion are directly linked to what is called the alliance security dilemma, that is, the dual and often conflicting concern of allies to be entrapped in an alliance on the one hand, or to be abandoned on the other.[12] When the hegemon perceives a stronger and more urgent threat than its secondary allies, they are likely to be concerned about entrapment. A powerful ally can find various ways to drag them into unnecessary conflicts, militarily, politically, or financially. Conversely, secondary allies who believe the hegemon is less interested in their immediate and vital threats are likely to be concerned about abandonment.

In a unipolar system both concerns are on the rise, due to the factors mentioned before, as well as the overwhelming power preponderance of the hegemon and the lack of the key strategic bargaining chips secondary allies held under bipolarity. This is a much greater challenge for secondary allies. If they had to worry mainly about abandonment, they would be better off investing all their energies in binding the hegemon or perhaps choosing to bandwagon. Bandwagoning may still be a good option in case threat divergence is low. When interests and threats are shared, the cost of bandwagoning is lower. If, on the other hand, they had to worry mainly about entrapment, then they would be better off investing all their energies in strategies such as leash slipping, to ensure the greatest autonomy possible. In the extreme scenario, if threat perceptions became contradictory, then balancing would become an option to consider. However, because all these different scenarios are possible under unipolarity—in different issue areas, different geographic regions, under different domestic political constellations—decision makers in secondary states need to design a flexible strategy to allow them to prepare for all these scenarios.

The development of regional cooperation arrangements that are linked to the alliance with the hegemon is a smart strategy to enable allies to mitigate both concerns. By developing regional capabilities to operate collectively in face of various threats, they can prepare for an unwanted yet possible scenario of abandonment. At the same time, by pooling their resources they are more likely to be able to offer meaningful burden-sharing for the hegemon, thus increasing their ability to influence it. A strategy of balking, for example, is meaningless if that support does not add too much. Increasing regional capabilities therefore facilitates restraining the hegemon by proving one's ability to offer or withhold a meaningful contribution.[13] All of this can be made possible only if regional allies succeed in cooperating effectively with one another. In this regard, Western Europe should face fewer challenges than other regions due to high level of preexisting regional cooperation via the EC and then the EU. Even here, as I shall note later, coordinating regional cooperation collectively vis-à-vis the United States was problematic.

REGIONAL COOPERATION, LEASH SLIPPING, AND BINDING IN EUROPEAN POST–COLD WAR STRATEGY

In the aftermath of the Cold War, Western European states were unclear about the future intentions of the United States. Many feared the United States would abandon Europe with the demise of the Soviet threat (as predicted by John Mearsheimer in 1990). Britain was concerned about U.S. abandonment of its special relations. Even France, the traditional advocate of an independent policy line, could not ignore the rising importance of the United States, with the shift to unipolarity and in face of the growing role of a united Germany. France, at the same time, was also concerned about entrapment in the Gulf, in light of its strong relations with Arab states.[14] The first Gulf War (1991) then served in part as a litmus test of U.S. intentions.

In face of the crisis in the Gulf, for both France and Britain, the working assumption was that military contribution meant political influence. This is the same logic that drives much of the current call to build greater independent capabilities in Europe.[15] The Europeans and Japan offered very significant financial burden sharing, as they covered most of the cost of the war.[16] However, despite initial hopes for a coordinated European military response, Britain and France ended up cooperating individually with the United States in the war. Germany, for its part, contributed with significant financial burden sharing. This inability to work collectively on the military front played an important role in pushing the Europeans at the time to consider seriously the need for a common security policy.[17]

The next major breakthrough in European military cooperation also came as a response, at least in part, to interaction with the United States. The experience during the Kosovo crisis and air campaign was formative for the Europeans. The United States did end up getting involved in the conflict via the NATO air campaign, and when it did it completely dominated. However, it was evident that this crisis was of much greater concern for Europe than for the United States, as was reflected in the U.S. reluctance to use ground troops and domestic public debate surrounding intervention. Threat perceptions here clearly diverged and were higher for the Europeans.[18] It was not at all certain that the United States would be willing to intervene in any such future conflict.[19] In other words, there was a growing concern of abandonment. At the same time, the huge military and technological power disparities between the United States and European armies also led to a sense of entrapment once the campaign began. Britain under Prime Minister Tony Blair, which headed the EU at the beginning of 1998 when violence in Kosovo erupted, came to a conclusion by the end of 1998 that an EU security policy would allow Europe to speak with a single voice, act alone if the United States was unable or unwilling to participate, and avoid burden sharing debates with the United States.[20] This was a dramatic shift for Britain, which always hesitated to enhance European security cooperation at the expense of its bilateral special relations. The shift found its official expression in the often cited Franco-British summit at Saint Malo in December 1998 and then was fueled by the events in Kosovo, to lead to the EU Council's summits in Cologne (June 1999) and Helsinki (December 1999), in which EU leaders pledged to improve collective military capabilities and to develop the European rapid reaction force. This shift is directly linked to the U.S. challenge.

The events of September 11, 2001, created in the very short run a sense of shared threat perceptions across the Atlantic, but in the longer run they accentuated the already diverging approaches to security by the Americans and the Europeans. Immediately after the attacks, the Europeans invoked NATO's article 5 and offered military support to the United States. This move stemmed from a real empathy with the United States but also from the desire to remain relevant. Consequently, when the United States politely refused to make use of the forces offered by its European allies at the outset of the war in Afghanistan, this raised concerns of irrelevance and hence possible abandonment in the future. The famous "axis of evil" speech of President Bush in 2002, as well as the consequent U.S. behavior, only served to highlight to the Europeans the growing gap in their threat perceptions and interests. Once again this had a dual implication. On the one hand, as the United States became more preoccupied with the "War on Terror," it was becoming less likely that it would be willing or able to offer military support in case of a future European crisis.[21] On the other hand, its aggressive unilateralism also raised concern over entrapment in America's military adventures.

The significant European contribution to the ISAF should be seen in light of these two challenges as a means to offer meaningful burden sharing so as to remain relevant. Perhaps most dramatic in this regard was the shift in German security policy. For the first time since the end of World War II, Germany decided to deploy troops in the Enduring Freedom operation and in ISAF. In March 2002 Germany took command of the ISAF. By December 2009 Germany had 4,280 troops in ISAF, more than the French (3,750).[22] If in 2001 the Americans viewed the European offer of help as merely a political token, the realities of today suggest otherwise. Already in 2003 Secretary of Defense Rumsfeld requested that NATO expand its role in Afghanistan. NATO took over control of ISAF and gradually began to expand its operations from the capital of Kabul to other areas of Afghanistan. ISAF, which began as a small 5,000-troop operation, has grown to over 80,000 troops. NATO forces today (that is, beyond U.S. troops) are a very important element in the war in Afghanistan that cannot be easily dismissed. When the French defense minister addressed in 2004 the five-nation Eurocorps (German, French, Spanish, Belgian, and Luxemburgian troops), which took over as the lead contingent in ISAF, she noted that "your presence is proof that Europe exists and is capable of bringing its weight to bear on the great crises shaking our planet."[23]

It is extremely important to remember that these developments occurred along the vocal feud surrounding Iraq and in the aftermath of the failure of the strategy of using NATO to restrain the United States in its decision to invade Iraq in 2003. Much has been written about the Franco-German attempt to prevent the attack and restrain the United States via the United Nations, as well as through NATO indirectly (the refusal to commit in advance to help Turkey). In framing these responses in the context of the differing responses to hegemony, several points should be made here. The case of Hussein and the mysterious "weapons of mass destruction" (WMDs) exemplified in full strength the divergence in threat perceptions and in foreign policy style. Whereas the United States believed this was indeed a serious threat warranting military action, France and Germany were convinced that war was simply a bad policy to deal with this (less vital) threat. Strong opposition to the United States, therefore, did not reflect any attempt to balance in principle U.S. power but rather reflected a sincere dispute over means.[24] Variations in threat perception divergence among the European states also help explain their differing policies. France clearly did not view Hussein as the threat the United States claimed he was and also had much to lose in terms of its economic and political ties in the region. Consequently, for France, concern about entrapment was much higher. Britain, on the other hand (or more precisely, Blair), shared the U.S. threat perception. Blair did try to influence the United States to operate through the United Nations but, when the time came, made the choice to offer military participation. When divergence in threat perception is low, cooperation is likely. In the context of such wide power disparities cooperation can be easily interpreted as bandwagoning. The distinction lies in the motivation behind cooperation. This may be empirically hard to establish. In this case as well, there is evidence that Blair's decision to support Bush stemmed from his moral perspective on international politics. At the same time, he also believed that he could influence U.S. policy via the special relations. Indeed, Posen argues that Britain adopted a strategy of "strategic bandwagoning"[25] (one could also argue this is a bonding response). Blair's policy turn in 1998 reflected the logic advanced in this chapter, that this influence can only be enhanced via the strengthening of Europe and of Britain's role in Europe. Ironically, the strong support for the United States during the Iraq war served to undermine this very goal.[26]

IMPACT OF REGIONAL AND DOMESTIC POLITICS

What role did the particularities of the regional power distribution and domestic politics play? The driving force behind the changes in European security strategies has been the systemic shift to unipolarity. While not determining policy, it created a new set of pressures as well as new opportunities for Europe. However, the broad systemic change needs to filter down via regional particularities. This suggests that, while we are likely to find similar dilemmas for America's partners around the globe, their implications and eventual strategy choices may be different, depending on different regional and domestic constellations. Furthermore, as I argue at the outset, one of the main implications of the shift from bipolarity to unipolarity has been a less constraining international security environment, which then in turn gave a potentially greater impact to domestic factors and other particularities of specific states.[27] If threat perceptions under bipolarity were more easily deduced from the system's structure, the current divergence of threat perceptions between the United States and Europe (and different European states), especially after 9/11, is a function both of the different power positions of the United States and Europe but also of the specific cultural and historical conditions of individual states.[28] Put differently, the change in global material power distribution has made nonsystemic factors more relevant than ever in understanding the dynamics of hegemony.

On the regional level one cannot ignore two crucial factors. One has to do with the central role of Germany. Much of the drive for European integration since the end of World War II has been linked to the need to bind a peaceful Germany into a wider European framework. The end of the Cold War and the reunification of Germany served to intensify the importance of this goal, despite the fact that West Germany had already been well integrated before that. Also, the growing active role of Germany in issues of European defense and out-of-area operations is a function not only of the broader systemic changes but also of its own increased power within Europe and its changing self-understanding that an increasingly powerful Germany had a growing responsibility to world peace.[29] The second and related factor has to do with the high level of regional institutionalization that had already occurred before the systemic shift. While the Maastricht treaty and the EU were born only in 1992, clearly this was a culmination of a longer process that predated the systemic change. Why is this important? The potential success of a regional burden-sharing/autonomy building/leash-slipping strategy depends on the ability of regional states to cooperate effectively with one another. Given the standard difficulties of cooperation under anarchy, the thick net of preexisting regional institutions and the habits of cooperation associated with them should have made it much easier to adopt this strategy in Europe. However, as we have seen, even in this relatively benign environment, by the time of the war in Iraq the Europeans could not find a way to operate collectively. Skeptics of ESDP point to the fact that despite the growth of security institution building, the ESDP project remained strictly intergovernmental. It is extremely unlikely that "Europe" could develop a coherent military force and strategy. Even if individual states like France wish to balance the United States, this remains a national aspiration rather than a European one.[30]

Domestic politics had an impact on the strategies European states chose to adopt or not (explanatory framework 3). Perhaps the most crucial domestic factor is the lack of public support for increased military spending since the end of the Cold War. The inability to invest any additional resources in military buildup or military technological developments to narrow the gap with the United States suggests that power balancing is unlikely in the foreseeable future.[31]

The role of domestic public opinion has come to the center stage in light of the war in Iraq, which generated massive public opposition in all European capitals, including those of states that participated in the wartime coalition. Schuster and Maier demonstrate that, despite these clear public opinion polls, governments did not end up following public opinion. Public opinion did not influence their policy stances but did influence their decisions to use their own military forces.[32] This in turn means that governments' ability to actually follow the strategy I presented in the preceding discussion is limited. One cannot ignore the fact that, for example, both Blair in Britain and Aznar in Spain paid a high political price for their active support of the U.S. mission in Iraq. Schuster and Maier also find that with the (significant) exception of France and Britain, in all Western European states there was a correlation between the ideological orientation of the ruling party and its support for the war, where right-wing parties were more pro-American. In East Europe, however, there was no such correlation, where six out of seven left-wing governments supported the United States.[33] These types of variations can be expected in a unipolar system.

Linking domestic politics to the concept of abandonment so central to this chapter, one can argue that both European and American governments, given their democratic nature, also play a significant two-level game. Both need to consider also the option of the other's involuntary abandonment (defection). The Americans, especially after Iraq, are aware of this constraint facing their European allies from their local constituencies. Conversely, part of the concern of the Europeans since the early 1990s stemmed from their reading of the dynamics within the U.S. Congress. Congress has traditionally been very sensitive to the high costs of international involvement and demanded that such costs be incurred also by its allies. Such calls after Kosovo were particularly alarming to Europeans. If hegemony is in part about the will to lead, these domestic factors cast some doubts regarding the resilience of this will.

"NORMATIVE POWER EUROPE" AND ALLIANCE STRATEGIES

European strategy can also be understood as an attempt to reconcile two competing approaches in Europe to its proper international role. The notion of "Normative Power Europe" suggests that it should seek to promote common liberal-democratic principles, such as liberty, democracy, respect for human rights and fundamental freedoms, and the rule of law—without using physical force to impose them.[34] Enhancing military capabilities while maintaining the principles of Normative Power Europe is tricky. Conversely, a different argument suggests that for Europe to be able to promote its normative agenda it has no choice but to develop significant material capabilities. Otherwise, it will remain difficult to disprove Kagan's argument that Europe's declared normative agenda is merely an outgrowth of its weakness compared to the United States.[35] By enhancing regional military capabilities as part of a burden-sharing operation with the United States, this can be achieved while trying to uphold the principles of a normative power.

Finally, I will put up front the opposite argument, suggesting that despite the prolonged crisis in transatlantic relations since the war in Iraq, there is in fact an underlying shared normative and cultural base to the alliance.[36] While clearly this is not an issue that can be dealt with properly here, if we adopt this approach, then current European strategies to deal with the United States seem very sensible. Europe and the United States are still together on a long walk in the global park. The leash may be slipping, but no one is running off.

NOTES

1. Christopher Layne, "The Unipolar Illusion Revisited: The Coming End of the United States' Unipolar Moment," *International Security* 31, 2 (Fall 2006): 9.

2. Seth Jones, *The Rise of European Security Cooperation* (Cambridge, UK: Cambridge University Press, 2007).

3. Brian Crowe, "A Common European Foreign Policy after Iraq?" *International Affairs* 79, 3 (May 2003): 534–536.

4. Galia Press-Barnathan, "The Changing Incentives for Security Regionalization: From 11/9 to 9/11," *Cooperation and Conflict* 40, 3 (2005): 281–304.

5. Jolyon Howorth and Anand Menon, "Still Not Pushing Back: Why the European Union Is Not Balancing the United States," *Journal of Conflict Resolution* 53, 5 (2009): 736–737.

6. Crowe, "A Common European?": 539–540.

7. For data see "Troops Contributing Nations," NATO, International Security Assistance Force; retrieved on January 26, 2010, from www.isaf.nato.int/ec/troop -contributing-nations-3.html. This number includes the contribution of Turkey (1,755), which is a NATO member but not a member of the EU.

8. Kenneth N. Waltz, *Theory of International Politics* (New York: McGraw Hill, 1979).

9. Galia Press-Barnathan, "Managing the Hegemon: NATO under Unipolarity," *Security Studies* 15, 2 (April–June 2006): 271–309.

10. Emil Kirchner and James Sperling, "The New Security Threats in Europe: Theory and Practice," *European Foreign Affairs Review* 7 (2002): 434–435; Sven Biscop, "In Search of a Strategic Concept for the ESDP," *European Foreign Affairs Review* 7 (2202): 480–487; Alfred van Staden, Kees Homan, Bert Kreemers, Alfred Pijpers, and Rob de Wijk, "Toward a European Strategic Concept" (paper presented at the Netherlands Institute of International Relations, Clingendael, Netherlands, November 2000): 28–30.

11. Christopher S. Chivvis, "Recasting NATO's Strategic Concept: Possible Directions for the United States," *RAND Project Air Force* (2009): 29. See also, "National Security Strategy," White House; available at www.whitehouse.gov/nsc/nssalll.html; The White House, "A Secure Europe in a Better World: European Security Strategy," Brussels, December 12, 2003; available at www.consilium.europa.eu/uedocs/cmsUpload/ 78367.pdf.

12. Glenn Snyder, "The Security Dilemma in Alliance Politics," *World Politics* 36, 4 (1984): 461–495; and Glenn Snyder, *Alliance Politics* (Ithaca, NY: Cornell University Press, 1997).

13. Paul W. Schroeder, "Alliances, 1815–1945: Weapons of Power and Tools of Management," in *Historical Dimensions of National Security Problems*, ed. Klaus Knorr (Lawrence: University of Kansas Press, 1976): 259–277.

14. Joseph Lepgold, "Britain in Desert Storm: The Most Enthusiastic Junior Partner," in *Friends in Need: Burden Sharing in the Persian Gulf War*, eds. Andrew Bennet, Joseph Lepgold, and Danny Under (New York: St. Martin's Press, 1997): 74–75; Isabelle Grunberg, "Still a Reluctant Ally? France's Participation in the Gulf War Coalition," in *Friends in Need: Burden Sharing in the Persian Gulf War*, eds. Andrew Bennet, Joseph Lepgold, and Danny Under (New York: St. Martin's Press, 1997): 118–124.

15. Lawrence Freedman and Efraim Karsh, *The Gulf Conflict 1990–1991: Diplomacy and War in the New World Order* (Princeton, NJ: Princeton University Press, 1993).

16. Andrew Bennet, "Sheriff of the Posse: American Leadership in the Desert Storm Coalition," in *Friends in Need: Burden Sharing in the Persian Gulf War*, eds. Andrew Bennet, Joseph Lepgold, and Danny Under (New York: St. Martin's Press, 1997): 42.

17. Trevor C. Salmon, "Europeans, the EC and the Gulf," in *Iraq, the Gulf Conflict and the World Community*, ed. James Gow (London: Centre for Defense Studies, Brassey's, 1993): 97–101.

18. Anne Deighton, "The European Union and NATO's War over Kosovo," in *Alliance Politics, Kosovo, and Nato's War: Allied Force or forced Allies?* eds. Pierre Martin and Mark R. Brawley (New York: Palgrave, 2001): 61–66, 117.

19. Charles A. Kupchan, "Kosovo and the Future of US Engagement in Europe: Continued Hegemony or Impending Retrenchment?" in *Alliance Politics, Kosovo, and Nato's War: Allied Force or Forced Allies?* eds. Pierre Martin and Mark R. Brawley (New York: Palgrave, 2001): 77.

20. Emil Kirchner and James Sperling, "Will Form Lead to Function? Institutional Enlargement and the Creation of a European Security and Defense Identity," *Contemporary Security Policy* 21, 1 (April 2000): 42; Richard G. Whitman, "NATO, the EU and ESDP: An Emerging Division of Labor?" *Contemporary Security Policy* 25, 3 (December 2004): 436.

21. I. H. Daalder, "The End of Atlanticism," *Survival* 45 (2003): 147–166.

22. Scott Brunstetter, "A Changing View of Responsibility? German Security Policy in the Post–9/11 World," in *Old Europe, New Europe and the US: Renegotiating Transatlantic Security in the Post 9/11 Era*, eds. Tom Lansford and Blagovest Tashev (Farnham, UK: Ashgate, 2004); Troop data from NATO, International Security Assistance Force: Afghanistan; available at http://isaf.nato.int/en/troops-contributing-nations-3.html.

23. Beverly Crawford, *Power and German Foreign Policy: Embedded Hegemony in Europe* (New York: Palgrave-McMillan 2007): 98.

24. Philip H. Gordon and Jeremy Shapiro, *Allies at War: America, Europe, and the Crisis over Iraq* (New York: McGraw Hill, 2004).

25. Barry Posen, "European Union Security and Defense Policy: Response to Unipolarity?" *Security Studies* 15, 2 (April–June 2006): 167–169.

26. Steven Phillip Kramer, "Blair's Britain after Iraq," *Foreign Affairs* 82 (July/August 2003): 90–104.

27. David Andrews, "Is Atlanticism Dead?" in *The Atlantic Alliance under Stress: U. S.–European Relations after Iraq*, ed. David M. Andrews (Cambridge, UK: Cambridge University Press, 2005): 259–261.

28. Francis Fukuyama, "Does the 'West' Still Exist?" in *Beyond Paradise and Power: Europe, America and the Future of a Troubled Partnership*, ed. Todd Lindberg (London: Routledge, 2004): 156–157.

29. Crawford, *Power and German Foreign Policies*: 96.

30. Jolyon Howorth and Anand Menon, "Still Not Pushing Back": 738–740.

31. See the excellent volume by Steven E. Lobell, Norrin M. Ripsman, and Jeffrey W. Taliaferro, eds., *Neoclassical Realism, The State and Foreign Policy* (Cambridge, UK: Cambridge University Press, 2009).

32. Jürgen Schuster and Herbert Maier, "The Rift: Explaining Europe's Divergent Iraq Policies in the Run-Up of the American-Led War on Iraq," *Foreign Policy Analysis* 2 (2006): 232.

33. Ibid.: 233.

34. Ian Manners, "Normative Power Europe: A Contradiction in Terms?" *Journal of Common Market Studies* 40, 2 (2002): 238–244; Ian Manners, "Normative Power Europe Reconsidered," *From Civilian to Military Power: The European Union at a Crossroads?* CIDEL Workshop, Oslo (October 22–23, 2004): 4–5.

35. Robert Kagan, "Power and Weakness" *Policy Review*, 113 (June and July 2002); Tanja A. Börzel and Thomas Risse, "Venus Approaching Mars? The European Union as an Emerging Civilian World Power," Berlin Working Paper on European Integration, No.11 (April 2009): 32.

36. Gordon and Shapiro, *Allies at War*: 187.

8 PAKISTAN

Anatomy of a Hegemonic Malcontent

John R. Dreyer

PAKISTAN IS A STATE locked between two extremes. Pakistan has a secular and democratically elected government cooperating with the United States and its allies to rid the region of terrorism in the guise of the Taliban and Al-Qaeda. Yet there are elements within Pakistan that seek to support and enable the same terrorist elements to survive as a path to the goal of more control of Afghanistan and furthering the competitive edge over India. This dichotomy leads to the view that Pakistan is a particular type of hegemonic malcontent: a passive-aggressive state that is neither a malcontent nor truly a follower of U.S. hegemony in the region. The government is torn between domestic cleavage and regional security demands, as well as the need for economic stability. Pakistan's reaction to U.S. hegemony can best be categorized as alternating between times of compliance (bandwagon) and resistance, typically through balking and leash slipping.

Framework 1 (realism) accounts for Pakistan's overall motivation and responses to the hegemon. Yet domestic factors (framework 3) explain the short-term strategies such as leash slipping, balking, and complying. Examples are elites' desire to remain in power by cooperating with the United States, public opinion that opposed U.S. involvement in what many see as a regional situation, and, I argue the most important, the military acting in its own, specific long-term interests in building a power base in the region with the focus on India.

I first examine the two major policies influencing Pakistan's policy. Next I build a history of Pakistan's relationship with the United States and pre-9/11

fallout over nuclear weapons. The next section looks at the post–9/11 landscape and the influences on the choices and decisions by the government, the
army and other domestic players in the war on the Afghanistan border. Finally, I examine the lack of change in policy toward the U.S.-led war on terror
after the February 2008 elections and the U.S. reaction toward Pakistan.

Pakistan's policy alternatives after 9/11 were limited as events overtook the
ability to plan and execute foreign policy. The initial choice of General Per-
vez Musharraf's regime had been to act as a bridge between the Taliban and
United States. The declaration by the Taliban leadership on Osama bin Laden's
status as a guest in Afghanistan eliminated this option.[1] Not only would the
United States view Pakistan as part of the problem, but its allies would possibly cut their support as well. The United States would then begin to support India as the primary ally in the region against the Taliban. Pakistan thus
chose a middle ground, emphasizing the government's cooperation while the
long-term strategy of grooming the tribes, Islamists, and Taliban was carried out by the Inter-service Intelligence Agency (ISI) and army. The middle-
ground policy decision allowed Pakistan to keep its long-term interests intact
regionally while cooperating with the United States for the short term. The
major policy choice for Pakistan is the maintenance of regional relationships
that promote the strategy against India.

I conclude that, while acting as a very strong force in Pakistani society,
Islam is also a political tool wielded to the benefit of foreign and domestic
policy. The lessons of the 1980s and the proxy fight between the USSR and the
United States in Afghanistan led Pakistan to use Islam as a weapon to balance
the playing field against India. After 9/11 many elements in the government
continued to support and nurture militant Islam in the rugged terrain of the
Northwest Frontier Province (NWFP). This led the United States, especially
after the presidential election of 2008, to take measures to increase cooperation and control over Pakistan's effort to combat militant groups domestically.
By tying aid and other support to this increased control, the United States is
reasserting itself in the domestic politics of Pakistan. The danger is that such
actions will likely cause further discontent and see elements of the Pakistani
military and government oppose the hegemon.

TWO STRAINS OF INFLUENCE

The relationship the United States built with Pakistan after the September 11,
2001, attacks is based on convenience. Pakistan proved to be an expedient ally

in the U.S. fight against the Taliban, which provided support to Al-Qaeda. With U.S. troops came aid—economic and military assistance desperately needed by the Musharraf government. The ability to stabilize the economy and add new weapons to his arsenal made Musharraf a willing ally in the fight against the Taliban and Al-Qaeda.

Pakistan's conflict with India represents the very core of policy for any government in Islamabad (see Chapter 11). Many of the most important policy decisions stem from a desire to trump India's numerous advantages in military strength and economic development. This strain of policy influences far more than the wishes of any outside force, such as a global hegemon, the United States, or a regional hegemon, China.

PAKISTAN AS A FOLLOWER

Pakistan is neither a full follower state nor a full malcontented state. Instead, Pakistan alternates between appeasing the United States and using subtle resistance, a pattern that I call "a passive-aggressive malcontented state." A passive-aggressive malcontent has been forced into a position of compliance with hegemonic goals but actively seeks to pursue its own self-interested goals; often these goals are directly opposite to what the hegemon seeks to build and enforce. Domestic cleavage fuels the passive-aggressive behavior. One part of the state wants to cooperate with the hegemon for reasons that range from purely national to systemic in nature (frameworks 1 and 3). The elite dictate just enough of the policy and hold just enough of the power that cooperation and followership are sustained for a period of time. The other part of society is disgruntled with the hegemon and feels under pressure, preferring instead to pursue national goals distinct from the hegemon.

Pakistan emerged as a follower of U.S. hegemony during the Cold War. America saw Pakistan as a valuable ally against Soviet ambitions in the South-Central Asia region. Throughout the 1950s and 1960s, Pakistan found its relationship with the United States useful as the feud with India continued. This escalated in the 1970s to include nuclear weapons, a fact that the United States could not ignore. By seeking nuclear weapons capability, Pakistan put itself in a position that directly contradicted U.S. policy, and subsequently all military aid was suspended, starting in 1979.[2] Arms sales resumed shortly afterward as the Soviet invasion of Afghanistan quickly became a focus of U.S. foreign policy. Pakistan was, once again, an important ally against the USSR. The United States not only sold arms directly to Pakistan but also began using Pakistan as a base to supply rebel Afghans with arms and aid in their guerilla war against the Soviets.

U.S. economic and military assistance was key in helping Mohammad Zia ul-Haq stabilize his military coup and legitimize his government in the early 1980s.[3] Even with U.S. support, ul-Haq encountered domestic resistance, which was secular and opposed to the former general. Seeking to undermine this resistance, the regime began to forge closer links to militant Islamists, which in turn saw the reincorporation of elements of Islamic law into Pakistan's civil codes as well as the establishment of Islamic *madrassas* with the help of Saudi funds.[4] Ul-Haq's compromises with the Islamists domestically would have ramifications later. This is a consistent story in Pakistan: The army seeks to stabilize its position through domestic compromises that ultimately become liabilities. By seeking a compromise with militant Islam, ul-Haq gave the Islamists the legitimate foothold they had sought since Pakistan's creation in 1947. Likewise, the U.S. effort in Afghanistan was built on two pillars: military aid and the concept of jihad.[5] The idea of jihad ensured that the effort against the USSR was something larger; indeed the idea of a Muslim-wide war against the Soviets was beneficial to U.S. interests as well as domestic stability in Pakistan.

The army sought to change permanently the balance of domestic power. After ul-Haq took power he amended the constitution so that the presidency, the position that he occupied after his coup in 1977, held the ultimate power.[6] The eighth amendment to the constitution gave the person holding the position of president the power to dismiss the prime minister and parliament. Ul-Haq realized that power needed to be restored to the civilian government, but he was unwilling to give up his new authority.[7] The army supported this shift in the balance of domestic power; it gave them a check on the authority of the civilian government without resorting automatically to martial law. The only authority to balance the power of both the executive and legislative arms of the government was the judiciary. Throughout the 1980s and 1990s the judiciary strove to play this role.[8]

Because of Pakistan's position in the Cold War and the U.S. effort in Afghanistan against the USSR, the changes ul-Haq made were not challenged. The United States needed a stable ally in the region, and Pakistan fit the bill perfectly; it was a far more reliable follower than India. The end of the Soviet effort in Afghanistan in 1989 changed America's attitude, however. There was already a strain of anti-Americanism running throughout Pakistan. America's global stance against Islam and support of Israel and military dictators like ul-Haq all played to the distrust of U.S. interests in Pakistan domestically.[9] After the Soviet defeat in Afghanistan, suspicion of the United States was further reinforced by the hard line suddenly taken on Pakistan's possession of a nuclear arsenal. The image of America had never really been stellar, and after 9/11 the positive view of Americans was less than 1 percent.[10]

NUCLEAR AMBITION

Pakistan's foreign policy is, in part, based on India. This is essential to understand certain decisions, including the acquisition of nuclear weapons (see Chapter 11). The Pakistan–India issue is central to tensions in South Asia, tensions that finally included a nuclear option in the spring of 1998 with the official testing of Pakistan's nuclear arsenal. The nuclear program began secretly in 1977 and led to a break in U.S.–Pakistani relations in 1979.[11] However, the Soviet effort in Afghanistan gave a reprieve to the ul-Haq government, and U.S. scrutiny of Pakistan's nuclear research program ebbed low. After the end of the Soviet–Afghan war the United States once more became interested in the progress of the nuclear program. Renewed U.S. concern about Pakistan's arsenal in 1989 led to the suspension of all military aid, including a promised delivery of F-16 fighters.[12] Pakistan had always suffered from a disparity in conventional forces against their much larger adversary, India.[13] The possession of nuclear weapons was Pakistan's effort to level the playing field: A nuclear arsenal would serve as an effective deterrent. The United States and most of the international community saw quite the opposite: A nuclear Pakistan further escalated an already tense regional situation.

Pakistan largely ignored U.S. demands to tame its nuclear arsenal. The need to balance against India was a far more pressing foreign policy concern. The Pressler Amendment was applied in 1990; it was the source of the suspension of military aid as well as all bilateral economic aid. Only humanitarian assistance and ongoing economic programs were allowed to continue.[14] By the mid-1990s, the United States began to shy away from a strict nonproliferation stance to a position that emphasized risk avoidance and restraint. Pakistan was going to possess nuclear weapons, and a total collapse of the state would bring chaos to the region. Under this assumption, the Clinton administration changed its position, at least on the matter of economic aid and trade. Economic concerns throughout the region weighed more heavily than nonproliferation, seemingly a lost cause.

India tested its first nuclear device in May 1998. Pakistan did likewise, against U.S. wishes, later that month.[15] The direct result of this was a response that tightened economic sanctions that had been loosened previously. Pakistan pledged to sign the Comprehensive Test Ban Treaty. In addition it promised to suspend any further testing plans as well as not to transfer nuclear plans and materials abroad.[16] There was a dichotomy at work within Pakistan's foreign policy. International support and trade were desperately needed by the government. Yet the tension with India demanded a response that did not show Pakistan bowing under any international pressure.

The resurgence of a positive U.S.–Pakistan relationship as a result of the U.S. War on Terror helped gloss over Pakistan's nuclear policy. But India–Pakistan tension still ran high, and in 2002 a deployment of Indian short-range nuclear weapons came as a result of Pakistan's alleged support of Islamist militants within India. The possibility of war was at an all-time high as the United States mediated between the two states. As a result of this U.S.–sponsored bargaining, the government banned the identified militant groups.[17] America eased up on Pakistan in regards to its nuclear weapons in exchange for a greater array of cooperation domestically.

With its nuclear arsenal, Pakistan engaged in a strategy of both balking and leash slipping. The more U.S. interest in the area, the less scrutiny applied. This allowed Pakistan to continue to develop its nuclear arsenal. By balking, Pakistan was also leash-slipping against U.S. interests in the region. There was little fear of military action by the United States; instead, most of the pressure was economic. An independent foreign policy that allowed Pakistan to present a strong front to India was essential, and a nuclear arsenal was deemed a cornerstone of this policy regardless of U.S. interests.

MUSHARRAF AND ISOLATION

Musharraf's military coup in 1999 replaced the legitimately elected government. By the time he moved himself into the president's office he was presiding over a state and civil society suffering through economic and political instability. The democratically elected Sharif government in 1999 had been the fifth one since 1988 and had won power with a strikingly low voter turnout.[18]

Musharraf's coup highlights a particular problem of Pakistani domestic analysis: the power of the army within civilian politics. The 1990s saw the exponential increase in a strain running through the army where the cult of professionalism was supplemented by militant Islam. The Islamists believed that a higher power was the only power worth pledging oneself.[19] Thus, by 1999 radical Islam was becoming a problem. The idea of jihad, which had proven so useful in the 1980s, had been allowed to establish deep linkages through society. By the summer of 2001, sectarian bloodshed throughout the country demanded action on his part against the most violent of the Islamists.[20] This wave of violence challenged the army as Musharraf used them as a tool against the most militant groups. The army performed as he needed, demonstrating that, despite some rumblings by Islamists in its ranks, the army was still responsive to the secular government.[21] The fighting in Pakistan in the summer of 2001 was, as he called it, to restore the "writ of the state" and, more importantly, stabilize his regime. He used his victory as a chance to purge many high-ranking Islamists.

While Musharraf was in a politically more stable position, the country suffered other problems. The poor economy and the lack of substantial aid packages made many international observers believe that Pakistan was entering a downward spiral from which it might never recover.[22] The pursuit of nuclear weapons and the rise of radical Islam had put Pakistan into a forced sort of isolation. The United States, once a valued ally, considered economic aid only in the form of loans and minor assistance.

FROM PARIAH TO FRONTLINE STATE

September 11, 2001, was a rebirth for U.S.–Pakistan relations, as U.S. policy now made the destruction of the Taliban and Al-Qaeda a priority. Pakistan underwent a transformation from isolation to a frontline ally in the U.S. War on Terror, a windfall for Musharraf and Pakistan. The nuclear arsenal was easily overlooked, and the U.S. desire to purge the area of militant Islam was perfectly in line with his own policies. The new status did present a problem for both him and the ISI. Both the government and the ISI had invested in a long-term strategy to build and nurture the Taliban in their role as the government of Afghanistan.[23]

The ISI is powerful enough to retain an independent standing from both the army and the government, reporting to both. The ISI, which functions as an independent intelligence arm of the military, has been referred to as a "state within a state" and a "kingdom within a state" by observers.[24] It was this autonomy that allowed the ISI into Afghanistan after the collapse of the Soviet-backed government in the early 1990s. The power vacuum was filled by the Taliban with assistance from the ISI. This gave the ISI, and thus Pakistan, deep roots in Afghanistan.[25]

Influence in Afghanistan was intended to gain an edge over India on the issue of Kashmir. Fundamentalist Islam was a tool to be used against India.[26] Emphasizing ties to the Pashtun peoples of the Northwest Frontier and Islam was hoped to put pressure on India. The Taliban would, in the eyes of the ISI, function as a proxy in the Indo–Pakistan conflict over this region, in effect cultural and religious ties would enable Pakistan to trump any Indian advantage. The Taliban provided a safe haven, a base for insurgents from which to operate. Al-Qaeda's camps provided the training the ISI needed for the militant Islamic terrorists to fight against India in Kashmir. It was a win-win situation for the ISI and Pakistan.[27]

After 9/11 the deep roots in the Taliban became a liability for Musharraf. For a short while Pakistan clung to a belief that the Taliban and Al-Qaeda were separate and distinct; Pakistan had put in far too much effort simply to condemn the Taliban outright. Musharraf sought to act as a bridge of sorts between the Taliban and the United States.[28] In doing so, he sought to preserve the legitimacy of the Taliban and consequently Pakistan's advantage over India. This policy ultimately ended when Mullah Omar declared that bin Laden was a guest of the Taliban and that Afghanistan would shelter him from the United States. Overnight the work Pakistan had put into making Afghanistan a proxy seemed to disappear. Further, failure to cooperate with the United States could potentially see America shift power to India to help eliminate the Taliban.[29] A stark reality left little choice for Musharraf: The Taliban was disowned.

Even as Musharraf officially denounced Pakistani involvement with the Taliban, the ISI continued to actively support it. Thanks to deep involvement in Afghanistan during the Soviet conflict, the ISI could navigate the networks of Islamic schools and tribal societies.[30] The links between Pakistan and Afghanistan through radical Islam were further complicated by the shared ethnicity of Pashtun tribes in the area of the NWFP. The Pashtun shared roots in both states, and a strong part of Pakistan's policy was dedicated to ensuring that the border areas were unified and stable. It was in the best interests of the ISI to continue their involvement on the border.

Even as the Taliban was ejected from power, its ideas, doctrine and concepts of jihad spread throughout the Pashtun tribal areas on the NWFP.[31] However, the Taliban could not have done this without the assistance of the ISI. Here the "kingdom within a state" fully manifested itself. Musharraf had fractured the long-term strategy of Pakistan and the ISI when he aligned with the United States. The ISI continued to use the pre-9/11 strategy of securing the border even as the United States and its allies hunted down any Taliban and Al-Qaeda they could find. The Taliban and Al-Qaeda found support among the Pashtun tribes based on the resurrection of jihad against the United States and its efforts to create a secular state in Afghanistan.[32]

Thus, while the ISI supported the fundamentalist Islam that flourished throughout the region and had little intention of abandoning the Taliban, U.S. interests were exactly the opposite, marking the Taliban for destruction. Musharraf made an attempt to rein in the ISI and even forced out their leader, General Mahmud Ahmed, in October 2001.[33] Ahmed had been a key figure in Musharraf's coup in 1999 but had begun to use ISI contacts and power to promote his own brand of fundamentalist Islam. After Ahmed was gone, many others in the organization who shared his goal were forced out as well. This did little to tame the influence and power of the ISI in Afghanistan. As late as 2008 the ISI was helping Taliban insurgents cross the border areas and protecting them from the army and the Americans.[34]

Pakistan's status after 9/11 as a frontline state placed a dividing line between regional and global policy and commitments and domestic policy. For Musharraf the best policy was to distance Pakistan as far away from the pre-9/11 Afghanistan policy as possible. Pakistan needed to heel to U.S. demands to ensure regional power and to keep aid flowing. Yet Pakistan engaged in another strategy of resistance to U.S. interests, blackmail. It is easy to see how Musharraf could exploit his situation: If America did not support him, Pakistan would collapse. The strategy played an essential role in how Pakistan acquired and used U.S. aid and influence. Without such, he would lose control of his state and open it up to Islamists and possibly even the Pakistani Taliban. Overplaying the threat posed by these groups domestically could only work in his favor.

EXIT MUSHARRAF

Domestic pressure against Musharraf's rule reached critical levels by late 2007. The dismissal of the Supreme Court's chief justice led to an uprising of Pakistani lawyers.[35] This exercise by the core of Pakistan's civil and political society proved a turning point. Further, he had been under pressure from the United States to open Pakistan up to democracy far more than he had been since 2001. It was under these pressures that the National Reconciliation Ordinance (NRO) was drawn up. The NRO had Musharraf resign as army chief of staff but retain the civilian presidency.[36] His dismissal of the Pakistani chief justice, the terror attacks on the Red Mosque in Islamabad by pro-Taliban elements, and his November state of emergency declaration all worked against him as Pakistan took to the polls in the presidential election. The Pakistan Peoples Party (PPP) took the majority of votes, with Musharraf's own party, the Pakistan Muslim League (PML-N), taking a distant second place. Initially, he stayed in power, a new chief justice was appointed, and many policies, including those that stressed a close working relationship with America, stayed in place. By August 2008, he reached a point where both the PPP and the PML-N had formed a coalition that announced impeachment proceedings against the president. This action led to Musharraf resigning that same month, leaving Pakistan in the hands of a democratically elected government for the first time since 1998. His departure from government opened up a window of official discontent with U.S. involvement in the NWFP border areas against the Taliban.

The new president of Pakistan, Asif Ali Zardari, the widower of Benazir Bhutto, was the leader of the PPP. The PPP rode to power based on an anti-Musharraf policy and a tinge of anti-Americanism. Very little changed: Cooperation with U.S. interests and policy continued. Zardari worked with America to target elements of the Taliban and Al-Qaeda along the border areas of the NWFP. Domestically such concessions to U.S. wishes splintered the PPP's coalition and allowed Musharraf's old party, the PML-N, now to built around former Prime Minister Sharif to offer opposition to Zardari and his cooperation with U.S. interests. The tribes in the NWFP were in a competition that included U.S. and Pakistan support against other tribes that housed insurgents and Taliban. The strictly military approach pursued by the United States and the Pakistani army was a major source of domestic discontent. The approach of diplomacy, talk, and negotiation advocated by the PPP and Zardari quickly faded once the political reality of America's desire became clear. Like his predecessor, Zardari faced a stark choice of carrot or stick when faced with U.S. policy choices in the border regions.

The national election also included local changes in the NWFP. The MMA had been voted out in favor of the nationalist Pashtun ANP party. This was to some a rejection of religious conviction for national ideals, but some read the vote as a rejection of the MMA's cooperation with the United States.[37]

The Awami National Party (ANP) took steps to secure Pashtun tribal areas against Taliban insurgency, up to and including arming vigilante groups with Chinese weapons.[38] Not only could the local tribal units protect themselves against Taliban insurgents, but the newly armed groups began to fire on U.S. forces as they crossed the border areas hunting down Taliban and Al-Qaeda forces.

BETWEEN A ROCK AND A HARD PLACE

Pakistan has never fully abandoned its Afghan strategy. Domestically it wants to distance itself from a U.S. strategy that is expensive, destructive, and bad for relations on both sides of the border. Regionally, Afghanistan is still an important piece of Pakistan's foreign policy.

The issues surrounding the NWFP and the seeming inability of Pakistan's government to control the actions of the ISI and elements of the army have led to a shift in U.S. foreign policy in the region. The U.S. presidential election in 2008 saw a change of leadership that gave a window for a change of strategy. The Bush administration had emphasized the war in Iraq, which had taken attention from the Afghan conflict and consequently Pakistan. The Obama administration began to focus more attention on Afghanistan.[39] The renewed focus brought a more determined hunt for Al-Qaeda that would also include Pakistan. The administration also began to hint that U.S. aid would no longer flow as freely as it had under Bush. Long-term plans for a stable economy were made as well as commitments from America for rebuilding and reviving democratic and civil society. These were coupled with military aid made conditional on the ability and success of Pakistan to eliminate terrorist groups domestically.[40]

The U.S. Congress passed the Kerry-Lugar bill in September 2009, which outlined a U.S. policy that took a far greater role in Pakistan's politics and tied aid packages to goals and oversight.[41] These goals included the ability of Pakistan to fight domestic terrorist groups through increased accountability from both the secretary of state and the secretary of defense to Congress. The bill represents a rather late, though powerful, attempt by America to counter leash slipping by elements of the Pakistani military and the ISI. If the aid packages were to keep flowing, Pakistan would have to share its strategy and policy planning with U.S. officials. Kerry-Lugar introduced language that emphasized "close cooperation" while many Pakistani officials, many of whom were in the military, saw such provisions as violating national sovereignty and national security.[42]

CONCLUSION

Passive-aggressive malcontents put national interests ahead of hegemonic desire, and in this respect Pakistan is no different. For Pakistani elites, cooperation with America is based on self-interest. Following the policies and wishes of the United States gives not only valuable aid but also an advantage against India; not following would possibly put India in a better position internationally. For the elites, cooperation is a positive situation, at least systemically. There is little room for actions such as leash slipping and balking. U.S. support is essential to a stable regime. However, this plays into the strategy of blackmail, which both Musharraf and Zardari used to their advantage. Without U.S. support, Pakistan could potentially collapse and become a haven for radical Islam. This is a future America wished to avoid, and accordingly it is generous with aid and support.

Domestically, the Pakistan public is at odds with the decisions made by the ruling elite. Many Pakistanis reject U.S. interference in the NWFP region. The view of America as an interloper that seeks cooperation only when U.S. interests are of importance is common in all levels of Pakistani society. The nuclear controversy demonstrated that America was concerned with only its hegemonic goals in the region; once those were completed, Pakistan was no longer exempt from serious examination of its nuclear arsenal.

Many within Pakistan, especially organizations like the ISI and elements of the army, view America as strangling long-term strategy as well as valued allies in the form of the Taliban. The presence of ISI agents in harboring and protecting insurgents in the NWFP region is not overt support for the Taliban. Instead it is the protection and continued nurturing of an ally valuable for long-range strategy in the region, especially in opposition to India.

The ISI and the Pashtun tribes in the NWFP region represent the other side of Pakistan's passive-aggressive status. The elites in Islamabad are unable to bring these domestic forces to heel, and while official policy supports U.S. policy such official proclamation has little reach into the hills and backrooms of the NWFP and the ISI. It is here that the most effective form of leash slipping occurs. The terrain and culture of the NWFP make control by a national entity very difficult. Islamabad is very far away, and local commanders can trump national policy in favor of a policy that strengthens the concerns of the ISI and the army.

Religion, while a very strong factor in Pakistani society, plays a small role. Militant Islam is viewed by many policy makers as a tool to further national policy goals. Islam is a tool of the ruling elites to stabilize the national government and to unite the electorate domestically. The Taliban, both in Afghanistan and Pakistan, is not welcomed in most regions. The extremist views of the Taliban run against the religion of many of the tribes and cultures on Pakistan's border regions.

The United States seeks a stable peace in the region, and its strategy is based on increased cooperation and partnership aimed at steering Pakistan on a course that builds democracy and civil society leading to a position where a dialogue with India can be established and sustained. In turn, this will enable the two rivals to become former rivals and work on establishing a stable regional partnership. All of this requires greater U.S. penetration in Pakistani politics, a role that many Pakistanis are reluctant to see. American money is needed, but American oversight is not wanted, and pre-9/11 national goals still hold sway over the forces that play a primary role in fighting militant groups all throughout Pakistan. Only as these forces lose power will U.S. goals be realized.

NOTES

1. Nasreen Akhtar, "Pakistan, Afghanistan and the Taliban," *International Journal on World Peace* 25, 4 (December 2008): 61.

2. Richard F. Grimmett, *U.S. Arms Sales to Pakistan.* CRS Report for Congress (Washington DC: Congressional Research Service, 2007): 1–2.

3. Samina Ahmed, "The United States and Terrorism in Southwest Asia: September 11 and Beyond," *International Security* 26, 3 (2001–2002): 82.

4. Hamza Alavi, "Pakistan between Afghanistan and India," *Middle East Report* 222 (2002): 25.

5. Alavi, "Pakistan between Afghanistan and India": 2–6.

6. John Bray, "Pakistan at 50: A State in Decline?" *International Affairs* 73, 2 (1997): 316.

7. Ibid.

8. Kamran Asdar Ali, "Pakistani Islamists Gamble on the General," *Middle East Report* 231 (2004): 4–5.

9. Hamid H. Kizilbash, "Anti-Americanism in Pakistan," *Annals of the American Academy of Political and Social Science* 407 (1988): 67.

10. Matthew Gentzkow and Jesse Shapiro, "Media, Education and Anti-Americanism in the Muslim World," *The Journal of Economic Persepctives* 18, 3 (2004): 120.

11. Grimmett, *U.S. Arms Sales to Pakistan*: 2.

12. Samina Ahmed, "Security Dilemmas of a Nuclear Armed Pakistan," *Third World Quarterly* 21, 5 (2000): 786.

13. Ibid.: 782.

14. Hasan-Askari Rizvi, "Pakistan in 1998: The Polity under Pressure," *Asian Survey* 39, 1 (1999): 183.

15. Ibid.

16. Ibid.: 184.

17. Ian Talbot, "Pakistan in 2002: Democracy, Terrorism and Brinkmanship," *Asian Survey* 43, 1 (2003): 201.

18. Bray, "Pakistan at 50": 320.

19. Alavi, "Pakistan between Afghanistan and India": 28.

20. Iftikhar Malik, "Pakistan in 2001: The Afghanistan Crisis and the Rediscovery of the Frontline State," *Asian Survey* 42, 1 (2002): 207.

21. Alavi, "Pakistan between Afghanistan and India": 28.

22. Bray, "Pakistani at 50": 315.

23. Tim McGirk, Hannah Blach, and Massimo Calabresi, "Has Pakistan Tamed Its Spies?" *Time Europe* (May 6, 2002): 54.

24. Ibid.: 55.

25. Lawrence Ziring, *Pakistan: At the Crosscurrent of History* (Oxford, UK: Oxford University Press, 2003): 280–286.

26. Juan Cole, "Pakistan and Afghanistan: Beyond the Taliban," *Political Science Quarterly* 124, 2 (2009): 244.

27. Ibid.

28. Ziring, *Pakistan*: 305.

29. Nasreen Akhtar, "Pakistan, Afghanistan and the Taliban," *International Journal on World Peace* (2008): 61.

30. Ibid.: 67.

31. Lawrence Ziring, "Unraveling the Afghanistan–Pakistan Riddle," *Asian Affairs: An American Review* 36, 2 (2009): 71.

32. Ibid.: 71–72.

33. McGirk et al., "Has Pakistan Tamed its Spies?": 55.

34. Ron Moreau, Mark Hosenball, John Barry, and Michael Hirish, "Pakistan's Dangerous Double Game," *Newsweek* (September 22, 2008): 44–45.

35. Matthew J. Nelson, "Pakistan in 2008: Moving beyond Musharraf," *Asian Survey* 49, 1 (2007): 18.

36. Ibid.: 16.

37. Ibid.: 21.

38. Ibid.: 21–24.

39. Syed Farooq Hasnat, "Pakistan's Strategic Interests, Afghanistan and the Fluctuating US Strategy," *Journal of International Affairs* 63, 1 (Fall/Winter 2009): 149.

40. Ibid.: 150.

41. *A bill to authorize appropriations for fiscal years 2010 through 2014 to promote an enhanced strategic partnership wth Pakistan and its people, and for other purposes.* S. 1707, 111th Congress, 1st Session.

42. Inter services Public Relations, 2009, Press Release (October 7, 2009); available at http://ispr.gov.pk/front/main.asp?o=t-press_release&id=914.

REGIONAL HEGEMONS

Part II

9 RESISTANCE IS ÚTIL (USEFUL)
Responses to Brazilian Hegemony

Nancy D. Lapp

WHEN THINKING OF HEGEMONY in the Western Hemisphere, the United States and its often overbearing relationship with Latin America are the first to come to mind. However, the United States is not the only influential state in the region. Though a secondary power in a hemisphere that has long been dominated by the United States, Brazil is a major power in its own neighborhood: "a regionally predominant, but not dominant, state," as described by Sean Burges.[1] Brazil fits the definition of a regional hegemon adopted by this volume. First, it is "significantly stronger than other states." In traditional measures of power, such as territory, population, GDP, number of military personnel, and size of defense spending, Brazil dwarfs its neighbors.

Second, Brazil "is aware of its power preponderance and is willing to use it." Within Latin America, it has sought to reduce conflict and to promote democracy, taking a prominent role in reacting to the 1995 war between Ecuador and Peru, and has opposed the ouster of Honduran President Manuel Zelaya from office in June 2009. Brazil has increasingly acted as a regional hegemon by asserting its leadership internationally and in the Western Hemisphere, taking the lead in international fora such as the World Trade Organization negotiations in Cancún in 2003 and the U.N. peacekeeping mission to Haiti.[2]

Third, Brazil "is active in the building, developing and sustaining of various international institutions." In the economic sphere, Brazil has been a major proponent of MERCOSUR (the Common Market of the South, MERCOSUL in Portuguese), while resisting the U.S.-sponsored Free Trade Area of the Americas (FTAA).[3] In the security sphere, it has sought to create institutions to reduce security threats and to coordinate security policy such as the South American Defense Council.

Brazil has been wielding its influence and belying the old adage that "Brazil is the country of the future—and always will be." This chapter explores how Brazil's neighbors have reacted to its hegemonic aspirations and focuses primarily, though not exclusively, on the politics in South America surrounding MERCOSUR and the increasingly assertive foreign policy of Venezuela. The frameworks used by this volume help explain the various reactions of Brazil's neighbors to its policies.

STRATEGIES OF RESISTANCE

Binding

MERCOSUR provides an excellent example of the binding strategy. Of course, Brazil has strongly supported MERCOSUR for its own benefit.[4] Burges considers MERCOSUR one of the three main endeavors that Brazil has used to promote its foreign policy agenda.[5] As Walt explains, "Weaker states may want to use institutions to bind the strongest power, but the dominant power will try to use the same institutions to magnify its power and to advance its own interests."[6] However, it was the smaller states that first pushed for economic integration. By formally linking their economies and creating a customs union (though still an "incomplete customs union"),[7] the member countries hoped to gain economic and political benefits.

MERCOSUR has survived against the odds and despite many crises and difficulties.[8] Overall, the record of integrationist schemes in Latin America has been poor. An earlier impulse toward free trade in the 1950s and 1960s, with such groupings as the Latin American Free Trade Association (LAFTA), the Caribbean Community and Common Market (CARICOM) and the Andean Pact, faltered in implementation; none increased intraregional trade to any significant extent, and the debt crisis of the 1980s distracted attention from these efforts.[9]

Argentina led the way in creating MERCOSUR. Argentine President Rafael Alfonsín made the first overtures to his Brazilian counterpart and initiated the crafting of cooperative agreements between the two states; economic integration was one of Alfonsín's highest priorities.[10] Continued negotiations resulted in multiple agreements on many issues, ranging from tariff reduction to surface transportation facilitation.[11] Negotiations also expanded to include other potential members. Uruguay, "a logical addition given its geographical proximity and traditional commercial ties with both neighbors" joined in discussions almost immediately and promised its support.[12] Further negotiations led to the signing of the 1991 Treaty of Asunción, which created MERCOSUR. By that time, Paraguay had joined the group. Again, the parties agreed to further important protocols, and the treaty entered into force January 1, 1995.[13] Eventually Chile, Bolivia, Ecuador, Peru, and Venezuela became associate members, although Venezuela has nearly completed the process of becoming a full member.[14]

The frameworks help explain the multiple factors contributing to the creation of MERCOSUR. First, security concerns provided some of the impetus. Negotiations between Argentina and Brazil beginning in the 1980s signaled a positive change in relations between the two military rivals.[15] Manzetti explains that both the Argentine and Brazilian leaders "favored demilitarizing the South Atlantic to keep it free of East–West confrontations."[16] Unprecedented agreements on the development of the two states' nuclear programs overlapped with the move toward economic cooperation.[17] "Both new governments reasoned that if they tied themselves more closely to each other's economy, a renewal of traditional conflicts and rivalries would be less likely."[18] Conscious trust-building measures coincided with the economic agreements. Reciprocal visits by Alfonsín and Brazilian President Sarney to inspect their respective nuclear plants, initiated by Alfonsín, were unprecedented efforts at reducing uncertainty and distrust; Manzetti reports that Argentina had never before allowed a foreign leader onto the premises of the Pilcaniyeu nuclear plant.[19] It probably helped motivate Argentina that the power gap between it and Brazil had been widening and that Argentina had fared miserably in the Falklands/Malvinas War.[20] As Sampanis notes (see Chapter 6), a larger gap in power between two states will make acquiescence by the weaker more likely. Changes in the *international* balance of power also facilitated coordination between Brazil and Argentina. The end of the bipolar confrontation between the United States and USSR reduced the value of Latin American states as U.S. allies and resulted in less attention to the region by both superpowers. It also raised the specter that Latin America could face alternative blocs of power, such as a resurgent Europe.[21]

In line with the second framework, in establishing MERCOSUR member countries attempted to constrain the regional hegemon and to realize the joint benefits of trade. Brazil, the regional hegemon, of course expected to benefit from institutions that reduced barriers to its exports. Thus, Brazil enthusiastically supported the creation of MERCOSUR and has sought its expansion throughout the continent. However, the smaller parties who signed onto the project also expected to benefit. Argentina, Uruguay, and Paraguay expected to gain reciprocal access to Brazil's market.[22] Institutions can "lock in" neoliberal economic reforms and head off backtracking by the domestic government.[23] MERCOSUR serves as a guarantee against a future Brazilian administration throwing up protectionist walls. Indeed, Gómez Mera argues that Brazilian presidents used MERCOSUR commitments as leverage to pressure their own domestic industries to accept reduction in trade protection and that Argentine President Carlos Menem used MERCOSUR commitments as support for his 1991 economic reform.[24]

Furthermore, the end of the Cold War, plus the devastation of the 1980s debt crisis, left a changed international economic climate that enhanced the attractiveness of free trade agreements. Globalization and neoliberal economic reforms reduced the attractiveness of previously in vogue autarchic economic practices. The debt crisis precipitated the end of import-substituting industrialization, the attempt to reorient developing countries' economies, and increased emphasis on foreign trade. At the same time, the states of Latin America feared they would face growing economic competition from the United States and Europe.[25]

Finally, understanding MERCOSUR necessitates employing the third framework. Domestic factors heavily influenced the leaders of Argentina and Brazil. Leaders sought to decrease tensions between countries to improve the stability of their own governments. Furthermore, the regime type affected the motivations of the leaders and their ability to strike an accord. Both were new democracies, with regimes that allowed sufficient autonomy in foreign affairs to enable the executives to initiate free-trade negotiations in the absence of significant societal support.

Experts concur that MERCOSUR was primarily initiated by the leaders of Argentina and Brazil and not spurred by public support or demand for integration. At the beginning, there was little public debate or instigation by economic interests within either state.[26] Subsequently, however, domestic interest groups influenced strategies later employed by member governments.

First, the return to democracy brought to power individuals who were interested in such agreements (unlike their military predecessors). In addition, the presidents saw integration as a means not only to reduce security threats and improve the economy but also to shore up their democracies.[27]

Both the Brazilian and Argentine presidents who initiated economic integration in the 1980s were the first civilian presidents their countries had seen for many years. The Brazilian military had been in power for twenty years after the 1964 coup. The Argentine military held power from 1976 to 1983. The new civilian presidents looked to bolster their new democratic regimes by reducing security threats and decreasing the influence of the military. Argentina redemocratized before Brazil and led the way when "the March 1985 emergence of simultaneous transitional democracies in Uruguay and Brazil provided a critical mass of committed democratic institutions in the Southern Cone."[28] Dávila-Villers points to Alfonsín's desire to remove any rationale for the military to intervene in politics. Repeated attempts at military insurrection in the 1980s were constant reminders of the threat.[29] Aldo Zilli argues that redemocratization was a critical factor because it was only when Argentina democratized that "Raul Alfonsín took power and produced a shift in the identity of Argentina as democratic leaders sought to clearly distinguish themselves from their authoritarian predecessors."[30] Foreign minister Dante Caputo made the democratically elected government's goals clear:

> The way that Argentina inserts itself into the world plays a fundamental role. Notably because external linkages will serve to integrate the democratic memory of the world into Argentina in a kind of accelerated apprenticeship of democratic forms. . . . Therefore, our foreign policy is articulated so as to strengthen our democratic system.[31]

The need to reinforce democratic institutions extended beyond Argentina and Brazil. Uruguay was included in pre-MERCOSUR negotiations because it had redemocratized in 1985. Significantly, Argentina, Brazil, and Uruguay excluded Paraguay from negotiations until it redemocratized in 1989.[32] Later MERCOSUR leaders played a significant role in shoring up the elected Paraguayan government during an attempted coup in 1996.[33] Afterward, MERCOSUR made democratic government a condition for membership.[34] Concerns about undemocratic actions by President Hugo Chávez delayed Brazil's approval of full membership for Venezuela.[35]

Societal pressure has since affected the evolution of MERCOSUR. Domestic interest groups have supported its continuation but have also at times lodged complaints against harmful effects of decreased protectionist practices. But despite opposition, eventually "substantial portions of the business community actively supported integration, which made it more difficult for policymakers to turn back."[36] Furthermore, Gómez Mera argues that social-ization between executives in member states has strengthened personal ties and made the union able to withstand crises.[37] Pertinent to Argentina's inter-ests, the country has benefitted from access to Brazil's market, which became the largest importer of Argentina's industrial products in the 1990s.[38]

Even Venezuela, which frequently engaged in oppositional strategies, has sought full membership in MERCOSUR rather than remain an associate member. The prospect of cheaper oil from Venezuela provided an incentive for other members to admit it to the group. On Venezuela's part, the coun-try is dependent on oil exports and on Brazilian and Argentine imports. For Chávez, MERCOSUR also provides the possibility of influencing MERCO-SUR's economic policies from within.[39]

Blackmail

One way to extract better deals is through a blackmail strategy. South Ameri-can states wanting to extract benefits from Brazil have used blackmail strate-gies to get greater concessions from Brazil than they otherwise would have received.

The disproportionate economies of MERCOSUR's member states create friction between them. Argentina, Uruguay, and Paraguay fear that competi-tion from Brazilian manufactured goods might overwhelm their own econo-mies and result in a lack of industrial development and trade imbalances. For example, that Argentina's industries are generally less efficient than Brazil's has raised questions of compatible interests.[40] Statements like former Brazil-ian President Cardoso's that he foresaw "Brazil becoming the industrial pow-erhouse" of the region, while Chile would be "a ready source of capital" and "Argentina the breadbasket" could not have helped alleviate concerns.[41]

Argentina and Brazil have had multiple disagreements because of their economic disparity. Several times Argentina has gained concessions, some-times through threats. One area of contention has been occasions where an unequal balance of trade between the two countries has adversely affected Argentina. Even before the signing of the Treaty of Asunción, Argentina ex-perienced a negative trade surplus with Brazil. Domestic pressure then arose from Argentine business to redress this inequality, which was having dire ef-fects on the Argentine economy. In addition to new economic agreements, Brazil in 1988 agreed to buy Argentine aircraft and to build an oil pipeline so it could import Argentine natural gas.[42] Another instance early in the process of creating MERCOSUR illustrates the ability of Argentina to use the threat of "undesirable actions" to get Brazil to change its policy. In the early 1990s, after the signing of the Treaty of Asunción, a trade imbalance again became a serious issue. Argentina had instituted a neoliberal austerity program and, more significantly, had moved to cut hyperinflation by pegging the peso to the dollar in 1991. Brazil, however, did not begin an effective anti-inflation plan, the *Plan Real*, until 1994. This disparity led the Argentine peso to become overvalued compared to the Brazilian currency, which led to an influx of Brazilian products into Argentina and a serious trade deficit. Argentina moved to address this issue by implementing what was effectively a tariff, which resulted in Brazil agreeing to buy more Argentine products (wheat and oil) in exchange for Argentina dropping the tariff.[43] Argentina thus violated its agreement to reduce protectionist practices, risking Brazil's ire. But it correctly calculated that its action would result in concessions from Brazil.

In these cases, Argentina faced serious economic and political consequences if the imbalance in trade continued unabated. Argentina took the risk of provoking Brazil, gambling that the perpetuation of MERCOSUR was important enough to Brazil that the country would make concessions. In these cases, as well as in later crises, Brazil initially rejected compensating for Argentina's problems but ultimately relented. Brazil did not abandon MERCOSUR and instead sought to repair the damage to its relationship with Argentina. Gómez Mera notes that this is puzzling because, economically, MERCOSUR "had fading economic relevance."[44] But Brazil saw MERCOSUR as a stepping-stone to greater South American integration, with Brazil as the economic head. In the cases described here, the binding of international institutions helped a weaker country protect itself in its relationship with a larger economy, simultaneously providing an opportunity to blackmail the larger country.

Balking

Balking is a potentially effective strategy, though less extreme than blackmail. Again, relations with MERCOSUR provide examples of this approach. Although Chile was invited early on to join MERCOSUR, ultimately it decided to become an associate member, rather than a full member. Overall, its economic interests would likely have been hurt by adopting MERCOSUR's common external tariff. Chile is oriented toward free trade and had a low tariff of 11 percent, which it has since lowered to 6 percent for most products.[45] Chile also sought to negotiate its own bilateral free trade deal with the United States and others.

Chile had been repeatedly invited to join MERCOSUR negotiations in the early 1990s.[46] Chile rejected these overtures; it had grander plans than linking itself too closely to its closest neighbors. As the economy minister proclaimed, "Our goal is the world."[47] Most immediately, Chile hoped to join NAFTA; at the 1994 Miami Summit U.S. President Bill Clinton extended an invitation to Chile to do so. However, the "fast track" to membership in a North American free-trade area was derailed by Congress's rejection of a "fast track" for the U.S. president. Instead, Chile turned back toward its neighbors. It sought bilateral free-trade agreements with several countries and became an associate member of MERCOSUR in 1996. Although Chile has from time to time indicated that it still desires full membership in MERCOSUR, it has acceded to a free-trade agreement only with the bloc thus far. In doing so, it has gained preferential access for its products without having to adopt its common external tariff.[48] In late 2000 Chile finally began free-trade negotiations directly with the United States, a move that was criticized by Brazil.[49] Certainly one reason for resistance by Chile was the divergence between its lower tariffs and MERCOSUR's common external tariff—Brazil has resisted lowering MERCOSUR's tariff further.[50] Also, Brazil took the position that, as a full member of MERCOSUR, Chile would have to follow requirements that it negotiate with other members of MERCOSUR when negotiating with other trade blocs.[51] Chile, on the other hand, would not "think of sacrificing our trade autonomy."[52] Instead, Chile finally obtained its free-trade agreement with the United States, and thoughts of joining MERCOSUR have stalled.

After finally securing the agreement, though, Chile endangered that very agreement over the U.S. decision to go to war in Iraq. The United States pressured both Chile and Mexico, who were occupying seats on the U.N. Security Council at the time, to support its 2003 resolution for the invasion of Iraq. Chile successfully balked—it refused to vote in favor of the resolution, despite insinuations from the United States that this decision could derail its free-trade agreement, which had been signed but not yet approved. Although approval of the agreement was delayed because of Chile's stand, it ultimately was approved and went into effect at the beginning of 2004.[53]

In both cases of balking, Chile acted to protect its own economy. One reason for balking is that "there is a genuine conflict between their interests."[54]

Clearly because of the free-trade orientation of its economy, the benefits of further integrating with MERCOSUR were uncertain. Associate member status continues to provide sufficient benefits without excessively tying Chile to the economic bloc. It also had options—free-trade agreements with other, wealthier countries. One major country, of course, is the United States. Europe presented another lure. At the same time Chile was being pressured by the United States over the 2003 U.N. Security Council resolution, it had another free-trade agreement pending with the EU. Caving in to the United States would have likely offended the Europeans and in turn endangered that agreement.[55]

However, domestic factors have had some impact on Chile's strategy. As Cason and Burrell describe, in early MERCOSUR negotiations Chilean domestic groups remained apathetic about joining the customs union, and the government had a free hand. However, by the mid-1990s, domestic business groups had begun to agitate in favor of MERCOSUR and helped influence Chile's decision to become an associate member.[56] Businesses feared the effects of a MERCOSUR customs union that excluded or discriminated against their exports.[57] Public opinion also now favors closer ties to Chile's neighbors rather than to the United States: A Chilean poll conducted in 2001 found that, given a choice, 45 percent favored full membership with MERCOSUR in contrast to 31 percent favoring a U.S. trade accord.[58]

Public sentiment was even more pronounced in the 2003 Iraq War decision. Chilean public sentiment opposed the war and submitting to U.S. pressure. The leaders of the major parties in the governing coalition publically stated their opposition to a war with Iraq at that time.[59] In the end, though, Chile successfully employed the balking strategy vis-à-vis two stronger states: It remains an associate member of MERCOSUR and got its free-trade agreement with the United States.

Soft Balancing

South American countries have used soft balancing to oppose gently, or not so gently, Brazil. For example, Argentina has opposed Brazil's ambitions for a permanent seat on the U.N. Security Council.[60] Soft balancing includes opposition to Brazilian candidates for positions in international institutions. In addition to leading opposition within the WTO, Brazil has put forward its own candidates for WTO director-general. While the ultimate failure of these candidates to become president is not especially surprising, what is more noteworthy is that other South American states opposed Brazil's candidate. In 1994, Argentine President Menem voiced his support for former Mexican President Carlos Salina de Gortari's candidacy over that of Brazil's Rubens Ricupero. Later papered over as a "misunderstanding," diplomatically it remained a snub. In 2005, Argentina and other Latin American countries supported the candidacy of Uruguay's Carlos Pérez del Castillo over that of Brazilian Luiz Felipe de Seixas Corrêa.[61] Brazil presented its own candidate because of Uruguay's promotion of Pérez del Castillo, who had written a text for the Cancun meeting undercutting Brazil's position in agricultural negotiations.[62] Other countries, especially Argentina, refused to renounce their support for the Uruguayan candidate.

While overall Brazil's neighbors seek cordial relations, this soft diplomacy is a reminder that they also can oppose a potentially overambitious state with subtle means. And Brazil's actions are sometimes seen as overambitious, as evidenced by Argentina's then-President Nestor Kirchner complaining, "If there is a vacancy at the WTO, Brazil wants it. If there is a space at the UN, Brazil wants it . . . they even wanted a Brazilian pope!"[63] Thus, soft balancing can be a "shot across the bow" to remind Brazil that it cannot take the support of its allies for granted.[64] At the same time, for the most part South American countries are not in a position to strongly challenge Brazil. However, in addition to engaging in a binding strategy, Venezuela has also attempted more oppositional strategies.

Hard Balancing

States also use hard balancing to oppose a threatening state. President Hugo Chávez created the Bolivarian Alliance of the Peoples of the Americas (ALBA). According to Burges, this "can be read as a fuzzy attempt at a counter-hegemonic project."[65] The aim of ALBA was to provide an alternative to the FTAA proposed by the United States, but it also competes directly with Brazil's own counter-FTAA ambitions. So far Venezuela has garnered support only from states that are small or led by ideologically sympathetic leaders: Cuba, Bolivia, Nicaragua, Dominica, Honduras, Ecuador, St. Vincent and the Grenadines, and Antigua and Barbuda.[66] Initially ALBA was proposed as a means to foster economic, social, and political cooperation within Latin America. To attract support, "Chávez has dangled the proverbial carrot before regional countries saying that there were significant benefits to be had from the planned expansion of oil refineries, bauxite and alumina facilities and petro chemical industries under ALBA" as well as other kinds of assistance.[67] Although there have been some attempts to make ALBA a military alliance as well, these suggestions have been rejected by most member states.[68]

At the heart of Venezuela's balancing is security. Relations between Venezuela and the United States have been hostile, as illustrated by the favorable view the United States took of the attempted coup against Chávez in 2002. Tensions continue to simmer between Venezuela and Colombia as well. Chávez's goal as a "small major power" in South America also conflicts with Brazil's own ambitions. Venezuela's relationship with Brazil has been less antagonistic than with other countries, but Brazil remains suspicious of Venezuela's actions.

Venezuela also has the means to balance. Venezuela's oil wealth makes its internal military buildup possible and offers an enticement for possible allies. The increase in oil prices allowed Venezuela to balance internally by significantly increasing its arms purchases and to attract allies by offering foreign aid.[69]

However, the third framework also helps explain Venezuela's actions. Venezuela's foreign policy became defiantly assertive only after the election of Chávez in 1998. He has an alternative economic and social vision for Latin America and will see it accomplished only if Venezuela takes the lead in shaping that vision.[70] Thus, the ideology of the leader explains Venezuela's assertive foreign policy, and that ideology lies behind Chávez's affinity with like-minded leaders such as Bolivia's President Evo Morales, Ecuador's President Rafael Correa, and Cuba's Fidel Castro. Chávez also has overcome stiff domestic opposition to his presidency, having survived a coup attempt and a recall effort by an at-times intense domestic opposition. Given that Chávez has vanquished his foes and packed the legislature with his supporters, he has had a free hand in conducting his foreign policy. Venezuela's choice of allies does not just include those with similar ideological predispositions, but his ideological goals have in part motivated his search for strong extrahemispheric friends.

Despite the relative rarity of wars in Latin America, conflict and militarized disputes have been ever present. States have increased arms and military might in reaction to perceived or real threats from their neighbors. Disputes over territorial boundaries have been particularly pernicious.[71] Significantly, though, with the end of the Cold War and redemocratization, hard balancing between some traditional rivals has lessened. The discussion of MERCOSUR has already pointed out factors that have resulted in increased cooperation and decreased antagonisms. Argentina and Brazil made a significant policy shift when they reached agreements to stop their nuclear weapons programs. As described earlier in this chapter, they engaged in other strategies to reduce security threats and reap economic gains. Furthermore, hard balancing is costly, and the benefits are often uncertain. Venezuela's decision to join MERCOSUR may provide it with increased leverage to influence the institution from within. But it may also simply be an acknowledgment that, despite its oil wealth, Venezuela cannot afford extravagant military expenditures forever. Brazilian President Luiz Inácio Lula da Silva supposedly chastised Chávez for his military spending during one visit, "Christ, what do you want these weapons for? You can't even get milk for your coffee in the hotels."[72] The reality for Venezuela is that Brazil is stronger, is wealthier, and has effectively parlayed its strengths, becoming the regional hegemon that Chávez would have liked Venezuela to have become.

CONCLUSION

This chapter's examination of South America illustrates the two-way relationship between a hegemon and weaker states. To this end, Brazil has supported and promoted MERCOSUR among other institutional arrangements. Brazil has sought not only to achieve its economic goals but also to increase its influence within and outside Latin America. However, weaker states have the wherewithal to resist and subvert the hegemon's efforts through strategies such as binding, blackmail, balking, and balancing. Followers can take the initiative in "locking in" the hegemon, as Argentina did in proposing economic and security cooperation in the 1980s. States can use existing ties to blackmail the hegemon, as when Argentina unilaterally imposed tariffs in violation of their free trade commitments to stem a crushing wave of Brazilian imports. Following the example of Chile, a state can balk at acceding to a hegemon's wishes while reaping benefits of partial cooperation. States can get away with using soft or hard balancing to restrain the hegemon's ambitions. Although not specifically examined in this chapter, the behavior of South American leaders like Argentina's Alfonsín exhibit attempts at bonding by pursuing personal relationships and confidence-building measures. This chapter demonstrates that all three explanatory frameworks explain the behavior of the states in South America. While providing only an initial examination of strategies of resistance in South America, it is clear that resistance can indeed be useful for weaker states.

NOTES

I would like to thank Martha Castañeda, Suzana Palaska, Yna Shimabukuro, and Craig Swain for research assistance and for helpful comments on earlier drafts by Maria Sampanis and Kenneth Bender.

1. Sean Burges, "Consensual Hegemony: Theorizing Brazilian Foreign Policy after the Cold War," *International Relations* 22, 1 (2008): 65.

2. Ibid.

3. Ibid.

4. Jeffrey Cason, "On the Road to Southern Cone Economic Integration," *Journal of Interamerican Studies and World Affairs* 42, 1 (Spring 2000): 24.

5. Burges, "Consensual Hegemony": 42.

6. Stephen Walt, *Taming American Power: The Global Response to U.S. Primacy* (New York: W. W. Norton, 2005): 148.

7. Andrés Malamud, "Presidential Diplomacy and the Institutional Underpinnings of Mercosur: An Examination," *Latin American Research Review*, 40, 1 (2005): 141; see also Laura Gómez Mera, "Explaining Mercosur's Survival: Strategic Sources of Argentine-Brazilian Convergence," *Journal of Latin American Studies*, 37, 1 (February 2005): 110.

8. Gómez Mera, "Explaining Mercosur's Survival": 110.

9. Robert Maryse, "Toward Economic Integration," *Americas* 47, 4 (July/August 1995): 54.

10. Luigi Manzetti, "Argentine-Brazilian Economic Integration: An Early Appraisal," *Latin American Research Review* 25, 3 (1990): 114; David R. Dávila-Villers, "Competition and Co-operation in the River Plate: The Democratic Transition and Mercosur," *Bulletin of Latin American Research* 11, 3 (Sept. 1992): 265.

11. Manzetti, "Argentine–Brazilian Economic Integration": 117–120.

12. Ibid.: 118.

13. Malamud, "Presidential Diplomacy": 141; Dávila-Villers, "Competition and Co-operation": 272–273.

14. "Venezuela to Fully Join Mercosur," BBC News, October 17, 2005; retrieved from news.bbc.co.uk/go/pr/fr/-/2/hi/americas/4348730.stm on September 25, 2009.

15. Mônica Hirst, "Security Policies, Democratization, and Regional Integration in the Southern Cone," in *International Security and Democracy: Latin America and the Caribbean in the Post–Cold War Era*, ed. Jorge I. Domínguez (Pittsburgh: University of Pittsburgh Press, 1998): 103.

16. Manzetti, "Argentine–Brazilian Economic Integration": 115.

17. Dominique Fournier, "The Alfonsín Administration and the Promotion of Democratic Values in the Southern Cone and the Andes," *The Journal of Latin American Studies* 31, 1 (1999): 50.

18. Cason, "On the Road": 25.

19. Manzetti, "Argentine–Brazilian Economic Integration": 119, 138.

20. Dávila-Villers, "Competition and Co-operation": 264.

21. Gómez-Mera, "Explaining Mercosur's Survival": 116.

22. Dávila-Villers, "Competition and Co-operation."

23. Gómez Mera, "Explaining Mercosur's Survival": 113.

24. Ibid.: 113.

25. Cason, "On the Road": 27; Jeffrey Cason and Jennifer Burrell, "Turning the Tables: State and Society in South America's Economic Integration," *Polity* 34, 4 (Summer 2002): 469; Gómez Mera, "Explaining Mercosur's Survival": 116.

26. Cason, "On the Road": 24, 26; Cason and Burrell, "Turning the Tables": 467; Gómez Mera, "Explaining Mercosur's Survival": 114.

27. Gómez Mera, "Explaining Mercosur's Survival": 113–114, 123.

28. Fournier, "The Alfonsín Administration": 73.

29. Dávila-Villers, "Competition and Co-operation": 266.

30. Aldo Zilli, "Testing the Democratic Peace Theory: Argentina, Chile and the Construction of Civility in the Southern Cone" (M.A. Thesis, California State University, Sacramento, 2007).

31. Quoted in Fournier, "The Alfonsín Administration": 44.

32. Dávila-Villers, "Competition and Co-operation": 271.

33. Arturo Valenzuela, *The Collective Defense of Democracy: Lessons from the Paraguayan Crisis of 1996* (New York: Carnegie Corporation, 1999).

34. Riordan Roett, "A Full Plate," *World Link* (May/June 1999): 42.

35. "World Briefing/Brazil; Venezuela Gets MERCOSUR Nod," *Los Angeles Times,* Dec. 16, 2009: A28.

36. Cason, "On the Road": 29.

37. Gómez Mera, "Explaining Mercosur's Survival."

38. Ibid.: 113.

39. Paulo Prada, "South American Trade Bloc Moves to Admit Venezuela," *New York Times,* December 9, 2005: C5.

40. Cason and Burrell, "Turning the Tables": 467–468.

41. Sean W. Burges, *Brazilian Foreign Policy after the Cold War* (Gainesville: University Press of Florida, 2009): 38.

42. Manzetti, "Argentine–Brazilian Economic Integration": 120.

43. Cason, "On the Road": 28.

44. Gómez Mera, "Explaining Mercosur's Survival": 123.

45. Glenn W. Harrison, Thomas F. Rutherford, and David G. Tarr, "Trade Policy Options for Chile: The Importance of Market Access," *The World Bank Economic Review* 16, 1 (2002): 51.

46. Cason and Burrell, "Turning the Tables": 470.

47. Ibid.: 471.

48. Harrison, Rutherford, and Tarr, "Trade Policy Options": 49–50.

49. "Another Blow to MERCOSUR," *Economist* 358, 8215 (March 31, 2001): 33.

50. Rohter, "South American Trade Bloc."

51. "Chile Hardens Its Position Regarding Its Possible Full Membership of MER-COSUR," BBC Summary of World Broadcasts, November 11, 2000; available at www.lexisnexis.com.proxy.lib.csus.edu/hottopics/lnacademic/.

52. José de Gregorio, economy minister, quoted in "Chile Hardens Its Position Regarding Its Possible Full Membership of MERCOSUR."

53. Randall Newnham, "'Coalition of the Bribed and Bullied?' U.S. Economic Linkage and the Iraq War Coalition," *International Studies Perspectives* 9, 2 (May 2008): 189.

54. Walt, *Taming American Power*: 145.

55. Hector Tobar and Marla Dicerson, "The World; Showdown with Iraq; Mexico and Chile Walk a Tightrope," *Los Angeles Times,* March 13, 2003: 1.

56. Cason and Burrell, "Turning the Tables": 459, 472.

57. Ibid.: 472.

58. "Chile-Trade: Chileans Prefer Full Membership MERCOSUR to a U.S. Trade Accord," EFE News Service, January 4, 2001; retrieved from www.lexisnexis.com on March 4, 2002.

59. Manuel Delano and Juan Jesus Aznarez, "Lagos y Fox se inclinan por la abstención o el voto negativo en el Consejo de Seguridad," *El País,* March 14, 2003: 4.

60. "Suspicious Neighbours Start to resent Brazil's Global Ambitions," *Irish Times*, May 6, 2005: 13.

61. Burges, *Brazilian Foreign Policy*: 168; "Argentina apoya candidatura de uruguayo para dirigir OMC; Argentina apoya a Pérez del Castillo al frente do la OMC," *El Pais* (Uruguay) October 16, 2004; retrieved from www.lexisnexis.com.proxy.lib .csus.edu/hottopics/lnacademic/ on January 21, 2010; "Brasil prepara nome de Luis Felipe de Seixas Correa para OMC," *Jornal do Commercio* (Brazil), October 8, 2004; retrieved from www.lexisnexis.com.proxy.lib.csus.edu/hottopics/lnacademic/? on January 21, 2010.

62. Paulo Braga, "Argentina oficializa apoio ao candidato do Uruguai à OMC," *Valor Econômico*, March 31, 2005; available at www.lexisnexis.com.proxy.lib.csus.edu/hottopics/lnacademic/?.

63. "Suspicious Neighbours": 13.

64. Walt, *Taming American Power*: 128.

65. Sean W. Burges, "Building a Global Southern Coalition: The Competing Approaches of Brazil's Lula and Venezuela's Chávez," *Third World Quarterly* 28, 7 (2007): 1346.

66. Gobierno Bolivariano de Venezuela, "ALBA Pasa a ser Alianza Bolivariana de los Pueblos de América"; available at www.vtv.gob.ve/noticias-nacionales/19957.

67. "Dominica's membership of Venezuela's ALBA bloc stirs up storm," BBC Worldwide Monitoring Service, March 8, 2008; available at www.lexisnexis.com .proxy.lib.csus.edu/hottopics/lnacademic/?

68. "Bolivian Leader Proposes a Unified ALBA Bloc Military Force," *Los Tiempos* (November 10, 2009) from BBC Worldwide Monitoring Service, November 11, 2009; available at www.lexisnexis.com.proxy.lib.csus.edu/hottopics/lnacademic/?; Caribbean Media Corporation, "Suggestion of Military Alliance with Venezuela 'Laughable'–Dominican Minster," BBC Worldwide Monitoring Service, March 9, 2008; available at www.lexisnexis.com.proxy.lib.csus.edu/hottopics/lnacademic/?

69. Burges, "Building a Southern Coalition."

70. Ibid.: 1344.

71. Jorge I. Domínguez et al., *Boundary Disputes in Latin America* (*Peaceworks* no. 50) (Washington, DC: United States Institute of Peace, 2003); Beth A. Simmons, *Territorial Disputes and Their Resolution: The Case of Ecuador and Peru* (*Peaceworks* no. 27) (Washington, DC: United States Institute of Peace, 1999).

72. Mac Margolis, "The Crafty Superpower; by Turns Charming and Cagey, Cool to America and Close to Obama, Lula Is Building a Unique Regional Giant," *Newsweek* 153, 17 (Apr. 27, 2009).

10 REACTING TO RUSSIA

Foreign Relations of the Former Soviet Bloc

Shale Horowitz and Michael D. Tyburski

WITHIN THE FORMER SOVIET BLOC, Russia remains by far the greatest economic and military power. How well has Russia been able to translate this power into influence on former Soviet bloc countries, defined as former Soviet Republics or Eastern European satellite states? How have the secondary states responded to Russia's hegemonic position in the region? Which explanatory frameworks and responses best explain secondary state behavior?

We begin by discussing how national foreign policy interests, while broadly affected by objective factors such as economic and military power, geography, and ethnic composition and settlement patterns, are typically specified by regime type and related leadership preferences (explanatory framework 3—domestic politics). We use regime type to indicate not just political institutions but the main goals that leaders and influential constituents view those institutions as serving. In a given state at a given point in its development and in a given international environment, there are usually only a limited number of identifiable regime types that are serious contenders for state power. In the former Soviet bloc, the two main regime types have been liberal nationalist democracy and neo-Communist authoritarianism (although Islamist authoritarianism is also a possibility in some former Soviet Republics in Central Asia). Once regime type and leadership preferences have identified and prioritized external threats, the familiar balance-of-power logic emphasized by realists is helpful in understanding the choice of foreign policy strategies (first explanatory framework).

We describe briefly the changes in Russia's foreign policy goals and strategies under Boris Yeltsin and Vladimir Putin. Russia's main areas of concern have been territorial and national defense, economic prosperity, and regime and leadership security—although the relative importance of these areas has varied over time. Russia's chosen methods of pressure and influence have also changed. Turning to Russia's neighbors, the followers, we ask how they have responded. Last, we summarize our conclusions in relation to the explanatory frameworks.

LEADERSHIP PREFERENCES UNDER LIBERAL NATIONALIST DEMOCRACY AND NEO-COMMUNIST AUTHORITARIANISM

Within the old Soviet bloc, encompassing the former Soviet Republics and satellite states, there have been two main political regime types: liberal nationalist democracies and neo-Communist authoritarian regimes. These two types mix political institutions with substantive goals based on relations with the Soviet-dominated past.[1] Liberal nationalist regimes were formed and driven by a desire to overthrow the Soviet past. In addition to replacing authoritarian rule with democracy, state repression with personal and cultural freedom, and a planned or socialized economy with a market economy, these regimes sought true and secure national independence from Soviet domination.

In contrast, the neo-Communist authoritarian regimes were formed and driven by the desire of old regime elites to conserve their authoritarian power. These Communist-era elites were willing to adopt elements of anti-Communist, reform nationalist ideology—such as the self-determination ideology of the dominant national group, greater personal freedom and cultural pluralism, and market-based economic institutions. But they sought to do so in a way that conserved their power. Personal freedom and cultural pluralism did not generally extend to freedom of the press and political organization and to free elections. Market reform was used to transfer control of wealth and lucrative economic opportunities into the hands of personal and political clients and to minimize concentrations of wealth and influence outside of state control. Ideologically, nationalist reformism was tempered by a greater emphasis on the achievements of the Soviet past—so as not to cede the ideological high ground entirely to the anti-Communist opposition groups.

In foreign policy, liberal nationalist democracies sought to solidify their political independence, military security, political institutions, and market reforms by affiliating with Western Europe and the United States. This was pursued through bilateral diplomacy and economic policy but above all by seeking membership in international institutions, specifically NATO and the EU. NATO seemed to offer credible security guarantees against the perceived residual threat from Russia. The EU offered not just economic gains but a political community with informal security benefits. The liberal nationalist democracies also formed strong bilateral and regional ties with one another to pursue their goals in common. Also to safeguard these common goals, they sought to legitimize, conserve, and proselytize their political model throughout the post-Soviet space and particularly on their immediate borders.

In turn, the neo-Communist authoritarian regimes sought to conserve their political power by affiliating with one another. An effort was made to conserve Communist-era economic and political ties and to promote external military security in common. This also meant preserving a relative separation from surrounding centers of power and ideological influence—Western Europe, Muslim South Asia, and, to a lesser extent, China. The implicit norm was that the neo-Communist regimes would not question each other's legitimacy and would work to protect one another against common external threats— threats that might have ideological, military, or economic elements, which could combine to strengthen internal opposition groups. Beyond bilateral relations, the neo-Communist regimes have been the core of the Commonwealth of Independent States (CIS) and the Collective Security Treaty Organization (CSTO) and later of the Eurasian Economic Community (EAEC). The CIS, CSTO, and EAEC have weaker collective obligations and cohesion than NATO and the EU because they are based on the weaker instrumental goal of leadership survival.[2]

Post-Soviet Russia itself well exhibits such variation in regime types, leadership preferences, and foreign policy priorities and strategies. Yeltsin presided over an initial democratic period, in which Russia's foreign policy was closer to the liberal nationalist ideal type. Putin then transitioned to authoritarianism, with foreign policy taking on a neo-Communist cast and showing more of Putin's "personal touch"—including oil and gas cutoffs, economic sanctions, cyber attacks, restrictions on migration and travel, internal political subversion, and assassinations.

WHAT THE REGIONAL HEGEMON, RUSSIA, WANTS

Before assessing and explaining defiance and compliance by Russia's neighbors, we must ask what Russia has wanted from them. There have been three major foreign policy areas of vital concern to Russia's leaders: national military security, national economic interests, and leadership and regime security.

In terms of national military security, Russia is concerned about territorial security interests as well as the broader security interests of the Russian people at home and abroad. In a number of former Soviet Republics—Estonia, Latvia, Moldova, Ukraine, and Kazakhstan—ethnic Russians account for a significant percentage of the population and have regionally concentrated settlement. Russian leaders cannot easily ignore the living conditions of these large Russian diasporas. There are also the interests of ethnic minorities in Russia with cross-border ethnic kin, most importantly in the volatile North Caucasus region. Russia's conflicts with Georgia are part of the effort to suppress opposition in Chechnya and to prevent separatist violence from spreading to other North Caucasus peoples. Russia supports South Ossetian and Abkhazian separatism in Georgia to solidify the loyalty of North Ossetians and other cross-border ethnic kin groups in the Russian North Caucasus.

Moreover, many former Soviet Republics and satellite states have sought membership in NATO and the EU. These two institutions are not direct threats to Russia's territorial integrity. However, eastward NATO and EU expansion affects Russia's ability to influence neighbors with large ethnic Russian minorities. NATO and EU members have formal or informal commitments to assist other member states involved in disputes with Russia. To the extent that such commitments are credible, Russia's relative power and bargaining leverage suffer.

The second important foreign policy arena involves national economic interests. Russia's energy sector is most important as a share of gross domestic product (GDP) and for future growth prospects. Here Russia has important interests both as an energy exporter and as an energy transit country for the three major Caspian Basin producers—Azerbaijan, Kazakhstan, and Turkmenistan. Russia gains from maximizing the value of domestic oil and gas production, along with transit fees collected from other states. To this end, it is interested in preserving its Soviet-era monopoly on Caspian Basin transit, which allows Russia to charge higher transit fees, while preventing a large increase in competing Caspian gas exports to Western Europe.

Leadership and regime security also matter. Both the conduct of foreign affairs and the character of surrounding governments may affect the popularity and legitimacy of incumbent leaders. First, governments viewed as effective in pursuing national interests and prestige abroad are more popular at home. The literature on diversionary politics argues that this often leads to myopic foreign policies, with leaders pursuing more popular, confrontational policies in the short run, at the expense of longer-term national interests. Authoritarian leaders seem more likely to engage in such behavior.[3] Limited political opposition and press freedoms insulate authoritarian leaders from effective internal criticism of diversionary policies. Second, neighboring states often have regimes that favorably advertise influential domestic political alternatives. By showing off the possibilities for domestic political change, such regimes inherently threaten the popularity and legitimacy of incumbent leaders. Again, this is likely to be a greater threat to leaders of authoritarian regimes, which lack the institutionalized political competition and routine government turnover of democracies.

Yeltsin's foreign policy initially imitated those of Western European powers such as Britain or Germany.[4] The new, smaller Russia would shed its imperial past and become an ordinary European country, pursuing stable, friendly relations with its neighbors through consultation and compromise. Yeltsin put up little resistance to the Western integration efforts of the Eastern European satellite states and the former Soviet Baltic Republics of Estonia, Latvia, and Lithuania. However, neo-Communist Duma opposition and great-Russian nationalism increasingly pushed Yeltsin into rhetorical opposition to the integration efforts of "defector" states—particularly to NATO's eastward expansion. However, he did not act to sabotage the Western accession of the Baltic States. This would not have been difficult in Estonia and Latvia, with their huge ethnic Russian minorities.

By contrast, Putin's opposition to EU and NATO expansion quickly became strident. NATO and the United States, in particular, are portrayed as threats to Russian security. Putin also ratcheted up the pressure on late EU and NATO aspirants, such as the new Westernizing governments in Georgia and Ukraine from 2004. In Ukraine, Russia supported Russian-speaking neo-Communist parties against Westernizing parties. Against Georgia, a battery of economic and political pressures included mass distribution of Russian citizenship to Abkhazians and South Ossetians, effectively annexing the regions to Russia. In 2008, low-intensity violence baited Georgian president Mikhail Saakashvili into an ill-considered preemptive strike against separatist South Ossetia.[5] Putin responded not just by occupying Abkhazia and South Ossetia but by pushing Russian forces into the Georgian heartland in an overt effort to force Saakashvili out of office. In former Soviet Republics such as Moldova and the Baltic States, Russia has supported neo-Communist opposition leaders and parties against Westernizing parties and governments.

Overall, Putin has been much more aggressive than Yeltsin in trying to influence Russia's neighbors. Both leaders were concerned with protecting Russia's territorial integrity, particularly in the Caucasus region. Putin stood out in other areas. Russia's preexisting energy subsidies and supply monopolies were routinely used to blackmail its neighbors. Russia regularly supported neo-Communist oppositions in smaller neighbors governed by liberal nationalist democratic regimes and also adopted overtly hostile public rhetoric toward such regimes, accusing them of joining the West in threatening Russian security and interests.[6]

Yeltsin's Russia would not have been expected to have had much influence on its neighbors except in the Caucasus region, where he was willing to act more forcefully. Putin's Russia would be expected to have more influence. In specific cases, we expect such influence to depend on how much pressure Russia was able and willing to apply and on how much follower (secondary) states were able and willing to resist.

RESISTANCE AND COOPERATION: THE FOLLOWERS

How have the other former Soviet bloc states responded to Russia? What explains these patterns? We will review evidence in four key areas where Russia sought influence: protecting Russia's territorial integrity and cross-border ethnic kin and ethnic allies; limiting formal alliances and economic integration with the West; controlling energy supply and transit from the Caspian Basin to Western European markets; and fighting political and ideological contagion threatening the legitimacy of Russia's regime.

Russia's Territorial Integrity and Cross-Border Ethnic Kin

What determines defiance of Russian territorial security and ethnic kin interests—and of analogous Soviet interests before August 1991? During the late 1980s, opposition elements in Eastern Europe and many Soviet Republics challenged the Communist authorities. First-movers like the Polish opposition front, Solidarity, risked harsh, military-style crackdowns. In 1989, Soviet reform leader Mikhail Gorbachev made it clear that force would not be used to prop up the satellite Communist Parties in Eastern Europe. Opposition movements spread out of control, and Communist governments fell like dominoes. Even before 1989, the same process had already begun in many

Soviet Republics. Here the first-movers were Estonia, Latvia, and Lithuania, and also Armenia, Georgia, and Moldova. Unlike in Eastern Europe, Gorbachev was willing to use force to preserve the Soviet Union—either in direct interventions by federal forces, as in Azerbaijan, Georgia, and Lithuania, or by using local ethnic minorities as proxies, as in Moldova. Opposition leaders and protesters often risked their lives.

Whether across Eastern Europe or across the Soviet Republics, why were anti-Communist oppositions much more aggressive in some countries than in others, when they faced similar crackdown threats? Oppositions were larger and better organized when led by leaders that made far-reaching demands for national revival, envisioned as wholesale replacement of the Soviet system with independent, democratic regimes, embracing civil liberties and market economies. These ideological movements are not easily explained in terms of economic interests and appear to be generated largely by historical comparisons between pre-Communist political and economic achievements and those of the Communist period. Whatever their source, these nationalist movements took greater risks because of their stronger ideological commitments to reform.

Almost without exception, the countries and Soviet republics with the stronger anti-Communist nationalist movements developed into liberal nationalist democracies in the post-Soviet period. On the other hand, the Soviet republics with the weakest nationalist movements, again almost without exception, were transformed into neo-Communist authoritarian regimes in the post-Soviet era. The few former Soviet republics that teetered between the two types of post-Soviet regimes mostly had Soviet-era reform nationalist movements of intermediate strength—like Azerbaijan, Kyrgyzstan, and Ukraine.

Under Yeltsin, Russian territorial security interests were defined more narrowly to exclude the former satellites and Soviet republics and even to exclude direct representation of large ethnic Russian minorities abroad. On the other hand, Yeltsin was determined to defend the territorial integrity of the new Russian Federation—the former Russian Republic of the USSR. This integrity was most directly threatened by the violent secessionist movement in Chechnya, led by a former Soviet general, Dzhokar Dudayev. During the late 1980s, Gorbachev sought to rein in Georgia's nationalist opposition by supporting Abkhazian and South Ossetian separatist movements. Chechen separatism maintained this incentive for Yeltsin. Georgian president Zviad Gamsakhurdia openly voiced support for Dudayev, and Yeltsin's Russia responded by supporting an internal coup that deposed Gamsakhurdia. Gamsakhurdia was succeeded by the veteran colleague of Gorbachev, Eduard Shevardnadze. In the conflict between Armenia and Azerbaijan over the Nagorno-Karabakh region, Gorbachev had sided with Azerbaijan's more loyal Communist party. Incentives were reversed after the Soviet collapse. Armenia's government carefully sought to restore good relations with Russia. In 1992, however, Azerbaijan's Communist government was replaced by a reform nationalist regime, led by President Abulfaz Elcibey, which looked to Turkey and the West. Russia duly supported another successful coup in 1993, which led to the rise of the more cautious Soviet-era leader, Heidar Aliev. Both Shevardnadze and Aliev understood that Yeltsin would tolerate no support—active or passive—for the Chechen cause. More generally, both came to understand that defying Russia in any significant way would lead Russia to support internal opposition elements that might overthrow their rule. Shevardnadze was forced to live with the de facto independence of Abkhazia and South Ossetia. Both Shevardnadze and Aliev struggled to consolidate power against internal opponents seeking Russian patronage. In this way, Yeltsin not only secured the allegiance of the North Caucasus ethnic kin of the South Ossetians and Abkhazians but also made sure that Chechen fighters would have no safe havens or material support networks operating in the South Caucasus rear of Chechnya.

Outside of the South Caucasus, Yeltsin's direct involvement in the former Soviet Republics was limited to Moldova and Tajikistan. In Moldova, Yeltsin continued Russia's support for the ethnic Russian-dominated Transnistrian separatist regime—largely because of its popular legitimacy in Russia and its support from within the Russian military. In Tajikistan, Russia cooperated with local neo-Communists to consolidate an authoritarian regime and to contain the mutually threatening Islamist opposition.

Putin has been more aggressive with Georgia—effectively adopting Abkhazia and South Ossetia as satellite territories of Russia, even prior to crushing Saakashvili's response in South Ossetia. Putin has also more strongly supported the Transnistrian regime's efforts to gain an equal legal status with the Moldovan government.

The pattern of responses to Russian military intervention has been consistent.[7] Where Russia or its local proxies have used decisive military force, target governments such as Georgia and Moldova have made tactical withdrawals from contested regions. However, far from formally conceding Russian demands, they have loudly rejected them. This political defiance is due both to their own ideological commitments to their country's territorial integrity and to their fear that kowtowing to Russia would provoke a nationalist backlash benefitting their internal political rivals.

Bonds with Other Great Powers: Hard Balancing

What determines when and how successfully former Soviet bloc states seek a Western geopolitical orientation, as indicated by applying for EU and NATO membership and later gaining them?[8] During the years that Yeltsin fought the neo-Communists in the Russian Duma, almost all the former satellite states of Eastern Europe, along with the Baltic states (Estonia, Latvia, and Lithuania), were able to make credible commitments to enter the orbit of the NATO and EU countries. The states that most aggressively pushed internal liberal democratic and market reforms under the banner of nationalist revival—Poland, the Czech Republic, and Hungary—were the same states that first pursued and gained entry into NATO and the EU. Among the former Soviet republics, this vanguard role was played by the Baltic states.

By the time Putin came to power in late 1999, the Czech Republic, Hungary, and Poland had joined NATO, and the other former Eastern European satellite states, along with the Baltic states, were on the formal path to membership. This second group joined NATO in 2004. Most of the same countries, including the Baltic states, formally applied to enter the EU in the mid-1990s and also gained entry in 2004. Formal negotiations for entry into NATO and the EU, and especially actual entry, made it more costly and less effective for Russia to apply pressure on these states.

Putin has gone much farther than Yeltsin in interfering in internal Baltic politics in favor of neo-Communist opposition forces and has used economic sanctions, cyber attacks, and diplomatic rhetoric to attempt to bully Baltic governments on various issues. But Putin has so far avoided direct military intervention. This situation can be compared to those of Georgia, Moldova, and Ukraine. Both because of active or potential military conflicts with Russia or because of lagging internal reforms and political instability, or both, these three late aspirants to Western integration have not been granted entry. As a result, Putin's intervention has been much more forceful.

However, none of the governments in question has been forced to bend to Putin's will. The Ukrainian liberal democratic parties and leaders have arguably become more defiant. Putin has had the greatest success where, as in Abkhazia and South Ossetia, Russian troops directly occupied parts of Georgia in concert with its local ethnic proxies. More generally, by maintaining or increasing tensions, Putin has so far helped to block Georgia, Moldova, and Ukraine from joining NATO and the EU. But that had already been achieved for these countries during Yeltsin's rule, by weak internal reforms and the Western desire to avoid being drawn into direct conflict with Russia. Moreover, the internal reforms following the Rose and Orange Revolutions have belatedly led the West to allow Georgia and Ukraine to enter the formal integration process.

Largely for geographical and cultural reasons, EU and NATO membership is, for the foreseeable future, not possible for the Central Asian states and Mongolia. Even generous geographical definitions of Europe, which include the South Caucasus region (Armenia, Azerbaijan, and Georgia), nevertheless exclude Central Asia. Although NATO is not in principle subject to such restrictions, even faster-reforming countries (like Mongolia) are too unimportant strategically and too costly to protect militarily.

Yet the orientation of all the former republics can be gauged by examining their involvement in international security and economic organizations that sought to sustain cooperation in the former Soviet space—the CIS, CSTO, and the EAEC. The Baltic states, Mongolia, and Turkmenistan refused any involvement in these organizations. Mongolia and Turkmenistan embraced formal neutrality. The so-called GUUAM states (Georgia, Ukraine, Uzbekistan, Azerbaijan, and Moldova)—the other former republics with more difficult relations with Russia—resorted to "soft balancing" and held back from full participation in the CIS. With the exception of Uzbekistan, which had patched up relations with Moscow, they later remained outside the CSTO and EAEC.[9]

It is also worth noting that Russia has not tried to exclude China from significant influence. China was a core partner of the Shanghai Cooperation Organization (SCO), which formally recognized China's key role in regional security and economic cooperation. This enabled China to secure most of the benefits available through such cooperation, without committing to the potentially costly mutual defense obligations taken up by Russia in the CSTO.

Since September 2001, the United States has developed a number of military bases in Central Asia as part of the war in Afghanistan. Russia shares the U.S. interest in defeating radical Islamism in Afghanistan, but bristles at the unprecedented U.S. intrusion into Russia's traditional sphere of influence. At various times, U.S. bases were opened in Uzbekistan, Kyrgyzstan, Tajikistan, and Turkmenistan; and in 2009, Kazakhstan too offered to host U.S.

logistical facilities. The U.S. base in Uzbekistan was closed after the United States criticized a crackdown against internal opposition in Andijan. It was not done because of Russian pressure. Even had there been such pressure, the Uzbek government would probably not have complied if the U.S. presence had been viewed as a significant asset in the struggle against internal and regional Islamists or other political opponents. U.S. bases in Tajikistan and Turkmenistan remain open. In 2009, Kyrgyzstan's government announced that the U.S.'s Manar base would be closed. This appears to have occurred under Russian influence, as part of a buildup of Russian bases in Kyrgyzstan. Russia offered a significant bribe, well in excess of the basing fee paid by the United States. However, after negotiating an increase in U.S. fees, and a change in title from "air base" to "transit center," Kyrgyzstan agreed to allow the United States to stay at Manar. Even if Putin wanted to push all U.S. bases out of Central Asia, Russia's influence is limited. For example, Uzbekistan's Karimov might decide to restore U.S. access if Putin's pressure seriously imperiled the U.S. mission in Afghanistan.

Caspian Basin Energy Supply and Transit

What determines whether regional governments defied or complied with Russian efforts to preserve the Soviet-era energy transit monopoly in the Caspian Basin? Consider first the key alternative transit countries. Because the United States has successfully opposed transit through Iran, the main alternative transit corridor to Western markets can run only from the Caspian Sea through Azerbaijan and Georgia to the Black Sea and Turkey. Even after Azerbaijan's Turkish- and Western-oriented Elcibey government was overthrown with Russian assistance, the governments of Heidar and Ilham Aliev have continued to develop the oil and gas pipeline infrastructure. The same is true for Georgia's Shevardnadze and Saakashvili governments. All these governments view the pipelines as crucial economic assets, which in Azerbaijan's case also offer an outlet for its own considerable oil and gas reserves. Just as importantly, they view the pipelines as attracting a stronger Western commitment to the continued security and political autonomy of their countries—for Georgia in its conflict with Russia and local separatists, and for Azerbaijan in its conflict with Russian-backed Armenia.

Apart from Azerbaijan, the main potential regional sources of significant new oil and gas output are Kazakhstan and Turkmenistan. Kazakhstan's neo-Communist regime has always sought the closest possible relations with

Russia but, at the same time, has preserved Kazakhstan's freedom of maneuver. Western oil companies were admitted early on to develop Kazakhstan's promising energy deposits. And although Kazakhstan exports most of its output through the Russian pipeline system, it has emerged as a key supplier of the new pipelines through Azerbaijan and Georgia and, more recently, to China. Logistical barriers have so far prevented Turkmenistan from exporting large quantities of gas through Azerbaijan and Georgia. But Turkmenistan's government has had a number of transit fee disputes with Russia and has recently joined Uzbekistan in linking up to the Kazakhstan-China pipeline. It is also developing additional export agreements and infrastructure with China and Iran. The China outlet in particular has broken Russia's traditional control over Turkmenistan's energy exports—with exports to China surging ahead of those through Russia.[10]

Putin cannot easily impose his will on neo-Communist regimes in Central Asia. Here Islamism is increasingly more likely than liberal nationalism to supplant fallen neo-Communist regimes. If Putin were to push Russia's economic leverage too far or to use military force, the populations would be likely to rally behind existing leaders. If such leaders were deposed by economic chaos or military force, Putin might easily face more defiant regimes. Such regimes might even influence Russia's own far-flung Muslim internal minorities.

The old Soviet pipeline system supplying Western European markets goes through former Soviet republics such as Lithuania and Ukraine and former Eastern European satellites such as Poland and Hungary. Under Yeltsin, former Soviet republics such as Belarus and Ukraine continued to receive Russian gas at below-market prices, while transit countries negotiated fees for movement of gas across their territories to Western European markets. Putin has frequently used Russia's dominant gas-supply position to demand higher payments or lower transit fees, often after cutting off supplies. Russia has also sought to build alternative pipeline routes along the Baltic and Black Sea beds and to buy up national pipeline companies on existing routes. These measures aim to reduce Russia's transit fees, while preventing the pipeline infrastructure to the West from being linked up to alternative suppliers—such as pipelines through Azerbaijan and Georgia or liquefied natural gas terminals on the seacoasts. Putin has sometimes succeeded in raising gas prices or lowering transit fees, but this has been at the expense of alienating customers and driving them to look for alternative suppliers.

REACTING TO RUSSIA 173

Political and Ideological Contagion

Under Putin, democracy per se in the culturally and politically proximate former Soviet Republics is viewed as a threat. The threat was demonstrated in the aftermath of the 2003 Rose Revolution in Georgia, in which an opposition popular front returned to the mass mobilization methods of 1989–1991 to push aside Georgia's cautious, status-quo-oriented president, Shevardnadze. The example quickly spread to two other post-Soviet semidemocracies with similar problems of corruption and inefficient government. Most important was the Orange Revolution in Ukraine, in which the neo-Communist "Party of Power" regime was forced to rerun the presidential election, leading to the victory of liberal nationalist reformer Viktor Yushchenko. A similar episode brought down long-ruling Askar Akayev in Kyrgyzstan's Tulip Revolution.[11]

After failing to stop Yushchenko, Putin used Russia's leverage as Ukraine's gas supplier to disrupt the economy, while providing rhetorical and material support to Yushchenko's neo-Communist rivals, led by Yanukovych's heavily ethnic Russian Party of Regions. In Georgia, Saakashvili, the vocal leader of the international "color revolution" coalition, was Putin's particular obsession. Putin began with internal subversion and increased tensions in Abkhazia and South Ossetia. After swallowing Abkhazia and South Ossetia in 2008, he publicly demanded that Saakashvili step down. Putin was not able to topple the heretical regimes in either Ukraine or Georgia. Both governments survived, and his tactics seemed to backfire by strengthening liberal nationalist resistance ideologies among the younger generations. Russia's effort to support neo-Communists in the Baltic states have not fared any better.

Putin might have imposed his will by using military force directly. But he evidently shied away from the likely consequences. In both cases, relations with the West would have been hurt badly. There would have been greater pressure to diversify energy supply away from Russia and to limit new energy investments in Russia. In Georgia, Russia would have had to create a new satellite regime that depended on Russian military support. In Ukraine, any use of force would have split the country. Russia's local allies would be able to hold only the East and South, while turning the rest of the country into an enemy. Rump Ukraine would become a new Poland.

The basic constraint on Putin's attempt to keep liberal nationalist ideology at bay is that the preferred neo-Communist alternative, if not already in power, is not easily imposed without direct military occupation. Shying away from the associated costs, he has had to fall back on internal repression and, in foreign relations, diversionary politics. By getting into visible disputes with liberal nationalist democracies, in which local ethnic Russians and Russian national interests are associated with neo-Communism, he has sought to paint the liberal nationalist ideological alternative as the enemy of the Russian nation. Internal repression of the political opposition and state control of the mass media have undoubtedly made this strategy more effective. Until the world economic crisis of 2008, Putin also benefited from high energy prices and rapid economic recovery.

CONCLUSIONS

Divergent historical development paths, leading to different regime types and leadership preferences, laid the essential foundations for conflict or coopera-tion between Russia and the other former Soviet bloc states. In Russia itself, Yeltsin's weak liberal nationalist regime did not make strong demands on its neighbors except where, as in the South Caucasus, Russia's territorial secu-rity was at stake. Yeltsin, like Putin later, might have increased his internal legitimacy by cultivating external confrontations in which he postured as the defender of Russian interests and of ethnic Russians abroad. Yeltsin's own lib-eral nationalist ideology best explains why he hesitated to use such methods. With Putin's creation of a neo-Communist authoritarian regime in Russia, regime survival became the primary goal. This dictated a strategy of posing as the defender of Russian interests in conflicts that would discredit ideologi-cally threatening liberal nationalist regimes. Putin also pursued a more con-frontational foreign policy generally, whether in defense of Russian energy interests in bilateral relations, or in depicting NATO and the United States as the greatest threats to Russia through a series of visible disagreements on the world stage. This allowed Putin to tap into the widespread Russian yearning to restore some of the Soviet-era international prestige that had been lost under Yeltsin.

Whether responding to Yeltsin or Putin, liberal nationalist democra-cies tended to defy Russia in pursuit of their ideological goals, whereas neo-Communist regimes tended to make common cause with Russia for mutual benefit. With the liberal nationalist democracies, military force has been the most reliable way for Russia to impose its will. But Putin has avoided military occupation because of the likely costs: embittered relations with the West and stubborn liberal nationalist movements that would have to be suppressed on an ongoing basis. With the neo-Communist regimes, a shared emphasis on regime survival under conditions of ideological compatibility has minimized conflicts of interest. Relations remain strong even though secondary interests often diverge. Thus, Central Asian states have pursued their energy interests at Russia's expense and have looked to their own interests when deciding on U.S. basing rights. Use of force in such disputes would also be costly, again because Russia would face resistance and would have difficulty creating reliable client regimes.

Realist theories about balancing or bandwagoning against external threats have explanatory utility only once such threats are defined and prioritized. In many cases, they are defined and prioritized by specific regime types and leadership preferences and might easily be different under other regime types and leadership preferences. For example, Estonia, Kazakhstan, and Ukraine all inherited large ethnic Russian minorities, which potentially threatened their cultural identities and territorial integrity. In terms of objective economic and military power, Estonia is by far the weakest and Ukraine by far the strongest. Yet Estonia, as a liberal nationalist democracy, balances against Russia[12]; Kazakhstan, as a neo-Communist authoritarian regime, bandwagons or cooperates with Russia[13]; and Ukraine does one or the other depending on how well democracy is functioning and what ideological type of leader is in power.[14]

Nor is there much evidence that most international organizations can exert much restraint on leaders of any type (explanatory framework 2). Rhetorical postures taken in international organizations are usually extensions of rhetorical postures taken in domestic politics, and they often signify nothing more. The main exception to this rule is where international organizations deliver reasonably credible mutual defense obligations and significant increases in economic interdependence—as with NATO and the EU. As this chapter shows, regime type (framework 3) is central to understanding secondary state responses to the regional Russian hegemon.

NOTES

1. Shale Horowitz, "Structural Sources of Post-Communist Market Reform: Economic Structure, Political Culture, and War," *International Studies Quarterly* 48, 4 (2004): 755–778; Grigore Pop-Eleches, "Historical Legacies and Post-Communist Regime Change," *Journal of Politics* 69, 4 (2007): 908–926.

2. See, for example, Richard Sakwa and Mark Webber, "The Commonwealth of Independent States, 1991–1998: Stagnation and Survival," *Europe-Asia Studies* 51, 3 (1999): 379–415.

3. Ross A. Miller, "Regime Type, Strategic Interaction, and the Diversionary Use of Force," *Journal of Conflict Resolution* 43, 3 (1999): 388–402.

4. A. Kozhemiakinm, "Democratization and Foreign Policy Change: The Case of the Russian Federation," *Review of International Studies* 23 ,1 (1997): 49–74.

5. Independent International Fact-Finding Mission on the Conflict in Georgia // Council of the European Union, "Independent International Fact-Finding Mission on the Conflict in Georgia Report," September 30, 2009; available at www.ceiig.ch/Report.html.

6. Dina Rome Spechler, "Russian Foreign Policy during the Putin Presidency: The Impact of Competing Approaches," *Problems of Communism* 57, 5 (2010): 35–50.

7. P. K. Baev, "Conflict Management in the Former Soviet South: The Dead-End of Russian Interventions," *European Security* 6, 4 (1997): 111–129.

8. D. Averre, "NATO Expansion and Russian Interests," *European Security* 7, 1 (1998): 10–54.

9. Irina Ionela Pop, "Russia, EU, NATO and the Strengthening of the CSTO in Central Asia," *Caucasian Review of International Affairs* 3, 3 (2009): 278–290.

10. Gregory Hall and Tiara Grant, "Russia, China, and the Energy-Security Politics of the Caspian Sea Region after the Cold War," *Mediterranean Quarterly* 20, 2 (2009): 113–137.

11. Donnacha O. Beachain and Abel Polese, "What Happened to the Color Revolutions? Authoritarian Responses from Former Soviet Spaces," *Journal of International and Area Studies* 17, 2 (2010): 31–51.

12. Andrus Park, "Ethnicity and Independence: The Case of Estonia in Comparative Perspective," *Europe-Asia Studies* 46, 1 (1994): 69–87.

13. Reuel R. Hanks, "'Multi-Vector Politics' and Kazakhstan's Emerging Role as a Geo-Strategic Player in Central Asia," *Journal of Balkan and Near Eastern Studies* 11, 3 (2009): 257–267.

14. Filippos Proedrou, "Ukraine's Foreign Policy: Accounting for Ukraine's Indeterminate Stance between Russia and the West," *Southeast European and Black Sea Studies* 10, 4 (2010): 443–456.

11 SOUTH ASIA

Conflict, Hegemony, and Power Balancing

Srini Sitaraman

THE SOUTH ASIAN ASSOCIATION for Regional Cooperation (SAARC) includes eight states—Afghanistan, Bangladesh, Bhutan, India, Maldives, Nepal, Pakistan, and Sri Lanka. Until recently South Asian international relations did not typically include Afghanistan, but in 2007 it became a pivotal component of South Asian power competition, which is and has been dominated by one singular dynamic—India's enduring rivalry with Pakistan. The central dynamics of the South Asian balance-of-power struggle and consequential entanglements of extraregional hegemons, most importantly the United States and to a lesser extent China, are clearly evident with India and Pakistan. India is attempting to emerge as a hegemonic power both within and outside the subcontinent. Pakistan is attempting to challenge Indian aspirations by relying on its relationships with the United States and China and its strategy of using terrorism to weaken India's hold on Kashmir or at the very least draw India to the negotiation table (see also Chapter 8 in this volume). The strategy of banking on terrorism as a military strategy to weaken or soften India has now spread outside South Asia as a consequence of the Taliban's emergence in Afghanistan after the Soviet withdrawal from the region in 1989.[1] Direct military intervention by the United States in Afghanistan in October 2001 significantly altered the power quotient in the South Asian subcontinent, with Pakistan emerging as a frontline state in global politics because of its direct involvement as a supporter and detractor of U.S. operations in Afghanistan and in Pakistan. It has become the epicenter of global terrorism with direct ramifications for international security, U.S. foreign policy, and regional stability in South Asia. Despite the strenuous efforts on the part of the United States to remain neutral, it became deeply embroiled in the regional conflict because of its growing dependency on Pakistan as it attempted to rebuild Afghanistan before the scheduled withdrawal process beginning in 2014. Overt nuclearization of the military conflict between India and Pakistan through retaliatory nuclear tests in May 1998 and the subsequent military conflict in the high mountains of Kashmir (the 1999 Kargil War) adds another layer of complexity to the already fractious India–Pakistan hegemon–challenger competition. Pakistan's original motivation to acquire nuclear weapons was to balance against India following India's decision to conduct "peaceful" nuclear tests in 1974, but Pakistan's role in the illicit transfer of nuclear materials and technology to North Korea, Iran, and Libya[2] is not just a significant challenge to India's hegemonic designs but also presents a far more serious international security challenge and a direct national security threat to the United States.[3]

This chapter examines what strategies the South Asian states—particularly Pakistan—use to counter the presumed hegemonic designs of India. I argue that Pakistan has relied on hard balancing and bandwagoning to challenge India successfully. Both Pakistan and India (especially), but for the initial attempt to involve the United Nations in 1948 during the first Indo–Pakistani war, have eschewed international institutions, international law, and the intervention of third parties in the region. Both have relied on bilateral diplomacy to address some issues, but the core issues remain unresolved. Pakistan, in particular, has relied on its strategic alliance with the United States to profit in the form of military and economic aid, bandwagoning when necessary to check India's foreign policy gains.[4] In addition, Pakistan has used its special relationship with China to secure military assistance, chiefly in the form of covert and overt supplies of nuclear materials and technology.[5] Framework 1 (realism) best explains the India–Pakistan balance of power dynamics and, to a lesser extent, framework 3 (domestic politics) matters. Domestic constituents in both states will not tolerate their leaders surrendering any advantage to the other or allow them to make any concessions, limiting the maneuverability of the leadership in India and Pakistan and forcing them to conduct negotiations that do not yield any concessions.

In the subcontinent there are very few nonpower linkages such as liberal transnationalism, interdependence, and commercial ties or pluralistic security communities that seek to balance against the more urgent security competition. The economies of the eight South Asian states are not interdependent; there are very limited commercial and trade ties among them by design; and ethnolinguistic and religious divisions overwhelm the shared heritage and common identities. The South Asian sphere is characterized by hard balancing and attempts to blunt the soft power dimensions that limit interdependence and facilitate effective deployment of hard power assets. This chapter examines the India–Pakistan hegemon–challenger relationship in the context of India's ever-expanding global aspirations and the implications of this relationship for the South Asian region, including Afghanistan, and the primary extraregional hegemon—the United States.

IS INDIA A HEGEMONIC POWER?

The strategic elite in India have continuously asserted India's great nation status from its emergence as an independent republic in 1950. Prime Ministers Nehru and Indira Gandhi's move to build and support the Non-Aligned Movement (NAM), which became a significant voting bloc in the United Nations, was India's attempt to showcase its global presence.[6] As former U.S. Ambassador to Sri Lanka Teresita C. Schaffer puts it, "India came to see its natural place as being one of the world's major powers, and thus it redefined its relationships with other major powers."[7] During the last decade India has tried to secure a seat in the U.N. Security Council by launching a very public campaign by even reaching out to its strongest detractors such as China and the United States.[8]

In the subcontinent, India's status as a regional hegemon has been acknowledged by several of the smaller South Asian states: Nepal, Bhutan, Sri Lanka, Bangladesh, and Maldives. Although these states have slipped out of the Indian leash and challenged India on several occasions, they have largely conceded that they do not possess the strategic depth or the military or economic capacity to counter Indian hegemony, and neither has India been overtly concerned about these states as it is about Pakistan.[9]

Prior to India's decision to liberalize its economy in 1991, its power did not echo beyond the South Asian sphere of influence in certain arenas. China, Japan, other East and Southeast Asian states did not perceive India as a regional power and did not give much credence to India's military or economic capacity for a long time, especially during the Cold War. Japan has been cold to India's business and security overtures because of India's nuclear weapons program. Only recently have East and Southeast Asian states started inviting India to the Asian regional economic forums and Association of South East

Asian Nations (ASEAN) summits, which is an acknowledgment of India's emergence as a major economic power and its rising international stature.

During the Cold War, the United States and its NATO allies identified India as a regional player and did not see much strategic value in aligning with it due to its close association with the USSR and because of its anticolonial stance and ideological disengagement with the Western world. The end of the Cold War and the collapse of the USSR forced India to shift its strategy and pursue a policy of economic openness, which propelled it from international political obscurity to global prominence facilitated by the decision to liberalize its economy.

Steven Cohen argues that India is an emerging pan-Asian power, and its emergence will be conditioned by internal developments within India and South Asia more broadly.[10] Analysts at the leading global investment firm, Goldman Sachs, believe that Brazil, Russia, India, and China (BRICs) are emerging as serious global contenders to traditional U.S. and European economic hegemony.[11] According to the projections made in a widely circulated BRIC report, India is expected to surpass Japan's economy in 2032 and the expected real GDP growth rate for India for the next decade is likely to stay above 5 percent.[12] Several other noted South Asian scholars have pegged India as an emerging power.[13] India's elevation to the status of emerging power has less to do with its military and nuclear might (although an important component) and more to do with its growing global economic presence. As India began to slowly liberalize its economy starting in 1991, its GNP increased from less than half a trillion dollars at the end of the Cold War to $3.4 trillion in 2009 (measured in constant PPP dollars). The Indian economy has been growing at more than 8 percent during the last decade. Rapid growth in the information technology sector has made India one of the world's leading software exporters and information technology powerhouses.[14]

In terms of military power, India is ranked among the top five military powers in the world, behind only the United States, Russia, and China; India is also ahead of the United Kingdom, with 1.3 million active military personnel and equal numbers of paramilitary units and active military reserve. Military expenditure accounts for 2.6 percent of India's GDP, placing it in the top ten in the world but significantly behind the United States, which spends more than 4 percent of its GDP, or about $660 billion; China spends about $100 billion.[15] Geographically, India sits in the middle of the subcontinent with Nepal, China, and Bhutan to the north; Bangladesh and Myanmar to the east; Sri

Lanka to the south; and Pakistan to the west. India's geographic and demographic size has provided it with strategic depth and natural advantages in enabling it to establish dominant relationships with its neighbors, including Pakistan.

India has pursued opportunities to increase its power vis-à-vis its neighbors to expand and demonstrate that might and resolve are the best ways to get others to comply and follow. India has sought to modulate its behavior by appearing as a noninterfering benevolent hegemon, especially with smaller neighbors such as Sri Lanka and Nepal. The response has been to balance against India internally through arms buildup, which is the primary strategy pursued by Pakistan, and externally by joining alliances with other states, which Pakistan and India's other neighbors have followed. Pakistan has been most successful in balancing against Indian hegemony; recently Bangladesh, Nepal, and Sri Lanka have started to chip away at Indian attempts to assert control over them. Much of this challenge has manifested itself in three forms: (1) relying on extraregional hegemons to nullify or blunt India's hegemonic aspiration in the region (external balancing); (2) manipulating ethnosectarian conflict and domestic challenges to power across the borders to weaken Indian security through a tactic described by several analysts as "bleed India through a thousand cuts," and (3) using nuclear and conventional arms buildup as a deterrent. Pakistan has adopted all of these strategies.

India has not shied away from military adventurism in the region and beyond. It launched the Indian Peacekeeping Force (IPKF) operations in 1987, a military intervention to bring a peaceful settlement to the long-running Sri Lankan civil war between the Tamils and Sinhalas. The IPKF operations demonstrated India's willingness to exercise its military muscle beyond its territorial boundaries in a situation with no immediate strategic benefits. India has also been involved in peacekeeping operations outside the subcontinent, and it is the third largest contributor of soldiers and observers to various U.N. peacekeeping operations, including an all-women peacekeeping contingent dispatched to Liberia.[16] As of February 2011 India had contributed more than 8,000 personnel for several U.N. peacekeeping missions.[17] In Afghanistan, India has expanded its civilian presence and contributed over $1.2 billion toward reconstruction, deepening Pakistan's suspicion of India.[18] It is also actively engaging China in a head-to-head competition—not always successfully—for capturing new markets for its goods, and it has sought to secure vital mineral and petroleum resources in Central Asia, North and Central

Africa, and Latin America. It has allied with Russia, China, and Brazil under the aegis of the BRIC Forum to challenge the United States and the Europeans in WTO trade negotiations and in G-20 forums.[19]

EXPANSION OF INDIAN SOFT POWER
AND LEASH SLIPPING

The notion of soft power was popularized by Joseph Nye, who categorizes power into three categories: (1) coercion through threats; (2) inducements via payments; and (3) attraction or co-optation without demanding.[20] The third category, defined as soft power, is the ability to attract another state to change its behavior without coercion or inducements or having to command a suitable outcome. Nye describes soft power as the "indirect way to get what you want" in which other states choose to follow because of the hegemon's values, moral principles, and international legitimacy and seek to emulate it without reliance on coercion. Soft power, which is a measure of cultural and market power and the power of ideas, depends on the ability to attract other states. Former U.N. Undersecretary General Sashi Tharoor (presently a member of the Indian Parliament) argues that India's ability is similar to that of the United States in its exercise of soft power in several areas facilitated by the growing popularity of Bollywood movies;[21] serialized television dramas; varieties of Indian music, dance, and drama; and vibrant print, online, and television media that have a huge fan following across the world.[22] The dispersion of popular culture has largely been made possible by the increasing transmigration and growing strength of the Indian diaspora, particularly in key global centers such as London, Toronto, New York, San Francisco, Chicago, Dallas, Singapore, Perth, and Sydney; in parts of the Caribbean Islands, Nairobi, and Johannesburg; and of course in the Gulf and Middle Eastern states.[23]

Sensing the impact of soft power of Indian cultural exports, Pakistan has banned Indian movies in public cinema houses in Pakistan since the end of their second war in 1965. After the 2008 Mumbai terrorist attacks, a Pakistan Parliamentary Committee recommended that all Indian television channels be blocked in Pakistan,[24] but protests from cable operators who were pilloried by their customers enabled broadcasting of these TV dramas because of their enormous popularity.[25] Despite these official bans, consumers have been able to buy pirated copies of Indian movies, TV dramas, and music CDs on the streets of every major town in Pakistan.[26] Expansion of India's soft power is being felt in Indonesia and Malaysia, where Muslim clerics have issued fatwas (religious edicts) on practicing yoga because of its association with Hindu spiritualism and its ability to corrupt individuals.[27]

As Tharoor rightly points out, however, soft power alone is unlikely to stave off challenges to Indian hard power or forestall security threats from its regional or extraregional competitors. It is more likely that India will be viewed favorably that might generate unanticipated positive global perceptions.[28] In a Gallup poll conducted in America in February 2010, India received a favorability rating of 66 percent among U.S. residents, placing it in sixth place, ahead of France and just behind Israel.[29] Soft power is not a substitute for hard power, but it definitely provides an alternative mechanism for an emerging power such as India to leverage its hard power more effectively.[30]

KASHMIR AND INDIA–PAKISTAN HEGEMON-CHALLENGER DYNAMICS

Most narratives of the India–Pakistan relationship begin with the unresolved status of Kashmir. This rivalry in many ways preceded the conflict over Kashmir, and probably the conflict between India and Pakistan is less likely to conclude with the settlement of the Kashmir territorial dispute, assuming such a settlement is even conceivable in the near future. One could trace the genesis of the India–Pakistan conflict to the larger Hindu–Muslim tensions predating partition; some trace it to the origins of Islamic rule in India, and others trace it to the divide-and-rule colonizing strategy employed by the British. The proximate causes include the partition of British India based on the two-nation theory and the mass migration of Hindus and Muslims across the newly established border, which was tremendously traumatic to the body politic.[31] Partition resulted in the displacement of nearly 10 million people; over a million perished during the mass movement of Hindus and Muslims across the border. The attendant communal violence worsened the relationship between the newly established states, which exacerbated the cycle of violence that still persists and radiates to other spheres.[32]

Political competition and ego among the preindependence governing elite of India and Pakistan, and of course colonial connivance and the precipitous departure of the British, laid the foundation for sustaining the Indo–Pakistani rivalry, but there is no gainsaying that failure of partition and the accompanying territorial dispute are a few of the fundamental causes of protracted conflict. The belief that partition of India into Muslim and Hindu regions would make a "clean and surgical break that would lay the foundations for a peaceful and stable relationship, proved to be wrong" because the leadership in both states felt they did not receive a fair bargain in the sharing of resources and territory.[33] As a consequence, intense animosity persists, which has resulted in four wars (1948, 1965, 1971, 1999), several near wars (1955, 1987, 2002), retaliatory nuclear testing in 1998, jihadi terrorism, persistent low-intensity border conflict, continued tensions over Kashmir, and a wider strategic competition in an attempt to outmaneuver and displace each other, for example in Afghanistan, exacerbating the enduring conflict between these two states.

Kashmir represents the unfinished business of partition for Pakistan and reaffirmation of its identity and belief in the two-nation theory, which is at the heart of the extraordinary and tragic partition into Muslim Pakistan and Hindu India.[34] To India, Kashmir represents the negation of the two-nation theory and confirmation of the principle that Hindus and Muslims could peacefully coexist and be effectively accommodated within the framework of secular parliamentary democracy.[35] Kashmir fundamentally represents the competing conceptions of national identity, in which the process of identity consolidation is not complete for Pakistan without the assimilation of a critical piece of territory because of its symbolic significance.[36] Aside from this, the geostrategic value of Kashmir is not lost on either India and Pakistan or an opportunistic third party to the conflict—China.

India's position on Kashmir has always been that the entire state of Kashmir, including the parts presently under the control of Pakistan, rightfully belongs to India by virtue of the accession to India by Maharaja Hari Singh in October 1947. Pakistan regards the areas under India's control as disputed and subject to an internationally supervised plebiscite to determine the rightful jurisdiction.[37] The first Indo–Pakistani conflict began in October 1947 when the Pakistani army regulars and armed local tribesmen crossed into Kashmir, beginning with attacks on Indian positions and the terrorizing of the local population. Immediately following the attacks, Maharaja Hari Singh ceded to India on October 26, 1947, but the conflict expanded into other areas as India decided to counterattack in Western Punjab and other adjoining areas along the newly demarcated India–Pakistan international boundary. Eventually the U.N.-brokered cease-fire agreement led to the conclusion of hostilities in December 1948, but the outcome of this conflict was that Kashmir splintered: Pakistan occupied two-fifths of the area, and India controlled the remaining three-fifths. Efforts to launch a comprehensive offensive against Pakistan were blocked by the British, who were still officially in charge of the Indian military, thus preventing India from completely displacing Pakistani forces occupying parts of Western Kashmir. Subsequently, India mishandled its representation in the United Nations, in effect ceding two-fifths of Kashmir already under Pakistan's occupation. Pakistan was allowed to retain territory it had annexed through aggression, but Pakistan saw itself as the aggrieved party because it could not lay claim to the entire state of Kashmir. India was deeply concerned and surprised by the decision of the major powers, with the exception of the USSR, to side with Pakistan.[38]

COLD WAR AND EXTRAREGIONAL HEGEMONS

The conflict over Kashmir immediately following partition laid the foundation for the emergence of the India–Pakistan rivalry; the progression of this rivalry would not have been possible without the active intervention and participation of Britain and the United States (see Chapter 8 in this volume for a discussion of U.S.–Pakistani relations). Although the U.S. objective in South Asia was driven by the emerging Cold War concerns, the United States initially sought to remain unequivocal in its support for both states. However, when Pakistan openly threw its support in favor of the United States, the Truman administration assumed a distinctly pro-Pakistan slant, realizing its geostrategic importance.[39] From India's perspective it came away with the belief that both Britain and the United States were siding with Pakistan at the expense of larger and more important India. Combined with Nehruvian anticolonialism and prosocialism, this view gradually pushed India toward the USSR, which became India's major benefactor. This, in turn, reinforced Pakistan's role as an American client state, setting the stage for involvement of extraregional hegemons, and subsumed the rivalry between India and Pakistan under the rubric of the Cold War. As the Cold War intensified, so did the India–Pakistan rivalry. The rivalry, however, was driven by distinct local conditions, although it was surely influenced by the military and economic support provided by the superpowers and gradually worsened relations between India and the United States and between Pakistan and the USSR. The Eisenhower administration viewed Pakistan as a strategic asset because of its proximity to the Middle East (particularly Iran), Central Asia, and China. Pakistan formalized its alliance with the signing of the Mutual Defense Agreement in May 1954 and joined SEATO (the Southeast Asia Treaty Organization) in September 1954.[40]

U.S. military and economic assistance to Pakistan has been the biggest point of contention between the United States and India, which has attempted to contest and lobby against every major military sale, such as advanced F-16 fighter jets to Pakistan, because of legitimate concerns that these arms were aimed at India. While Pakistan used the fear of the Soviet threat during the Cold War and the need for advanced weapons and technology transfers from the United States to engage in counterterrorism, both U.S. and Indian defense planners are well aware that the purpose of these weapons is for Pakistan to balance against India. More recently, one of the promises elicited is that the United States will pressure India to move its armored divisions away from its western borders so that Pakistan can shift those divisions to the frontier areas bordering Afghanistan to aid the U.S. war effort.[41]

Pakistan's military and intelligence agency (ISI) facilitated the Taliban's takeover of Kabul and expansion of their reign to other areas of Afghanistan. In the 1990s the ISI began to divert Taliban and other jihadi assets against Kashmir and India.[42] Pakistan has always wanted a regime friendly to it in Afghanistan and the Taliban offered the perfect foil to achieve its goal of balancing against India. Although the United States was fully aware of Pakistan's activities, as its own intelligence documents suggest, it did not want to be involved because there was no immediate strategic interest in that area. Pakistan pursued its own policy in Afghanistan unencumbered, as Pakistan had bandwagoned with the United States during the Cold War.

The unfortunate by-product of Cold War entanglements in the broader South Asian theater was that the Pakistani army and the ISI began diverting jihadi groups against India in a strategy deemed as "bleeding by a thousand cuts."[43] With the exit of the Soviets from Afghanistan and the Americans from Pakistan, the number of terrorist attacks on India increased, showcased by the spectacular attacks on Mumbai (Bombay) in 1993 when a string of coordinated bomb blasts ripped through the city, shut down economic operations for several days, and resulted in nearly 1,000 casualties with over 250 dead. Prior to the 1990s the attacks were primarily in the Valley of Kashmir (dominated by infiltration by the *tribal lashkars* and periodic violation of the ceasefire line by the Pakistani army), but after the 1993 Mumbai blasts acts of terror spread to various Indian cities, including Delhi, and culminated in a brazen attack on the Indian Parliament in December 2001, followed by attacks on a Hindu temple in Gujarat in 2002.[44] During the first decade of the twenty-first century, India experienced twenty-eight major terrorist attacks outside of Jammu and Kashmir with the biggest attack occurring in Mumbai in 2008, where a luxury hotel, commuter railway station, and other key locations were attacked by the heavily armed Pakistani-supported terrorist group *Lakshar-e-Taiba*.[45] The Indian government directly implicated the ISI for its role in training and guiding the terrorist operations, including the purchase of a speedboat used in transporting terrorists from Karachi, Pakistan, to the shores of Mumbai.[46]

CONCLUSION

In essence, the basic dynamic of the hegemon–challenger relationship between India and Pakistan has not altered regardless of whether we are looking at the Cold War or post–Cold War periods, although the context within which this relationship has played out and the power balance between the hegemon and the challenger have periodically shifted, with India seemingly ahead during the immediate post-9/11 period.

Two primary factors drive the regional hegemonic competition: (1) lack of resolution over Kashmir and (2) the active and aggressive involvement of extraregional hegemons, namely, the United States and the USSR during the Cold War. After the Cold War China, to a lesser extent, and the United States more directly, have become more invested in the regional conflict, which has drawn other regional hegemons, namely Saudi Arabia and Iran. While the overarching U.S. goal has been to prevent a nuclear conflagration between India and Pakistan, China has sought to leverage the Kashmir issue to pressure India on other fronts. Saudi Arabia has played a more indirect role as a critical supplier of energy needs and much-needed hard cash, but importantly it carries moral and religious weight because of its status as a benefactor of Sunni Islam. Similarly, Iran has sought to safeguard its interests in the region by ensuring that the Shia minority in Pakistan and Afghanistan are protected. Although smaller states, such as Nepal, Bangladesh, and Sri Lanka, are not directly involved in this regional balance-of-power game, they have sought to check India's hegemonic potential by reaching out to China, with whom India has a deeply insecure and adversarial relationship following the disastrous 1962 border conflict in which India lost a substantial amount of territory to China. To some extent, Bangladesh and Sri Lanka have relied on Pakistan to balance against India's hegemonic power. Pakistan became one of the largest arms suppliers to Sri Lanka during its war against the Tamil Tigers.[47]

Pakistan also perceives an existential threat from India. Its entire foreign and military policy is obsessed with India.[48] Pakistan has relied on external balancing since the first India–Pakistan war in 1948, but this balancing has not always produced major results in terms of direct military assistance. In the wars that Pakistan initiated after 1948 it has not been able to wrest any territory from Indian control and lost East Pakistan (Bangladesh) in 1971. Given the size differential between India and Pakistan in terms of both economic and military power, undersized Pakistan feels overwhelmed in comparison and obsessed with the Indian security threat, which fits in exceptionally well with explanatory framework 1. Pakistan's deep insecurity forced it to seek extraregional hegemons to balance against India, and it has embarked on a strategy of using terrorist attacks to rattle India.

For its part, India has not been able to respond effectively to Pakistani provocations because of the concern not only that a full-scale military conflict would be economically disadvantageous to India but also that such an escalation could quickly lead to a nuclear exchange. While the United States relied on Pakistan to pursue its strategic objectives against the Soviet Union, China has used Pakistan to check India's extraregional hegemonic aspirations and relies on its partnership with Pakistan to force India to address the unresolved Indo–China border dispute. Meanwhile, the United States is increasingly viewing a stable, democratic, and prosperous India as a bulwark against the growing aggressive moves by China in the region. Both China and the United States have propped up Pakistan to support their varying strategic objectives both during and after the end of the Cold War. In turn, Pakistan has attempted to channel its alliance with China and the United States to challenge India's economic and military might, not only at the regional level but also at the international level. At the regional level Pakistan has tapped into the growing mistrust of India among its smaller neighbors, such as Nepal, Sri Lanka, and Bangladesh, and it has sought better relations with them on a more equal footing in contrast to India. Furthermore, these smaller South Asian states have also slipped out of the Indian leash and increased their trade and military linkages with China, furthering Indian anxieties over encirclement by China.[49] Though India has moved closer to the United States, which has equally reciprocated by honoring the Indian prime minister at the White House and has ceased calling for a plebiscite in Kashmir and nullified Pakistan's diplomatic advantage, the United States has not refrained from selling advanced weapons and funneling economic aid to Pakistan because of its own concerns over Pakistan's role in Afghanistan. To mollify Pakistan, the United

States has ensured that India would remain isolated from any serious engagement in the Afghanistan–Pakistan situation. However, Indian hopes that U.S. involvement in the subcontinent would effectively solve the "Pakistan Problem" have not come to fruition. Unless India is able to successfully address its outstanding issues with Pakistan it will forever remain an emerging or less than an emerging power or, as Cohen expertly puts it, India's "strategic role is likely to remain circumscribed, as India's net military power will remain the sum of its own capabilities minus those of Pakistan."[50]

NOTES

1. Pakistan's intelligence agency has been identified as fomenting trouble in many states. For a detailed discussion on this, see Ashley J. Tellis, "Pakistan's Record on Terrorism: Conflicted Goals, Compromised Performance," *The Washington Quarterly* 31, 2 (Spring 2008): 7–32.

2. U.S. Congress, *The A. Q. Khan Network: Case Closed? Hearings before Subcommittee on International Terrorism and Nonproliferation.* (Washington DC: 109th Congress, May 25, 2006).

3. K. Alan Kronstadt, *Pakistan–U.S. Relations.* (Washington DC, Congressional Research Service [CRS], July 1, 2009).

4. Rajiv Chandrasekaran, "Neighboring Countries Wary of Thaw in Afghan–Pakistan Relations," *Washington Post*, July 25, 2010: A15.

5. William Burr, *China, Pakistan, and the Bomb: The Declassified File on U.S. Policy, 1977–1997*, National Security Archive Electronic Briefing Book No. 114, March 5, 2004; available at www.gwu.edu/~nsarchiv/NSAEBB/NSAEBB114/index.htm; "Clouds of Hypocrisy: Pakistan, India and the Anti-Nuclear Rules," *The Economist*, June 24, 2010; Gordon Corera, *Shopping for Bombs: Nuclear Proliferation, Global Insecurity, and the Rise and Fall of the A. Q. Khan Network* (New York: Oxford University Press, 2006).

6. See Dennis Kux, *India and the United States: Estranged Democracies, 1941–1991* (Washington, DC: National Defense University Press, 1992): 387.

7. Teresita C. Schaffer, *India and the United States in the 21st Century: Reinventing Partnership* (Washington, DC: Center for International and Strategic Studies, 2009): 4.

8. Shairi Mathur, *Voting for the Veto: India in a Reformed UN* (London: The Foreign Policy Centre, September 2005); available at http://fpc.org.uk/fsblob/565.pdf.

9. Stephen P. Cohen, *India: Emerging Power: India* (Washington, DC: Brookings Institution, 2001). On leash slipping, see Christopher Layne, *The Peace of Illusions* (Ithaca, NY: Cornell University Press, 2006).

10. Cohen, *India*.

11. Roopa Purushothaman "Dreaming with BRICS: The Path to 2050," Goldman Sachs Global Economics, Paper No: 99 (October 1, 2003), available at www2 .goldmansachs.com/insight/research/reports/99.pdf.

12. Ibid.: 8.

13. Sumit Ganguly, *India as an Emerging Power* (New York: Routledge, 2003); Christophe Jaffrelot, *The Emerging States: The Wellspring of a New World Order* (New York: Columbia University Press, 2009); Ashley J. Tellis, *India as a New Global Power: An Action Agenda for the United States* (Washington, DC: Carnegie Endowment for International Peace, 2005); Kaushik Basu, *India's Emerging Economy: Performance and Prospects in the 1990s and Beyond* (Boston: MIT Press, 2004); Arvind Panagariya, *India: The Emerging Giant* (Oxford, UK: Oxford University Press, 2010); Nandan Nilekani, *Imagining India: The Idea of a Renewed Nation* (New York: Penguin Press, 2009).

14. NASSCOM, IT-BPO Sector in India: Strategic Review 2010; available at www .nasscom.in/Nasscom/templates/NormalPage.aspx?id=58661.

15. SIPRI Military Expenditure Database; available at www.sipri.org/databases/ milex (data are current USD and based on current exchange rates as of 2009).

16. Doreen Carvajal, "A Female Approach to Peacekeeping," *New York Times Online*, March 5, 2010.

17. United Nations, "Contributors to UN Peacekeeping Operations" (February 28, 2011); available at www.un.org/en/peacekeeping/contributors/2011/feb11_1.pdf.

18. Jayshree Bajoria, "India–Afghanistan Relations," Council on Foreign Relations, July 22, 2009; available at www.cfr.org/publication/17474/indiaafghanistan_ relations.html#.

19. Siddharth Varadarajan, "BRIC Debut puts the 'Political' Back into Economy," June 16, 2009; available at www.hinduonnet.com/2009/06/16/stories/2009061655481000 .htm.

20. Joseph Nye, *The Benefits of Soft Power* (Boston: Harvard Business School Press, 2004); available at http://hbswk.hbs.edu/archive/4290.html.

21. Maithili Rao, "Bollywood's Hegemony," *The Hindu*, August 12, 2007; available at www.hindu.com/mag/2007/08/12/stories/2007081250010100.htm.

22. Shashi Tharoor, *The Elephant, the Tiger, and the Cell Phone: Reflections on India: The Emerging 21st-Century Power* (New York: Arcade Publishing, 2007).

23. Jigna Desai, *Beyond Bollywood: The Cultural Politics of South Asian Diasporic Film* (New York: Routledge, 2003).

24. Khawar Ghumman, "Pakistan: Senators Propose Ban on Indian TV Channel," The Dawn.com, January 12, 2009; available at www.asiamedia.ucla.edu/article -southasia.asp?parentid=103299.

25. Steve Metcalf, "Pakistani Cable Operators Oppose Ban on Indian TV Channels," *BBC Monitoring Service*, January 24, 2006; available at www.redorbit.com/news/

technology/368080/analysis_pakistani_cable_operators_oppose_ban_on_indian_
tv_channels/index.html.

26. Gregory F. Treverton, *Film Piracy, Organized Crime, and Terrorism* (Santa Monica, CA: The RAND Corporation, 2009).

27. Ian MacKinnon, "Indonesian Clerics Ban Muslims from Practising Yoga," *The Guardian*, January 26, 2009; available at www.guardian.co.uk/world/2009/jan/26/ indonesia-bans-muslims-yoga; Robin Brant, "Malaysia Clerics Issue Yoga Fatwa," *BBC News*; available at http://news.bbc.co.uk/2/hi/asia-pacific/7743312.stm.

28. Tharoor, *The Elephant, the Tiger, and the Cell Phone*: 401.

29. Gallup Poll; available at www.gallup.com/poll/126116/canada-places-first-image-contest-iran-last.aspx.

30. Tharoor, *The Elephant, the Tiger, and the Cell Phone*: 402.

31. For detailed discussion, see the three-volume study of Anshu Singh, *National Movement and Communal Strife in India* (New Delhi: Kalpaz Publications, 2005); and Sugata Bose and Ayesha Jalal, *Modern South Asia: History, Culture, Political Economy* (New York: Routledge, 2003).

32. J. N. Dixit, *India–Pakistan in War & Peace* (New York: Routledge, 2002): 108.

33. Ibid.

34. Cohen, *The Idea of Pakistan*.

35. Howard B. Schaffer, *The Limits of Influence: America's Role In Kashmir* (Washington, DC: The Brookings Institution, 2009).

36. Ibid.: 1.

37. Ibid.: 1–5.

38. U.N. Security Council, *Resolutions and Decisions of the Security Council*, 1948, Official Records, Third Year (New York, 1964): 1–9.

39. On this point, see the first chapter of Robert J. McMahon's *The Cold War in the Periphery: The United States, India, and Pakistan* (New York: Columbia University Press, 1994).

40. Lubna Saif, "Pakistan and SEATO," *Pakistan Journal of History and Culture* 28, 2 (2007): 79–80.

41. U.S. Department of Defense, *Report on Progress toward Security and Stability in Afghanistan in Accordance with Section 1230 of the National Defense Authorization Act for Fiscal Year 2008*, April 10, 2010; available at www.defense.gov/pubs/pdfs/ Report_Final_SecDef_04_26_10.pdf.

42. Barbara Elias, *Pakistan: "The Taliban's Godfather"? Documents Detail Years of Pakistani Support for Taliban, Extremists Covert Policy Linked Taliban, Kashmiri Militants, Pakistan's Pashtun Troops Aid Encouraged Pro-Taliban Sympathies in Troubled Border Region*, United States National Security Archive Electronic Briefing Book No. 227; available at www.gwu.edu/~nsarchiv/NSAEBB/NSAEBB227/index.htm.

43. Navnita Chadha Behera, *Demystifying Kashmir* (White Plains, NY: Pearson Longman, 2007), 87.

44. Manas Dasgupta, "26 Killed as Terrorists Storm Gandhinagar Temple," *The Hindu*, September 25, 2002.

45. Data on terror attacks on India were gathered from South Asia Terrorism Portal; available at www.satp.org/satporgtp/countries/india/database/index.html.

46. Chidanand Rajghatta, "US Mum on ISI Role, Hillary Follows up Krishna Visit," *Times of India,* July 16, 2010; available at http://timesofindia.indiatimes.com/world/us/US-mum-on-ISI-role-Hillary-follows-up-Krishna-visit/articleshow/6177589.cms.

47. M Rama Rao, "Pakistan Makes a Killing in Arms Supplies to Desperate Sri Lanka," *Asian Tribune*, December 28, 2006; available at www.asiantribune.com/node/3892.

48. Blake Hounshell, "Pakistan's India Obsession," *Foreign Policy*, May 18, 2010; available at http://blog.foreignpolicy.com/posts/2010/05/18/pakistans_india_obsession; Husain Haqqani, *Pakistan: Between Mosque and Military* (Washington, DC: Carnegie Endowment for International Peace, 2005): 319; Cohen, *The Idea of Pakistan*: 205.

49. David Scott, *China Stands Up: The PRC and the International System* (New York: Routledge, 2007).

50. Cohen, *India*: 198.

12 CHINA AND ITS NEIGHBORS

Too Close for Comfort?

Alexander C. Tan

SINCE ITS ECONOMIC OPENING in 1979, China has become one of the fastest-growing economies in the world and the second largest by overtaking Japan. China is making its voice heard and presence felt in the economic, political, as well as the security sphere. The phenomenal economic growth of the last three decades has seen China build up the world's largest foreign exchange reserves and become one of the world's largest exporters of manufactured products and one of the world's largest importers of raw materials. Politically, China's rapid growth has enabled it to project confidence in its role in the region and the world. Militarily, China has not been shy about showing off its military strength. According to the Stockholm International Peace Research Institute data, in 2008 China had the world's second-largest expenditure with US$84.9 billion, next only to the United States. The modernization of the Chinese military has seen it show its muscles in disputed areas such as the East China Sea and the South China Sea. At the same time, the growth in Chinese defense expenditures is contributing to the growing quantitative and qualitative imbalance in the cross-Straits region of China and Taiwan.

As China continues to rise and searches for its place in the region and the world, leaders in capitals in the Asia-Pacific, from Tokyo to Canberra, are confronted with the decision of how to engage or not to engage with a growing, confident, and increasingly important China. How is China's rise perceived, and why are countries in the region reacting differently to its rise? In this chapter, I examine China's relationship with three of its "neighbors" in the Asia-Pacific area and specifically their reaction to China's ascendance:

Australia, Japan, and Taiwan. The choice of these three states in the Asia-Pacific region provides a picture of the variety of strategies that states used to engage a regional hegemon. Specifically, I examine two questions: How can we describe or characterize these countries' responses to China? And what factors can help us understand their responses to China?

AUSTRALIA: LEASH SLIPPING

Australia, the "lucky country" as it is called, has been fortunate due to its rich mineral resources and unprecedented postwar economic boom. Much of the economic and industrial competitiveness of the Australian economy can be attributed to the economic reforms and restructuring of the late 1980s, releasing its economy from stifling overregulation and heavy-handed government participation. However, its longest postwar economic expansion also coincided with China's emergence into the world economy and voracious appetite for resources to fuel its economic expansion. Australia's rich mineral resources, such as iron ore, have helped Australia's export revenues as China's insatiable demands have resulted in record high prices for these highly demanded minerals.

While China is not seen as a direct threat to Australian national security for historical and geographic reasons, one would expect then that the cozy economic relationship would spill over to create a much "tighter" political relationship between the two. Yet, despite the clear benefits of Sino–Australian economic interaction to both states (but most especially Australia), the bilateral relationship, while strong, friendly, and cordial, cannot be considered as "tight" or on par with U.S.–Australian relations. Instead, in 2009 Australia drafted a defense White Paper that paints a scenario requiring massive increases in defense modernization and substantial expansion of military capabilities. While no enemies or direct threats are explicitly named, there is concern within Australia of regional instability as well as China's ascendance in the area. As Layne's work suggests,

> States engaging in leash-slipping do not fear being attacked by the hegemon. Rather, they build up their military capabilities to maximize their ability to conduct an independent foreign policy. . . . it [leash slipping] is a form of insurance against a hegemon that might someday exercise its power in a predatory and menacing fashion.[1]

This describes well Australia's response to the rising regional hegemon, China.

Why is Australia reacting with a leash-slipping behavior? This strategic behavior can be attributed mainly to China's (and Asia's) perception of Australia's role in Asia as well as Australia's view of its own regional role and the acceptance of its neighbors to its participation. The issue of Chinese and Asian suspicions of Australia emanates from its strong alliance with the United States and the fact that it is a "Western" country. In a kind of vicious cycle, Asia's suspicions of Australia's intentions fuels Australia's own ambivalence about Asia and its concern about regional uncertainty, which makes it risk averse and hedges its security with the U.S. alliance.

The strong alliance with the United States notwithstanding, since the mid-1980s the Hawke Labour government has been reorienting itself toward the Asia-Pacific region. During this period, Australian foreign policy began to focus more on multilateralism as well as emphasizing a regional collective security framework.[2] The push-pull factor of Australian orientation toward the Asian region is partly geographic reality, partly wanting to partake in Asia's phenomenal economic growth, and partly a fear of being left out of regional trade and economic blocs.[3] Since then, Australia has slowly become involved in Asia-Pacific affairs as an active participant rather than an observer, including participation in Asian multilateral organizations such as the Asia Pacific Economic Cooperation (APEC), East Asia Summit (EAS), and the Association of South East Asian Nations (ASEAN). Beyond just participation in these regional organizations, Australia (with New Zealand) signed a free-trade agreement with ASEAN, which came into effect in January 2010.

While some in Australia would argue its being a part of Asia, some argue that it is more realistic for it to be a partner with Asia.[4] Regardless of what Australians think of their country vis-à-vis Asia, there are some in Asia suspicious of Australian involvement in Asia. As Mohan Malik suggests, Australia became the target of "derisory barbs by Malaysian leaders, who called them U.S. proxies and ethnically or culturally unfit to be part of the Asian community."[5] More importantly, China's government views Australia as representing U.S. interests and influence, making it a rank outsider in Asia.[6] Despite Australia getting a seat in the EAS, China was known to be in opposition to including Australia, New Zealand, and India in the EAS. Besides the Chinese government's position, a public opinion poll conducted in China also shows that Chinese views of Australia are not all positive. In a survey conducted by the Lowy Institute, 48 percent of Chinese respondents believe that Australia is a country that is quite suspicious of China.[7] While a large percentage of these respondents believed that Australia can participate in regional groups, 18 percent believed that Australia should not be a member of Asian regional groupings. More importantly, the strong U.S.–Australian relationship, particularly in the defense sphere, is seen by the Chinese as a detriment to the bilateral relationship between China and Australia. This is corroborated by the fact that a large plurality (48 percent) of Chinese respondents agreed that ANZUS (the Australia, New Zealand, U.S. Security Treaty) has a negative influence on Sino–Australian relations.

The perception in Asia of Australia's "odd-man out" position and Chinese suspicions of Australia's role and intentions in Asia serve only to strengthen Australia's own ambivalence of whether it is a part or a partner of the region. And as China grows in confidence, Australia's leash-slipping behavior is also affected by its own domestic politics. From an economic perspective, Australia is becoming more integrated into Asia's and, specifically, China's economy. Australia has greatly benefited from China's economic expansion. This has led Australia to start looking into the possibility of a free-trade agreement with China. Business groups such as the Australian Chamber of Commerce and Industry support a free-trade agreement with China. A 2001 publication stated that it is "very supportive of a bold and comprehensive FTA between Australia and China where the outcomes and net dividends are in our national commercial and economic interest."[8] The view of China's economic importance to Australia is not limited to business groups. In a national public opinion survey conducted by the Lowy Institute in 2009, 63 percent of the respondents chose China as most important to the Australian economy. As one observer of Australia's involvement in Asia notes, "Australia needs Asia, more than Asia needs Australia."[9]

Realizing China's economic importance to Australia is one matter; perceiving China's intentions is another. As with China's (and Asia's) ambivalent attitude toward Australia, Australia is rather suspicious of China as well. In a survey that asked respondents to rate other countries using a thermometer rating (degrees), on "feelings" about China, where the higher the number the warmer the feelings, Australians are rather lukewarm toward China in comparison to other large powers such as the United States and Japan. As China continues to become a major regional player, feelings toward China have become increasingly lukewarm—from 61 to 53 degrees.[10] A large percentage of Australians tend to believe that China will not act responsibly in the world—38 percent in 2006, 51 percent in 2008, and 40 percent in 2009. This is compared to countries like the United States and Japan where fewer than 20 percent in 2009 believe these two states will act irresponsibly. Increasing numbers of Australians view the development of China as a world power as a threat to Australia's vital interest—25 percent in 2006, 34 percent in 2008, and 40 percent in 2009. In the same survey, 50 percent believe that Chinese investments in Australia are too much.[11]

Australia's careful reorientation toward Asia and emphasis on multilateralism, as well as its deepening economic ties with Asia are factors that make Australia more engaged in Asia. But Australia's historically strong ties with the United States and the West cause China (and to some extent the larger Southeast Asian states) to be suspicious and cautious of its intentions. It does not help Sino–Australian relations that both share the same economic and political hinterland, only stimulating mutual suspicion and mutual caution. From the Australian perspective, despite deepening economic connections to China, its "odd-man out" status in the region requires it to hedge its security strategy by spending on its own defense as well as deepening security partnership with the United States.[12]

Indeed, observers of Australian involvement in Asia suggest that "whilst Australia should always be prepared to participate in regional forums, it cannot expect to play any leadership or 'insider' role. Australia and Australians need to learn to live with their 'odd man out' status in this region."[13] Living with this situation can help us understand the leash-slipping behavior that can aptly characterize Australia's reaction to China's rise.

JAPAN: BANDWAGONING AND HEDGING

Several factors inform Japan's reaction to China's regional ascendance—history, territory, geography, and nationalism.[14] Despite increasing economic interdependence, bilateral political ties between China and Japan have long been plagued by the legacy of World War II. More recently, the emergence and reemergence of a series of more specific territorial and maritime disputes have exacerbated historic grievances and forced both states to abandon the passivity and ambivalence that dominated their interactions during the Cold War. Japan eyes China's military spending and regional diplomatic maneuvering with a mounting sense of unease, aware that China has been converting its economic power into diplomatic influence, especially among the Southeast Asian countries that Japan has traditionally considered its own backyard. Although it would be wrong to portray their relations in terms of the political-military meltdown, the trend in Sino–Japanese relations is likely to be one of tensions in the politico-military sphere and attempts at maximizing the potential for closer economic ties.

Most of the current disputes afflicting relations between the two countries relate to their joint quest for strategic space in East Asia, particularly in relation to maritime power. The end of the Cold War has seen the revival of Japan's interest in maintaining its regional maritime superiority. Japan seeks to remain a vital link in U.S. strategies for the Pacific, but Tokyo's current naval policies are also focused on a desire to contest China's rising naval pressure in East Asia (as would be expected according to the first framework, a realist argument for a secondary state's response to the hegemon). Japan's leadership is particularly wary of China's maritime interests, especially in the context of its own energy insecurity, and concerns over the security of the sea-lanes through which its oil imports flow.[15] For its part, China is critical of Japan's continued use of Cold War rhetoric to justify what it views as an aggressive maritime strategy and is suspicious of Japan's concept of Ocean Peace Keeping (OPK).[16] The OPK is a concept promoted by the Koizumi government to foster cooperation in the area of counterproliferation and antipiracy, but China sees it as a veil for Japan to increase its naval presence in East Asia and to thwart China's influence over Sea Lines of Communication (SLOCs) in Southeast Asia.[17]

Relations with ASEAN have become a key area in the Sino–Japanese competition for regional leadership, with both states seeking closer and broader engagement through diplomatic initiatives. Despite having established formal ties with ASEAN some fourteen years before China, the trend in recent years has been for China to lead the way in broadening and deepening its ASEAN links, with Japan playing "catch-up." For example, in 2002, China and ASEAN issued a joint declaration on cooperation on nontraditional security issues, including piracy, terrorism, and arms smuggling. Japan followed this with the Tokyo Declaration of December 2003, which promotes cooperation in the same areas. In October 2003, China acceded to ASEAN's Treaty of Amity and Cooperation in Southeast Asia, committing itself to follow the core principles of ASEAN. This was closely followed by the accession of Japan to the same treaty on July 2, 2004. And in January 2010, the China–ASEAN Free Trade

Agreement came into effect. This game of diplomatic chase plays a key role in the Sino–Japanese competition for regional influence—a competition that Japan fears it may be losing.

Tensions between China and Japan in the East China Sea are also on the rise, with both countries competing for strategic space and resources in the region and Japan increasingly irritated by what it sees as repeated Chinese transgressions. Recent incidents include the reawakening of the territorial dispute over the Diaoyutai-Senkaku Islands, where rich fishing waters and the potential for valuable minerals and oil deposits have led to increasingly insistent territorial claims and diplomatic friction over parallel projects exploring for natural gas in the East China Sea. Thus the potential implications of the recent trend toward more serious developments in Sino–Japanese relations in the East China Sea and the Sea of Japan should not be underestimated.

Despite the unease in Japan about China's rise, the tense nature of the disputes over the Diaoyutai-Senkaku Islands, and competition for regional leadership, the nature of the post–Cold War maritime competition is subject to numerous interlocking interests that are likely to decrease the chances of all-out confrontation. Although suspicious of each other's intentions given their historic animosities and current contest for spheres of influence, China and Japan have growing incentives to cooperate with each other in the area of maritime security. The mutual reliance on open sea-lanes of communications for the passage of oil imports, as well as securing a stable environment to support expanding trade activities, is an incentive for both countries to manage bilateral relations carefully to reduce the likelihood of future conflict.

China and Japan also have broader strategic motivations to promote bilateral cooperation in the areas of traditional and nontraditional security. Both countries have been proactive in trying to resolve the North Korean nuclear crisis and have pledged to cooperate more closely on this issue in the future. Such steps are evidence of the changing regional security dynamics that force them to work more closely together on hard security issues, despite their current differences and historic antagonisms. Neither China nor Japan (despite its security relationship with the United States) can afford to allow regional security challenges on their doorstep to escalate, particularly where the activities of nuclear-capable states are involved. Whereas the United States, as a solitary and distant superpower, may be prepared to take risks in the region, the same is not true of China and Japan, neither of which is confident that the United States would be willing to intervene militarily if the nuclear crisis in

North Korea escalated to the point of major military confrontation.[18] This is one of the most powerful incentives for China and Japan to cooperate despite their troubled bilateral relations and to ensure that low-level regional disputes remain contained. Since the latter part of 2006, there has been some improvement in the Sino–Japanese relationship as successive prime ministers after Koizumi have sought to improve bilateral ties.[19]

Despite the electoral defeat of the LDP to the Democratic Party of Japan in the August 2009 elections and the promise of the new Hatoyama government to improve ties with China and revisit issues pertaining to U.S. bases in Japan, the potential for Sino–Japanese conflict has actually made Japan hedge its position by strengthening its alliance with the United States (balancing against China, which a realist argument—first framework—would call for). From U.S.-Japan cooperation on Theater Missile Defense, the continued strong U.S. military on Japanese soil, the enhancement of interoperability and joint military exercises of American and Japanese forces, the promotion of Japan's Defense Agency into a full-cabinet position, to pronuclear and remilitarization statements by prominent Japanese leaders: All these aptly signal Japan's concern about China's growing power and its effort to follow the United States to "manage" its relation with China. From China's perspective, this would be an extremely unwelcome development, dramatically increasing the risks associated with the Sino–Japanese rivalry.

TAIWAN: BANDWAGONING, COOPERATING, EVERYTHING BUT REUNIFICATION

Of the countries included in the case study for this chapter, Taiwan's position is probably the most precarious and delicate. As part of a contested polity, Taiwan is claimed by China as part of its sovereign territory. Under Chiang Kai-shek's Nationalist Party, or Kuomintang (KMT), the Republic of China (ROC) established a government-in-exile on Taiwan and continued to make territorial claims on the whole of China. Until 1971, Taiwan sat as a permanent member of the U.N. Security Council representing the whole of China. Contested claims of sovereignty between the Chinese Communist Party (CCP) on the mainland and the KMT on the island of Taiwan remained the source of continued tensions despite formal cessation of hostilities.

With Taiwan being removed from the United Nations, the acceleration of the recognition of the PRC by countries around the world isolated Taiwan internationally. In 1979, the United States formally recognized the PRC, cutting formal diplomatic ties with Taiwan but at the same time providing Taiwan's security through the passage of the Taiwan Relations Act of 1979. The derecognition of the ROC by the United States also coincided with the opening up of China to the outside world as Deng Xiaoping consolidated his control of the CCP and became paramount leader of China. Since then, the level of tension across the Taiwan Strait remains high, but the nature of the tension has evolved as China continues its phenomenal rise, and Taiwan continues to find an international space for itself while consolidating its democracy.

From 1949 to 1979, it was easy to characterize Taiwan's response to China's threat as allying with an outside hegemon. In this instance, the United States has performed the role of Taiwan's security guarantor. Prior to severing formal diplomatic relations with Taiwan, the United States had military bases throughout the island and extensive military cooperation with the ROC military. From 1979 onward, the United States has continued to be Taiwan's sole source of military hardware and is Taiwan's only overt and expressed supporter in the world today. In the last twenty years, however, both China and Taiwan have undergone tremendous social, economic, and political transformation. China has become a major player in world affairs, and Taiwan has changed from an authoritarian system to a democratic one. With these changes, how can we best describe and explain Taiwan's response to China's growth today? What factors explain Taiwan's response?

As part of a contested polity or a divided nation, Taiwan's response to China is primarily to ensure that it is able to defend against any military threat and aggression. Despite the United States's switching recognition to the PRC, Taiwan continues to maintain strong military links to the United States through weapons procurement programs and military exchanges. Balancing against China is an obvious and only strategy available for Taiwan as it fights for its international space and national survival. Although the relationship with the United States continues to this day, there have been some changes to Taiwan's response, due in no small part to the changes in Taiwan's domestic politics since 1986. These changes include the opening up of people-to-people contact in 1989, allowing Taiwanese to travel to mainland China; this program initially was restricted to military veterans with mainland China family ties but later was expanded for general tourism. Since then, Taiwan–China interaction has expanded to business and investment albeit in the absence of official sanctions or a legal framework. Up until 2008, Taiwanese wanting to travel to mainland China had to go through a third country or territory. In 2009, direct flights, shipment, and mail as well as the travel of mainland Chinese tourists to Taiwan were allowed. These changes can specifically be attributed to Taiwan's democratization, which has opened up the cross-Straits policy arena by including identity politics and public opinion. As in a two-level game, however, the ebbs and flows of Taiwan's response to China need to consider not only U.S. and relevant international actor position but also how its domestic political constituents react (explanatory framework 3).[20]

With the democratization of Taiwan, identity politics has become an important factor in Taiwan's engagement with China. In 1986, the mainlander-dominated KMT under President Chiang Ching-kuo (Chiang Kai-shek's son) liberalized the party system by allowing the formation of an islander-dominated and pro-Taiwanese independence political party, the Democratic Progressive Party (DPP). While the KMT is vehemently against Taiwanese independence (owing to its claim of the mainland and its version of one China), allowing the DPP to form crystallized the independence versus reunification cleavage as well as the mainlander–islander divide. The death of mainlander President Chiang Ching-kuo in 1988 and the accession to power of an islander president, Lee Teng-hui accelerated the indigenization of Taiwanese politics, that is, the opening up the political system to islander Taiwanese participation. The Taiwanization of domestic politics and the increasingly intense party competition moved national identity politics to the front and center of domestic politics and China–Taiwan relations.

Taiwan's democratization earnestly began with President Lee Teng-hui in 1988 and accelerated in the first direct presidential election in 1996, which Lee won. Emboldened by his ability to "read" public opinion and his deep concern for Taiwan's limbo status, he began to push the boundaries of Taiwan's restricted international space through various methods of creative diplomacy that he termed "substantive diplomacy." His claim that Taiwan and China are actually "two states" triggered a missile crisis in 1996 that forced President Clinton to respond by sending U.S. aircraft carriers to prevent an escalation of the confrontation between the PRC and Taiwan. Following the election of President Chen Shui-bian of the DPP in 2000, the proindependence stance of Chen and his party as well as his administration's de-Sinicization policies and saber-rattling political rhetoric have all contributed to tense cross-Straits relations. National identity politics deepened, contributing to even deeper distrust of China and more importantly spurring the growth of a distinctly Taiwanese identity separate from a pan-Chinese identity.

The Taiwanese preference for unification has been in decline since at least 2002. Despite the growth of China's economy and the improving living standards in the mainland, Taiwanese do not prefer to reunify with the mainland. In surveys, the number of respondents who state that they prefer independence has increased, although it is not a majority or even a plurality.[21] To date, most Taiwanese hedge their preferences by stating a status quo position that essentially agrees to maintain what economic and political status Taiwan currently has. This centrist position forces the two large political parties—KMT and the DPP—to a middle position and limits the flexibility and policy options for incumbent politicians.

The position on national status is reinforced by national identity politics as well. The survey respondents' answers to the question of whether they consider themselves Taiwanese, Chinese, or both show a dramatic decline in identification of "just" Chinese to below 10 percent by 2008. This figure correlates highly with the drop in "unification" advocates. The dramatic increase in Taiwanese identity and identifiers of "both" identities show how a native identity has developed as democracy consolidates in Taiwan. The "separatist" identity of being Taiwanese, tempered by a more "moderate" dual identity, is reflected in the modern party system. The DPP represents voters with stronger Taiwanese identity, while the KMT has become a party with a more dual identity.

Despite these identity politics, the absence of formal legal framework for cross-Straits relations, and the tense relations from 1996 to 2008, economic relations between China and Taiwan are burgeoning. Taiwan is one of China's largest investors, and such investors have set up manufacturing facilities in the information technology industry, labor-intensive industries, as well as service industries. It has been estimated that between a quarter of a million and one million Taiwanese work and live in China.

The relative decline in Taiwan's economy beginning in 2000, exacerbated by the global financial crisis in 2008, created a strong impetus for opening up to China. During President Chen's administration, Taiwan's economy faced stiff competition from its neighbors but, more importantly, from China. The high labor and production costs in Taiwan vis-à-vis China forced many Taiwanese companies to invest and move a substantial part of their manufacturing operations to the mainland. In spite of the Taiwanese government's concern of industrial "hollowing-out" and the fact that there are no formal legal frameworks that protect Taiwanese investors in China, a rapid increase in cross-Strait economic activities occurred during the Chen Shui-bian administration from 2000 to 2008. Since President Ma's inauguration in early 2009, the KMT-led government has earnestly begun the process of active engagement, including conducting several semiofficial meetings between China and Taiwan, sponsoring visits of high-level party officials, opening up Taiwan to mainland Chinese tourists, establishing direct flights and shipping links, and, more importantly, negotiating an Economic Cooperation Framework Agreement (ECFA) that will legalize, harmonize, and regulate cross-Strait economic activities, including investments by Chinese companies and individuals in Taiwan.

The increase in interaction with China in the last twenty years, however, has not done much to change Taiwanese perception of China. From 2002 to 2008, a majority of Taiwanese surveyed felt that China was very hostile to Taiwan. These years corresponded with President Chen's overt public support of a more independent position for Taiwan. With the inauguration of President Ma in early 2009, there has been a corresponding drop in perceived hostility toward Taiwan as he set in motion a process of rapprochement with China.

At the same time that Taiwanese national identity is intensifying and that a majority of citizens perceive China to be hostile, in excess of 30 percent of survey respondents in 2006 to 2008 also maintained that cross-Strait exchanges were "too slow." Under the current Ma administration, the rapprochement with China and other increase in cross-Strait interchange has also received a similarly large percentage of respondents asserting that the pace is "too fast," 10 percent claiming the pace is "too slow," and slightly over 40 percent claiming "just right."

This conflicting and complex picture of public opinion on how to manage properly cross-Strait relations is reflected in Taiwan's official cross-Strait position, that is, continued economic engagement with China, protecting its national sovereignty and national identity, and strong alliance with the United States. The imminent signing of ECFA will allow Taiwan and China to formalize bilateral economic activities skirting any discussion on national sovereignty. However, while Taiwan promotes economic cooperation with China, it continues to actively seek international space by promoting its participation in international organizations—both governmental and nongovernmental. Furthermore, Taiwan has not lowered its defense expenditures and continues to develop its own military hardware as well as purchasing some from the United States.

CONCLUSION

In a comparative analysis of Australia's, Japan's, and Taiwan's responses to the growing power and influence of China in the past twenty to thirty years, we can see that the reasons for not following or cooperating with a hegemon are complex and multivariate. There are varying reactions to the rising power of China—Australia's leash-slipping behavior; Japan's and Taiwan's varying styles of accommodation of the United States, thus sometimes balancing against China; and cooperation. From the analysis presented in this chapter, the strategies adopted by these countries are informed by the complex interaction and dynamics of history, geography, economics, and domestic political factors (which are related to explanatory frameworks 1 and 3). Reminiscent of Putnam's classic thesis on international diplomacy and domestic politics, the reactions of Australia, Japan, and Taiwan to the growing power of China in the region is patently a two-level game.

In answering the question posed in the title of this chapter: Is China too close for comfort? After examining the China's three "neighboring" countries in the Asia-Pacific region, the answer would have to be: It depends.

NOTES

1. Christopher Layne, "The Unipolar Illusion Revisited: The Coming End of the United States' Unipolar Moment," *International Security* 31, 2 (2006): 9, 30.

2. Gary Dean, "Australia's Place and Influence in Asia" (Jakarta: Okusi Associates, 2000).

3. Ibid.

4. Alan Oxley, "Australia's future in Asia," *Asia Times Online*, February 10, 2000; available at www.atimes.com/oceania/BB10Aho2.html.

5. Mohan Malik, *China and the East Asian Summit: More Discord than Accord* (Honolulu: Asia Pacific Center for Security Studies, 2006): 4.

6. Ibid.: 4.

7. Fergus Hanson and Andrew Shearer, *China and the World: Public Opinion and Foreign Policy* (Sydney: Lowy Institute, 2009).

8. Australian Chamber of Commerce and Industry, Australia–China Free Trade Agreement (Barton, ACT, 2001).

9. Dean, "Australia's Place and Influence in Asia": 4.

10. A Lowy Institute study rating Australians' feelings on a 0 to 100 degree thermometer scale shows that China scores a cool 53 degrees among Australians. Fergus Hanson, *Australia and the World: Public Opinion and Foreign Policy* (Sydney: Lowy Institute, 2009), 2–3.

11. Hanson, *Australia and the World: Public Opinion and Foreign Policy*.

12. Mohan Malik, "The China Factor in Australia–U.S. Relations," June 9, 2005, *China Brief* 5, 8 (April 11, 2005); available at www.jamestown.org/programs/chinabrief/single/?tx_ttnews%5Btt_news%5D=30249&tx_ttnews%5BbackPid%5D=195&no_cache=1; Dean, "Australia's Place and Influence in Asia."

13. Dean, "Australia's Place and Influence in Asia": 4.

14. Paul Smith, "China–Japan Relations and the Future of Geopolitics of East Asia," *Asian Affairs: An American Review* 35, 4 (Winter 2009): 230–256.

15. Naoki Tanaka, "Living with the Rising Dragon," *Japan Echo* 31, 4 (August 2004): 29.

16. OPK was first proposed by Japan's National Institute of Defense Studies in 1996 as a new concept of maritime security cooperation.

17. Christopher W. Hughes, *Japan's Security Agenda, Military, Economic and Environmental Dimensions* (Boulder, CO, and London: Lynne Rienner Publishers, 2004): 225.

18. Reinhard Drifte, "US Impact on Japanese-Chinese Security Relations," *Security Dialogue* 31, 4 (2000): 460.

19. Smith, "China–Japan Relations": 231.

20. Robert D. Putnam, "Diplomacy and Domestic Politics: The Logic of Two-Level Games," *International Organization* 42, 3 (Summer 1988): 427–460.

21. Surveys were conducted by the Election Study Center at National Cheng Chi University.

13 SOUTH AFRICA

Benign Hegemony and Resistance

Stephen F. Burgess

SINCE 1994, South Africa's relations with Southern Africa and the African continent have taken the form of "benign hegemony," featuring the effective use of soft power.[1] Especially in the last decade, South Africa has provided leadership in multilateral settings, promoted ideas for African progress and change, and persuaded many countries to commit to work toward good governance, democracy, and market liberalization. South Africa's hegemony in the generation of ideas and in the diplomacy to implement them led to the formation of new continental institutions, the African Union (AU), the New Partnership for African Development (NEPAD), and the African Standby Force (ASF).[2] Its hegemony is underpinned by a GDP that is twice that of the other fourteen Southern African Development Community (SADC) states combined and by South African companies that heavily invest in SADC states and the rest of Africa.

From 1994 to 1999, South Africa was poised to play an important role as regional leader in Southern Africa and Africa as a whole, especially with the rise to power of Nelson Mandela. However, with the end of apartheid and phased emergence of black majority rule, South Africa was not eager to play a leadership role, rather focusing on building consensus within SADC. Given the negative legacy that the apartheid regime had built in the region, the Mandela administration proceeded cautiously. In 1999, the cosmopolitan Thabo Mbeki came to power and dramatically expanded South Africa's role in Southern Africa and Africa. South African diplomacy helped to end wars in Burundi and the Democratic Republic of the Congo (DRC) and to create the AU, NEPAD, and ASF. In 2008, Mbeki played the leading role in bringing a power sharing agreement to Zimbabwe.

South African benign hegemony and soft power were attractive to many African leaders and states, including Mbeki's concept of an "African renaissance" and the prospect of increased aid and investment. However, a number of leaders and states resisted South African hegemony. Most notable was Zimbabwe's Robert Mugabe, who had been the most powerful leader in SADC during the 1980s. He pushed back against Mandela and Mbeki's attempts to assume a dominant role in SADC, Mandela's disapproval of Zimbabwe's 1998 intervention in the DRC "in the name of SADC," and Mbeki's "quiet diplomacy" to end the crisis that gripped Zimbabwe from 2000 onward. Angola's Eduardo dos Santos also resisted South African efforts to bring a negotiated end to his country's civil war and 1998 intervention in the DRC. Resistance also came from autocratic leaders who were fearful of South Africa's promotion of free-market democracy and the right to intervene to stop massive human rights abuses, as occurred in the 1994 Rwandan genocide.

This chapter analyzes how benign hegemony and soft power have been employed, how states have responded, and resistance to hegemony. Insight is provided into how South Africa was able to build consensus in SADC and Africa. The analysis is divided into three periods: South Africa before the end of apartheid, the transitional period of the 1990s, and the decade of South African activism in the 2000s. A chronological approach is employed to compare and contrast hegemony and resistance in the three periods and the legacy that flowed from the apartheid period. Emphasis is placed on reaction to benign hegemony, especially the resistance of a handful of states that have employed various strategies, including soft balancing, balking, and leash slipping, to resist.[3] Explanation is provided as to how and why this resistance arose and the strategies that were adopted using the explanatory frameworks set out in Chapter 1.

WHITE SOUTH AFRICAN HEGEMONY AND NATIONALIST RESISTANCE

The British Empire created the Union of South Africa in 1910, and the new state soon played a dominant role in the Southern African subcontinent. The subcontinent was tied to South Africa through mining companies, most notably the Anglo-American Corporation, as well as through railroads and a migrant labor system. In the First World War, South African troops fought on the side of the British Empire and helped drive the Germans out of Southwest Africa/ Namibia and Tanganyika/Tanzania. Britain remained an active power in the subcontinent, as evidenced by the power of British corporations and by its veto of South African efforts to annex Bechuanaland/Botswana, Basutoland/Lesotho, and Swaziland. In 1948, the Afrikaner National Party came to power and instituted apartheid, distanced South Africa from the declining British Empire, and developed its own strategy for maintaining dominance in the subcontinent. In 1961, with the "winds of change" sweeping Africa, South Africa broke with the British Commonwealth and created the Republic of South Africa, with the aim of perpetuating apartheid and resisting the rising tide of African nationalism sweeping southward from the heart of the continent.

From the 1960s until the 1980s, South Africa acted as an interventionist regional power in an effort to maintain white minority rule in the subcontinent against African nationalism and newly independent African states. On the one hand, South Africa used hard power and counterinsurgency campaigns to defend its control of South West Africa/Namibia, to assist Portugal in maintaining its colonies in Angola and Mozambique and the white minority Rhodesian regime in the 1960s and 1970s, and to intervene in Angola and other "Front Line States" in the 1970s and 1980s. On the other hand, South Africa used soft power and nonreciprocity in attracting more conservative African states. For example, in the 1980s, the South African Development Bank was formed to attract potential African partners. South African hegemony and soft power led Malawi, Cote d'Ivoire, and other conservative states to engage and bandwagon with the apartheid state.

In the 1960s, resistance to South African hegemony was led by the African National Congress (ANC)-in-exile and newly independent African states, especially Tanzania and Zambia, which provided bases for guerrilla training and operations. The ANC exhibited skill in building a network of support and diplomacy in Africa and abroad, including an observer position in the Organization of African Unity (OAU).[4] In the 1970s, revolutions in Mozambique and Angola and the formation of the Group of Front Line States (GFLS) increased African nationalist solidarity and resistance against South African hegemony and created new bases for the ANC that were contiguous with South Africa and its colony in Southwest Africa/Namibia. During the 1980s, the hosting of ANC personnel in Southern African states brought South African military intervention.

Inside South Africa, a strong movement against apartheid grew from the 1970s onward, and protests and uprisings against the apartheid regime intensified. The government's ban of the ANC led to the formation of new organizations under the umbrella of the United Democratic Front.[5] By the time the ANC was unbanned in 1990 and began the process of negotiating a transfer of power, it had reestablished itself inside South Africa as the most popular movement for change. The ANC power base was important in providing backing for the postapartheid regime's practice of benign hegemony and use of soft power in Southern Africa and Africa as a whole from 1994 onward.

In 1980, the Southern African Development Coordination Conference (SADCC) was formed with the aim of strengthening political and economic resistance to South African hegemony and to enable Southern African states to engage in soft balancing. While SADCC was unable to isolate South Africa economically, it provided the basis for regional cooperation after the end of apartheid. Also in 1980, the independence of Zimbabwe, with a semi-industrial economy and a well-trained military, strengthened Southern African resistance against South African hegemony. In the 1980s, the ANC developed close relations with the Mugabe regime that persisted after the ANC took power in South Africa.

Apartheid South Africa remained dominant in terms of hard power, but the forces of resistance were able to exercise soft power by enlisting support of African states, the Soviet bloc, and the Non-Aligned Movement (NAM) and sanctions from the United States and West European states. The ANC-in-exile prepared for leadership by opposing the apartheid South African security state and actively participating as an observer in SADCC, the Group of Front Line States, the NAM, and the U.N. General Assembly.[6] By the late 1980s, South Africa proved unable to dictate the rules in the region and maintain dominance in the face of African nationalist uprisings and insurgency, soft balancing by Southern African states, and U.S. and European sanctions and diplomatic isolation. With the end of the Cold War and Soviet backing for white South Africa's enemies, the elite decided that the time was ripe for a transition from apartheid to black majority rule.

CAUTIOUS LEADERSHIP IN THE TRANSITIONAL PERIOD, 1994–1999

From 1990 to 1994, in a grueling negotiating process, power was passed from the white minority National Party regime to the ANC. Even in late 1993, when it was clear that power was going to pass to Nelson Mandela and the ANC, suspicion of South Africa lingered in Southern Africa, as the memory of assaults on the Front Line States by South African commandos did not fade easily.

In 1994, Nelson Mandela and the ANC came to power as senior partner in a power-sharing arrangement with the National Party in an interim government. During this period, the "new South Africa" was a reluctant regional power, trying not to emulate the "bully" profile of apartheid South Africa. Instead, the new transitional government focused its attention internally on implementing its Reconstruction and Development Programme and developing education, jobs, and housing for the millions of black victims of apartheid. Antimilitarist voices dominated government thinking in the 1990s, which was reflected in the 1996 Defence White Paper that called for the judicious use of military power, only when vital South African interests were at stake, and a broader definition of security to include human security.[7]

From 1994 to 1998, most Southern African and African states were attracted to South Africa, especially with Mandela as the president of the "new South Africa" and the "moral hegemony" that he established with his record of opposition to the evils of apartheid and magnanimous reconciliation with the National Party.[8] He also steered the ANC away from its decades-old commitment to socialism and the Soviet bloc and toward acceptance of free-market democracy and liberal internationalism.[9] The newly formed SADC (formerly SADCC) extended an invitation to South Africa, and the country soon became an active force in the organization. South African companies increased the intensity and scope of their investment activities on the continent.

South Africa quickly established a reputation for effectively using soft power. In the latter half of 1994, diplomacy helped to reverse a military coup in Lesotho and ensure the success of the U.N. peace and stability operation in Mozambique. In 1996, with Mugabe's founding of the SADC Organ on Politics, Defense and Security, Mandela and South Africa quietly worked to ease Mugabe's monopoly over the Organ. South Africa, Botswana, Tanzania, and Mozambique contended that the Organ should be primarily a peacemaking body, while Zimbabwe, Angola, and Namibia insisted on a military-oriented body that would be able to provide mutual defense.[10]

In 1996, Mandela challenged the brutal Abacha military dictatorship in Nigeria, after the hanging of human rights activist Ken-Saro-Wiwa, but South Africa was a lone voice unable to enlist much support from the rest of Africa.

In May 1997, Mandela took the lead role in trying to persuade Zairian President Mobutu to resign and in paving the way for the rebel leader, Laurent Kabila, to assume power.[11] In August 1998, Mandela opposed Zimbabwe and Angola's intervention in the DRC "in the name of SADC" and proposed a new round of diplomacy to put an end to the renewed civil war. South Africa was seen as "tilting" toward Rwanda partly as a result of guilt at South African inaction during the 1994 Rwandan genocide.

The first sign of South African use of hard power came in the September 1998 intervention in Lesotho, where the South African National Defence Force (SANDF) was deployed to preempt a military mutiny. The mistakes made in the intervention tarnished the image of the "new South Africa" as a benign hegemon and demonstrated that the country had much to learn in the use of hard power and military force.

In the trade realm, South Africa continued the nonreciprocal arrangements in the South African Customs Union (SACU) and the free and virtually unimpeded exchange of goods among SACU member states, Botswana, Lesotho, Namibia, and Swaziland. However, South Africa was not willing to extend nonreciprocal benefits to other SADC states, such as Zimbabwe, and continued to impose high tariffs on their exports. The government was concerned about preserving and creating South African jobs. Officials from several SADC countries demanded that South Africa invest more in their economies. South Africa was accused by several SADC states of offering too much support for domestic production, such as duty rebates on exports, which was hurting other economies in the region.[12]

In 1997, an agreement was concluded among the members of SADC, providing for the liberalization of trade and the establishment of a free-trade area (FTA) by 2008. Full implementation of the FTA agreement would bring zero tariffs on trade between SADC nations and a common external tariff. The agreement indicated that SADC was moving toward reduction of South Africa's dominance in the marketplace by giving other economies a competitive advantage. Until the FTA became fully operational, a SADC reciprocity agreement meant that South Africa would pay tariffs on exporting certain goods to other SADC countries, while weaker economies in the region would be exempt from these tariffs.[13]

Resistance to rising South African hegemony came from Zimbabwe, Angola, and Namibia. Zimbabwe resisted South Africa's inevitable rise to lead SADC, while Angola resisted South Africa's efforts to resurrect power sharing in Angola after the collapse of a peace agreement and elections in 1992. Angola was determined to achieve a military victory over the rebel movement, UNITA, and spent its oil revenues to acquire the necessary military capabilities. The government suspected that pro-UNITA elements in South Africa were continuing their activities without restrictions (thus, domestic politics played a significant role in the response to South Africa—as noted by explanatory framework 3).

Mugabe's control of the Organ on Politics, Defense, and Security (noted earlier) enabled him to lead the way in inviting Laurent Kabila and the DRC into the organization in 1997. DRC membership in SADC enabled Zimbabwe, Angola, and Namibia to accept Kabila's invitation in August 1998 to intervene in the DRC against the forces of Rwanda and Uganda that were trying to depose Kabila and claim that they were doing so "in the name of SADC." The intervention continued, even in the face of Mandela and South Africa's disapproval.[14] Mugabe and Zimbabwe challenged the inevitability of South African leadership in SADC, exploiting its reluctance to use hard power. Mugabe was able to maintain control of power politics within SADC for another three years until 2001. Angola continued its involvement in the operation to gain leverage in its fight against UNITA and to gain an ally in Kabila and the DRC. Namibia went along with its former patrons, Angola and Zimbabwe, who had supported the independence struggle of the 1980s.

ASSERTIVE BENIGN HEGEMONY, BANDWAGONING, AND RESISTANCE: MBEKI, 1999–2008

In May 1999, Thabo Mbeki became the South African president. He had spent much of the past three decades in exile, building ANC connections and soft power throughout Southern Africa, Africa, and the world.[15] As a result, he was more versed than Mandela in the dynamics and personalities of Southern Africa and Africa as a whole. His connections, cosmopolitanism, and ambition as well as the foreign policy team that he put together enabled South Africa to become more assertive in Southern African and African affairs.[16] One of his first initiatives was the launching of the "African Renaissance," which proposed regenerating Africa's potential for social and economic development based on African reform efforts. South Africa also led the way in transforming the ineffectual OAU into the AU, which contained stronger institutions, including in the provision of peace and security.[17] In 2003, an African Standby Force construct was created.

The African Renaissance developed into NEPAD in 2002.[18] One of the cornerstones of NEPAD was the concept of an African "peer review" mechanism, in which African states would provide transparent reports on their own governance and submit to peer review. In exchange, states expected increased flows of aid and investment from the West and multilateral financial institutions. Through the AU and NEPAD, South Africa was developing a continental mechanism to imposed standards of good governance and democracy, which would also apply to SADC states.[19]

Under Mbeki's presidency, South African diplomacy was assertive and successful in resolving the complex and turbulent DRC war, a conflict involving almost a dozen different nations and numerous guerrilla movements. South Africa provided peacekeepers to the U.N. Organization Mission in the Democratic Republic of the Congo (MONUC). Diplomacy in Burundi also was successful through the efforts of Mandela and then Jacob Zuma. South Africa backed the peace agreement with the deployment of a protection force in 2001; contributed peacekeepers to an AU mission (2002–2004) and then a U.N. mission (2004–2006);[20] and has continued to monitor and guarantee the peace-building process. Mbeki engaged in difficult negotiations in the Côte d'Ivoire peace process. South Africa also provided peacekeeping troops for missions in Darfur and Comoros and deployed election support contingents to the DRC, Mozambique, and Tanzania.

In SADC, South Africa led the way in convincing other member states to join a mutual defense pact in September 2003, which contained provisions on how the pact would be invoked, to avoid another squabble as occurred in 1998 over intervention in the DRC.[21] A SADC free-trade area was agreed on in August 2008 and has been slowly coming to fruition, with plans for a customs union, a common market by 2015, and a monetary union by 2016.[22]

Resistance in SADC to a more assertive South African hegemony came from Zimbabwe, Angola, and Swaziland, whose leaders were determined not to democratize. In Zimbabwe, a political and economic crisis—sparked by Mugabe's orders to seize white commercial farms for redistribution—spiraled downward, with hyperinflation starting in 2000 and worsening until 2008. Assaults on opposition party officials and white commercial farmers and the unfree and unfair March 2002 presidential elections led to EU and U.S. sanctions and to Zimbabwe's suspension from the Commonwealth. Mbeki opposed sanctions and argued that South Africa's "quiet diplomacy" would end the crisis. However, Mugabe remained in power, and Mbeki was powerless to remove him. In the meantime, Mbeki helped prevent Mugabe and Zimbabwe from holding any leadership positions within SADC.[23] The Zimbabwe crisis and Mugabe's undemocratic and economically disastrous behavior harmed the images of NEPAD, Mbeki, and South Africa. In 2008, parliamentary elections were won by the Movement for Democratic Change (MDC), as were the first round of presidential elections. After massive repression and fraud, Mugabe claimed victory in the second round. Finally, after fraudulent elections, Mbeki and other SADC leaders persuaded Mugabe and the opposition leader, Morgan Tsvangarai, to agree on a power-sharing arrangement, which has proven to be tempestuous and troubled.

Angola continued to oppose South Africa's liberal internationalist efforts to spread democracy, good governance, and market liberalization. The monarchy in Swaziland opposed democratization pressures from the South African government and civil society. Resistance to Mbeki came from further afield in Africa, including Libya and Sudan. In 1999, Moamar Qadhafi and Libya had initiated plans and provided funding for the AU, and soon afterward Mbeki and South Africa had taken over the initiative and driven it in a liberal internationalist direction, much to Qadhafi's dismay. The Sudanese military dictator, Omar el-Bashir, objected to South African support of the Sudanese Peoples Liberation Movement and criticism of massive Sudanese human rights abuses in Darfur. In addition, a number of leaders outside of SADC sided with Mugabe and opposed Mbeki and South Africa's efforts to remove him.

While Mbeki gained status for himself and South Africa as peacemakers, he lost the moral authority that Mandela had garnered. The biggest detraction was Mbeki's persistent denial that HIV causes AIDS. In September 2008, Mbeki was removed by the ANC from power and was replaced by an interim president. In May 2009, Jacob Zuma was elected president and has continued South African involvement in SADC and the AU, though with a more low-key style. South Africa has remained reluctant to use hard power and has continued to exercise benign hegemony and soft power through multilateral leadership.

ANALYSIS OF SOUTH AFRICAN BENIGN HEGEMONY

The pre-1994 South African state exercised imperialistic hegemony, while the post-1994 state practiced benign hegemony. Apartheid South Africa used hard power frequently and attempted to balance it with soft power. The new

South Africa rejected the apartheid model and looked to exercise multilateral leadership and employ soft power, which helped to create an image of benign hegemony. The ANC in Zambia, Tanzania, and other African countries built strong relations with local elites and generated favorable public opinion toward the ANC. Thus, when the ANC assumed power, it had cultivated good relations with SADC and the rest of Africa and had no real enemies. Another important factor was South Africa's long-standing integration into the global economy, as well as the country's liberal democratic transition in the 1990s. Mandela and the ANC abandoned socialism, accepted free market democracy and liberal internationalism, and began to spread the principles in African organizations and states. In SADC, Mandela and South Africa proceeded cautiously. However, they threatened the regional power that Mugabe had accumulated and the war that Eduardo dos Santos was waging to consolidate his dictatorship in Angola.

South Africa's disproportional power, with a GDP many times larger than the rest of the states in their region combined, provided a solid foundation for the practice of benign hegemony and enables one to deduce the degree of compatibility with benign hegemony that South Africa was able to elicit from most SADC secondary and tertiary states. However, with only 45 million people, external powers, such as the United Kingdom, United States, and China, also exercise influence, which has been a source of concern. South Africa continued to develop its mixed economy and interacted economically with Africa and the world. In the area of trade, postapartheid South Africa practiced nonreciprocity within SACU. In the 1990s, South Africa's main domestic imperative was job creation and preservation, which explains why it was unwilling to extend SACU arrangements immediately to the rest of SADC. However, in the 2000s, it gradually expanded nonreciprocity to the rest of SADC. In Africa, South Africa promoted free-market democracy through the NEPAD. The new international institutional setting divided those states and leaders who were willing to undergo peer review of governance and those who refused to move outside the shadow of sovereignty.

ANALYSIS OF RESPONSE AND RESISTANCE

In Southern Africa, most secondary and tertiary states, including Botswana, Lesotho, and Zambia as well as Tanzania, Mozambique, and Malawi, tended to follow and support and bandwagon with South Africa from 1994 onward. The ANC helped provide leadership in Southern Africa's struggle against white minority rule, and most SADC states expected the new South Africa to assist them in recovering from the antiapartheid era and help develop their economies. Several states had paid a high price for supporting the ANC and expected compensation. Most SADC states were bandwagoning with South Africa partly for anticipated benefits. The impact of power distribution factors— with South Africa so much larger—limited the ability and motivation of most SADC states to bandwagoning.

The most striking case was that of Mozambique, which had been a revolutionary Communist state in the 1980s and would have been expected to side with Zimbabwe and Angola against South Africa. However, after military pressure from apartheid South Africa and political and economic pressure from the West, the IMF, and World Bank, Mozambique's leaders jettisoned socialism in the late 1980s and adopted the neoliberal model of development. Mandela and South Africa helped the ruling party prevail in 1994 postconflict elections and consolidate power, and the regime maintained close ties afterward. Also, the capital of Mozambique—Maputo—had been the main port for South Africa's industrial heartland, and the regime sought to revive the connection. Mozambique cooperated with Mbeki and South Africa in undertaking "quiet diplomacy" with Mugabe and Zimbabwe. In sum, the ruling elite in Mozambique bandwagoned with South Africa to overcome domestic threats, consolidate power, and benefit economically (the third explanatory framework).

Opposition to South Africa's benign hegemony in the Southern African subcontinent (from Zimbabwe, Angola, Namibia, and Swaziland) has been heated but not adversarial. Mugabe and Zimbabwe's resistance to Mandela and South Africa's leadership of SADC was as much a matter of leaders' egos and business interests as it was a clash of national interests. Dos Santos and the Angolan ruling party were suspicious of what they saw as residual South African support for the UNITA rebel movement and efforts to revive power sharing. Dos Santos opposed South Africa based on fear of domestic threats from UNITA and other opposition factions as well as the rear areas that UNITA had established in the DRC. Namibia, led by President Sam Nujoma, followed the lead of Angola and Zimbabwe, who had been principal supporters of the country's independence struggle. The Swazi monarchy felt threatened by a domestic democratization movement with close ties to civil society in South Africa.

Zimbabwe, Angola, and Namibia used the international institutional setting of an international organization—SADC and the SADC Organ—in soft balancing against South African benign hegemony. Zimbabwe and Angola opposed South African hegemony as it was on the rise to prevent its spread and dominance over the entire SADC region. Their opposition was based on personal resentment of Mandela's charisma and on the desire to retain autonomy and voice in the Southern African system. In the Zimbabwe case, the policy toward the hegemon was driven by Mugabe's desire to maintain power in SADC. The Organ was used as an instrument to legitimize intervention in the DRC and for balking against pressures from South Africa to cease military operations "in the name of SADC." In the DRC intervention, Mugabe and his ruling faction had established business interests, which were threatened by South African disapproval.

In regard to Mugabe's resistance to Mbeki's quiet diplomacy in the 2000s, the former had built a strong patronage network based on billions of dollars of assets from minerals and other sources. This network proved resilient in the face of Western sanctions, hyperinflation, and South African pressures and enabled Zimbabwe to leash-slip. Mugabe's willingness to allow Zimbabwe to be destroyed economically and let the crisis spill over into South Africa became a form of blackmail, which prevented Mbeki from pushing too hard for change. Finally, in 2008, Mugabe was compelled to share power in the face of electoral defeat, economic collapse, and pressure from a number of SADC states.

In Angola, dos Santos had built a network based on billions of dollars of oil revenues and a strong military as a power base, which constituted a form of leash slipping. Angola had resisted South African efforts to bring about a negotiated settlement in the civil war against UNITA and Mandela's disapproval of the intervention in the DRC to save President Kabila. Angola built its own network of leaders and relations with China, which has enabled it to pursue its own agenda in the face of Western pressure and South African influence.

Normative disagreements persisted about democracy and free markets, especially South Africa's promotion of NEPAD and peer review and specifically South African pressure on Mugabe to end his dictatorship and move toward power sharing and genuine multiparty democracy. South African benign hegemony represented a commitment to free-market democracy and was opposed by Mugabe, dos Santos, the Swazi king, and other African dictators whose power was based on personal rule and massive patronage networks.

CONCLUSION

South African hegemony is exceptional compared to other regional hegemons, especially in regard to the effective use of soft power and the building of consensus. The fact that the ANC had spent thirty years in exile enabled its exiled leaders to cultivate good relations with the leaders of Southern African states in the struggle against white minority rule in South Africa, to develop soft power, and to establish largely harmonious regional relations once in power. South Africa's leaders, Mandela and Mbeki, empathized with their Southern African counterparts and the attacks they had suffered under apartheid and dealt with SADC leaders carefully and respectfully. At the same time, they inherited the South African state and economy, which had dominated the region and continued to offer incentives to neighboring states to cooperate.

In contrast, other regional hegemons confronted rivals and adversaries, which required the use of various instruments of coercion. Many rivals even feared for their survival and sought alliance and other instruments to deter the hegemons. Following the South African example, a few hegemons, such as Brazil, were able to offer attractive incentives to rivals to overcome animosities and hostility in order to build regional cooperation. However, most regional hegemons and rivals remain locked in security dilemmas.

The South African case demonstrates that even benign hegemony can engender resistance of various forms. The interests, agendas, and political orientations of rival regional states produced soft balancing, balking, and leash slipping. Leaders of rival states were driven by the desire to maintain and extend wealth and power to guarantee regime survival and personal rule. The inevitability of a far more powerful benign hegemon transforming smaller and weaker states into free-market democracies cannot be accepted.

NOTES

1. See also James J. Hentz, *South Africa and the Logic of Regional Cooperation* (Bloomington: Indiana University Press, 2005); and Adekeye Adebajo et al., eds., *South Africa in Africa: The Post-Apartheid era* (Pietermaritzburg: University of Kwazulu-Natal Press, 2007).

2. Peter Kagwanja, "Power and Peace: South Africa and the Refurbishing of Africa's Multilateral Capacity for Peacemaking," *Journal of Contemporary African Studies* 24, 2 (May 2006): 159–186.

3. Christopher Layne, "The Unipolar Illusion Revisited: The Coming End of the United States' Unipolar Moment," *International Security* 31, 2 (2006): 7–41; Stephen M. Walt, *Taming of American Power: The Global Response to U.S. Primacy* (New York: W. W. Norton, 2005).

4. Scott Thomas, *The Diplomacy of Liberation: Foreign Relations of the ANC since 1960* (London: I. B. Tauris, 1995): 164.

5. Ibid.: 4–5.

6. Ibid.: 164.

7. South African Department of Defence, *Defence in a Democracy: White Paper on National Defence* (Pretoria: Government Printer, 1996).

8. Kagwanja, "Power and Peace": 159–186.

9. Anthony McGrew, "Liberal Internationalism: Between Realism and Cosmopolitanism," in *Governing Globalization: Power, Authority and Global Governance*, eds. Anthony McGrew and David Held (Cambridge, UK: Polity, 2002): 267–269; G. John Ikenberry, "An Agenda For Liberal International Renewal" in *Finding Our Way: Debating American Grand Strategy*, eds. Michèle A. Flournoy and Shawn Brimley (Washington, DC: Center for a New American Security, 2008): 45–59.

10. Horst Brammer, "In Search of an Effective Regional Security Mechanism for Southern Africa," *Global Dialogue* (Braamfontein, South Africa) 4, 2 (August 1999): 21–22.

11. D. Venter, "South African Foreign Policy Decision-Making in the African Context" in *African Foreign Policies*, eds. Gilbert Khadiagala and Terence Lyons (Boulder, CO: Lynne Rienner, 2001): 174.

12. Stephen Burgess, "Regional Integration among Unequal States: The European Union and the Southern African Development Community Compared," in *Regions and Development: Politics, Security and Economics*, ed. Sheila Page (London: Frank Cass: 2000): 131–132.

13. Ibid.: 131–132.

14. Sandra J. Maclean, "Mugabe at War: The Political Economy of Conflict in Zimbabwe," *Third World Quarterly* 23, 3 (2002): 513–528.

15. Mark Gevisser, *A Legacy of Liberation: Thabo Mbeki and the Future of the South African Dream* (New York: Palgrave Macmillan, 2009).

16. Laurie Nathan, "Consistency and Inconsistency in South African Foreign Policy," *International Affairs,* 81, 2 (April 2005): 361–372. See also South African Department of International Relations and Cooperation, *Strategic Plan, 2003–2005*, Department of Foreign Affairs, South Africa; available at www.dfa.gov.za.

17. T. Tieku, "Explaining the Clash of Interests of Major Actors in the Creation of the African Union," *African Affairs* 103 (2004): 249–267.

18. At the February 2010 AU summit, NEPAD was replaced by the Nepad Planning and Coordinating Agency (NPCA).

19. Adekeye Adebajo and Christopher Landsberg, "South Africa and Nigeria as Regional Hegemons," in *From Cape to Congo: Southern Africa's Evolving Security Challenges*, eds. Mwesiga Baregu and Christopher Landsberg (Boulder, CO: Lynne Rienner, 2003): 171–204.

20. Kristina A. Bentley and Roger Southall, *An African Peace Process: Mandela, South Africa and Burundi* (Pretoria, South Africa: Human Sciences Research Council, 2005).

21. Gilbert M. Khadiagala, "Foreign Policy Decision-Making in Southern Africa's Fading Frontline," in *African Foreign Policies*, eds. Gilbert Khadiagala and Terence Lyons (Boulder, CO: Lynne Rienner, 2001): 131–158.

22. Trade Law Centre for Southern Africa, "SADC's Free Trade Area Slow to Pick Up"; available at www.tralac.org/cgibin/giga.cgi?cmd=cause_dir_news_item&news_id=80217&cause_id=1694.

23. Nathan, "Consistency": 361–372.

14 CONCLUSION

Christopher Layne

A WEEK, IT IS SAID, is a long time in politics. For sure, the last few years have been a *very* long time in international politics. When this book project was conceived, the United States was generally regarded as a global hegemon, and it was hard to find a major book or article on American foreign policy that failed to observe that the United States was the most powerful international actor since imperial Rome.[1] Indeed, since the Cold War ended and the "unipolar moment" was proclaimed, the linked issues of hegemony and unipolarity have preoccupied American IR scholars, policy makers, and foreign policy analysts.[2]

Although the chapters in this volume do not focus exclusively on the relations between a hegemonic United States and "follower" states, this book was inspired by the reactions of other states to American primacy. Today, however, it is evident that U.S. power is waning and that the post-1945 *Pax Americana* is drawing to a close. In a world dominated by U.S. power, the question as to why followers would choose to follow or resist the United States was of obvious interest. If, however, the curtain indeed is falling on the era of American hegemony, a rather different question arises: What do the followers do when the leader no longer can lead?

In this chapter, I argue that the era of American primacy effectively is over. I begin by reviewing the post–Cold War debate about U.S. hegemony. Second, I examine the economic, institutional, and ideational foundations of U.S. hegemony and posit a set of indicators—or signposts—that suggest that American dominance is eroding. Third, I discuss some of the implications of American hegemonic decline for the future of the international system. I argue that America's hegemonic decline has created space for followers to break free from its hegemonic embrace and for rising powers—China especially, but also India, Brazil, and Russia—to challenge the United States. I suggest that as the United States retreats from its role as regional stabilizer in key regions like Europe, the Middle East, and—possibly—East Asia, international politics in the twenty-first century's early decades will be characterized by the return of great power politics. As I conclude, the decline of U.S. hegemony paradoxically enhances rather than diminishes the contribution of this volume. While U.S. hegemony is ending, the problem of hegemony will remain and will be played out in the twenty-first century in the regional geopolitics of Europe, South Asia, East Asia, and the Middle East. This underscores the importance of the contributions of the chapters in the volume that discuss hegemony in a regional context.

THE PROBLEM OF (AMERICAN) HEGEMONY

The Soviet Union's collapse vaulted the United States into a position of seemingly unchallengeable dominance in the international system. To be sure, American hegemony was not just a by-product of the Cold War's end. At the end of World War II, the United States established its dominance in key regions of the non-Soviet world—Western Europe, the Middle East, and East Asia. During the Cold War, many states in the U.S. sphere (France under Charles De Gaulle is a good example) had misgivings about America's preponderant power but accepted it because the United States secured them against the Soviet threat and brought them economic prosperity. For the nonaligned nations, the Cold War presented the opportunity to play off the United States and USSR against one another and thereby increase their diplomatic maneuvering room and extract benefits—foreign aid, for example—from the superpowers.

With the demise of its superpower rival, however, U.S. hegemony acquired a new dimension. Bipolarity had allowed for the possibility of contesting not only America's hegemony in its own sphere, but also Moscow's dominance in the Soviet sphere (an opportunity capitalized on in varying degrees by Romania and Cuba as discussed in this volume). In the post-1991 unipolar world, however, it was not readily apparent how other states could resist U.S. hegemony, much less counterbalance against it.

Following the Soviet Union's implosion, a conventional wisdom about U.S. hegemony quickly emerged. "Hegemonic optimists" held that the post–Cold War era of American primacy would last for a very long time. To be sure, amid the triumphalist euphoria that swept the U.S. foreign policy community when the Cold War ended, a cautionary note was sounded by a few neorealists who argued that U.S. dominance would give way to multipolarity as other states counterbalanced against the United States.[3] This claim rested on the historical pattern of modern international history—a pattern also predicted by neorealist theory—that would-be hegemons invariably are defeated by countervailing coalitions formed by other states and/or by becoming overextended.[4] For most of the two decades since the Cold War's end, however, the hegemonic pessimists were on the wrong side of a one-sided debate that focused on two main questions: How long would American hegemony last, and were other states actually counterbalancing against U.S. hegemony (or contesting it by other means)?

Drawing on neorealism, hegemonic stability theory, balance-of-threat theory, and liberal international relations theory, a number of prominent American international relations and security studies scholars have advanced several explanations of why U.S. hegemony lasted nearly two decades without any major challenge and have suggested that the United States can prolong its primacy far into the future. One strand of thought in the hegemonic optimist camp was promoted by "unipolar stability" realists who made a two-pronged argument. First, they argued that the post-1991 unipolar distribution of capabilities in America's favor was insurmountable. That is, in terms of military and economic power, the gap between the United States and the rest was so large that no state could hope to close it. Second, they claimed there were no incentives for other states to counterbalance American power because they derived important security and economic benefits from U.S. hegemony.[5] Invoking balance-of-threat theory, other realists in the hegemonic optimist camp claimed that the United States could negate counterhegemonic balancing by adopting accommodative and benign policies that allayed others' fears of American dominance.[6] Liberal IR theorists and balance-of-threat realists joined forces to assert that the United States was successful because it was a "benevolent" hegemon.[7] Other states, they said, would acquiesce in U.S. hegemony as long as it displayed self-restraint by exercising its predominance multilaterally through international institutions. Moreover, some of them argued, the United States' soft power (the purportedly singular attractiveness of its political and economic institutions and its culture) drew other states into its orbit.[8]

THE GREAT RECESSION AND THE GREAT TRANSFORMA-
TION OF TWENTY-FIRST-CENTURY GEOPOLITICS

Since the Soviet Union's collapse, there have been occasional expressions of unease about U.S. preponderance in the post–Cold War international system. Russia, China, India, and France frequently have spoken of the need for a multipolar world to offset what then-French foreign minister Herbert Vedrine referred to as American "hyperpower."[9] While the consensus view among IR scholars is that other states did not engage in hard balancing against the United States, the followers experimented with many of the strategies discussed in Chapter 1 in an attempt to "tame American power."[10]

The reaction of followers to the Iraq War focused new attention on the dangers of unchecked American power. The ability of France, Germany, Russia, and China to prevent the United States from obtaining U.N. Security Council approval of the March 2003 invasion of Iraq *seemed* to confirm the efficacy of new diplomatic techniques—like soft balancing—for restraining the United States. Of course, there is another way to interpret the story. After all, notwithstanding the balking of big powers like France, Germany, China, and Russia—and many smaller states as well—the United States went ahead and invaded Iraq anyway. Simply put, the opposition of others, the refusal of followers to follow, had no discernable effect on U.S. foreign policy preferences. From this vantage point, therefore, it is unsurprising that the mainstream view of the hegemonic optimists was unaffected by Iraq. Indeed, between 2006 and 2008 a spate of books appeared, including Fareed Zakaria's with the grossly deceptive title *The Post-American World*, arguing that American hegemony was beneficial, necessary, and destined to last indefinitely.[11] And, in January 2009, the prestigious journal *World Politics* devoted an entire special issue to the topic of unipolarity premised on the assumption that unipolarity and U.S. hegemony would be enduring features of international politics well into the twenty-first century.[12] Similar views continue to persist in the U.S. foreign policy apparatus. In September 2010, for example, Secretary of State Hillary Clinton proclaimed a "new American moment" that will lay the "foundations for lasting American leadership for decades to come."[13]

It is becoming increasingly evident that the ground beneath these defenses of U.S. hegemony is shifting. There are several reasons for this. First, as discussed in this volume by Tan (Chapter 12) and Sitaraman (Chapter 11), the rapid rise of China and India—not to mention the resurgence of Russia and the (as yet unfulfilled) potential of the EU as a pole of power in international politics—demonstrates that the international political system is in the midst of a transition from unipolarity to multipolarity (and has provoked a round of secondary balancing, such as by Pakistan, as discussed in Sitaraman's Chapter 11 and Dreyer's Chapter 8). Second, the dramatic shift in global economic power from the Euro-Atlantic world to Asia not only underscores this geopolitical transformation but also highlights the relative decline of U.S. power. Third, China's breathtaking rise is evidence that a new peer-competitor rapidly is emerging. China is on course to overtake the United States as the world's largest economy. While analysts disagree on the date when this will happen, the most recent projections by leading economic forecasters have advanced the date dramatically over what was being estimated just a few years ago. For example, in 2003 Goldman Sachs predicted that China would surpass the United States as the world's largest economy in 2041, and in 2008 it advanced the date to 2028.[14] However, the most recent forecasts now are that China will pass the United States much sooner than 2028. The Economist Intelligence Unit (2009) predicts China will become the world's largest economy in 2021; Pricewaterhouse Coopers (2009) says 2020, and *The Economist* magazine (2010) says 2019 (measured by market exchange rate).[15] More strikingly, according to a 2011 International Monetary Fund study, in terms of purchasing power parity (PPP), China will overhaul the United States in 2016.[16] In fact, also using PPP, economist Arvin Subramanian of the Peterson Institute for International Economics has calculated that China already is the world's largest economy.[17] What could be clearer proof of U.S. relative decline than the fact that China—if indeed it has not already done so—soon will wrest from the United States the title of world's largest economy?

The interaction among four key drivers is causing America's hegemonic decline: the rise of new great powers; imperial overstretch; the erosion of U.S. economic dominance; and a looming fiscal crisis that imperils the dollar's reserve currency role. Although the Great Recession is not the cause of America's hegemonic decline, it has had three important effects. First, by propelling China's rise it accelerated the relative decline of the United States. Second, it exacerbated America's economic problems and worsened the (already poor) U.S. fiscal outlook. Third, the Great Recession has had a major perceptual impact. Policy makers do not make decisions about grand strategy on the basis of the objective distribution of power in the international system. Rather, they act on their *perceptions* of the balance of power.[18] In this respect, the Great Recession has fueled the increasingly widespread belief, both in the United States and abroad, that America is in decline. Thus, the Great Recession has made clear that the foundations on which the *Pax Americana* rested are crumbling.

THE DECAYING FOUNDATIONS OF AMERICAN HEGEMONY

American hegemony has rested on four pillars: military power, economic leadership, the institutional structures that the United States created after World War II, and the appeal of its political and economic model (soft power). The weakening of these pillars would be the best indicator that U.S. hegemony is declining. In this section, I show that such weakening indeed is occurring (focusing on how U.S. hegemony is eroding in the realms of economics, ideas, and institutions; I leave aside discussion of U.S. military power).

The Erosion of U.S. Economic Hegemony

The first signpost to examine to determine whether U.S. hegemony is eroding is whether the United States is still able to fulfill the hegemon's role as system leader and provider of public goods. One of the hegemon's key tasks is to manage the international economy. Specifically, the hegemon provides public goods by opening its domestic market to other states, supplying liquidity for the global economy, and providing a reserve currency (lender of last resorts, market of last resorts, and defender of the high seas).[19] As the economic leader, the hegemon runs the international economic system in a way that confers absolute benefits on all its members (or at least those states which agree to play by the rules—rules largely established by the hegemon). Economic leadership also means, as Lobell points out in Chapter 5 in this volume on U.S.–Jordan relations, that the hegemon can employ economic statecraft to influence followers' policies by giving them access to the U.S. market and bestowing other economic advantages on them. However, in the Great Recession's aftermath it is no longer obvious that the United States is able to provide leadership for the international economy. Similarly, U.S. economic decline arguably is constraining its ability to practice economic statecraft as many followers now look elsewhere, especially to China, for economic advantage.

The Great Recession dramatized the United States's inability to play the role of economic hegemon. An economic hegemon is supposed to solve global economic crises, not cause them. However, the freezing up of the U.S. financial system that began with the subprime mortgage crisis plunged the world into economic crisis. The hegemon is supposed to be the lender of last resort in the international economy. The United States, however, is the borrower of first resort—the world's largest debtor. When the global economy falters, the economic hegemon is supposed to take responsibility for kick-starting a recovery. However, the U.S. economy proved too infirm to lead the global economy back to health, and others (notably a rising China) had to step up to the plate to do so. This, in itself, was a remarkable reversal of fortune. After all, from World War II's end until the Great Recession, the international economy had looked to the United States as the locomotive of global economic growth.

As the world's largest market, America's willingness to consume foreign goods has been the traditional bulwark against global economic downturns. When economic slowdowns occur, the United States is expected to lead the way to recovery by buying other nations' goods. This has not happened during the Great Recession, and America's inability to galvanize global recovery suggests that in key respects it no longer has the capabilities of acting as an economic hegemon. President Barak Obama said as much during the April 2009 Group of 20 (G-20) meeting in London. There, Obama acknowledged that the United States is no longer able to be the world's consumer of last resort and that the world will need to look to China (and India, South Africa, Brazil, and other emerging market states) to be the motors of global recovery.[20]

America's relative economic decline is likely also to restrict its opportunities to practice economic statecraft. At the same time, a rapidly rising China is flexing its economic muscle to advance its geopolitical ambitions in the Middle East, Latin America, and Africa, as well as to foster its economic growth. Finally, as Sampanis argues in Chapter 6 of this volume, as U.S. hegemony wanes, in multilateral institutions there is more opposition and the followers are likely to pursue soft balancing strategies.

Challenges to the *Pax Americana*'s Institutional Framework

A second indicator that sheds light on the durability of American primacy is the robustness of the framework of international institutions that have underpinned the *Pax Americana* since World War II's end. To maintain its post-1945 hegemony, the United States created a web of security, political, and economic institutions to bolster and legitimate the *Pax Americana*. Today, many analysts—including Ikenberry, Brooks and Wohlforth, and Zakaria—believe that these "legacy" international institutions can help perpetuate U.S. dominance.[21] By strengthening them, it is said, the United States can "lock in" the hegemonic order that it built after the war and thereby ensure that it persists after unipolarity ends.[22]

Partly as a result of the Great Recession, there is a growing consensus that existing international institutions need to be overhauled (or even new ones created, in the security sphere, such as the Shanghai Cooperation Organization). The impetus for change is coming from China and India and the other emerging powers. This became evident during the run-up to the April 2009 London meeting of the G-20 when China and other rising powers argued that international institutions need to be revamped to give them a greater voice and also that the international privileges enjoyed by the United States and Europe need to be rolled back. In addition to the birth of the G-20, other signs that a new international order is emerging to replace *Pax Americana* include the institutionalization of the BRIC relationship and the demands by China and other rising powers that the IMF be restructured to increase the voting weight of the rising powers and diminish that of the United States and Europe.[23] Moreover, because of the perceptions both that its hard power is declining and of the hit its soft power has taken because of the financial meltdown, there is a real question about whether America retains the credibility and legitimacy to take the lead in institutional reform.[24]

The Crumbling Ideational Foundations of American Hegemony

A third indicator of the durability of U.S. hegemony is the robustness of America's ideational power. Here, there are two specific metrics: does the United States retain ideational legitimacy, and is the (purported) universality of the U.S. model of political and economic development being challenged by rival models? In addition to resting on the bedrock of American military and economic supremacy, U.S. primacy has also rested on an ideational foundation, namely the attractiveness of the U.S. model of political and economic development: democracy and free markets. In other words, American hegemony has been based on both hard and soft power. Whether the ideational foundations of U.S. primacy remain solid is, however, an open question.

Some analysts answer this question affirmatively. For example, Zakaria claims that by wielding its soft power, the United States can maintain its role as the "pivotal" nation in international politics far into the future.[25] He argues that the United States will remain at the center of the international system for a long time to come because there is "still a strong market for American power, for both geopolitical and economic reasons. But even more centrally, there remains a strong ideological demand for it."[26] There are reasons to believe that his view is too sanguine.

The robustness of the United States's soft power is being eroded by two factors. First, the global financial and economic crisis has discredited one of the pillars of U.S. soft power: American free-market capitalism. As former U.S. Deputy Treasury Secretary Roger Altman puts it, the meltdown has "put the American model of free market capitalism under a cloud."[27] Indeed, liberalism itself, in both its economic and institutional guises, has been compromised. Second, the United States is not the only country that possesses soft power. China, especially, has become a major soft power player.[28]

In its *Global Trends 2025* report, the National Intelligence Council (NIC) noted that the superior economic performance of authoritarian governments such as China's might discredit both democracy and economic liberalism.[29] Given the prevailing belief in U.S. foreign policy circles that American values are universal and that the U.S. model of economic and political development has worldwide applicability, the rise of alternative models perforce would undermine its soft power. As the NIC observes:

> The state-centric model in which the state makes the key economic decisions and, in the case of China and increasingly Russia, democracy is restricted, raises questions about the inevitability of the traditional Western recipe— roughly liberal economics and democracy—for development. Over the next 15–20 years, more developing countries may gravitate toward Beijing's state-centric model rather than the traditional Western model of markets and democratic political systems to increase the chances of rapid development and perceived political stability.[30]

These trends suggest that the American brand of liberalism, the so-called Washington Consensus of free markets and democracy, is losing its appeal. Moreover, the Great Recession has inflicted a big hit on liberalism generally.

The reactions of the EU to the Great Recession and to the sovereign debt crisis that was triggered by the financial meltdown are examples of how

liberalism has been discredited. The EU has often been cited as the paradig-
matic case of liberal theories about institutions, cooperation, and economic
integration. However, when the recession hit, instead of putting multilateral
cooperation first, the EU's key members (Britain, France, and Germany)
sought economic security by adopting self-help policies.[31] Similarly, during
the Greek sovereign debt crisis, the Eurozone was imperiled by Germany's
inclination to pursue its narrowly defined national interests instead of bailing
out Greece and bolstering confidence in the euro. As the Eurozone crisis has
spread to Italy and Spain, Germany, the Netherlands, Finland, and Austria
remain opposed to taking the one step, creation of a fiscal union, that could
resolve the Eurozone's sovereign risk crisis. This is unsurprising. We still live
in a world of nation-states, and nationalism—not multilateral cooperation—is
always the default policy option. Moreover, with states around the world (including the United States) trying to extract themselves from the financial and
economic crisis by intervening heavily in their economies and engaging in
full or partial nationalization of key sectors, the state has been brought back
into international and domestic economics in a big way.[32] At the same time,
the immense distress caused by the crisis had serious political consequences,
including the fall of governments and public protest. If the sovereign debt crisis in the Eurozone's periphery reintensifies, the affected countries could be
engulfed by political instability.[33]

Concerns about the appeal of the American model were percolating even
before the current global and financial crisis struck with full force. However,
the crisis made these worries about the future of U.S. soft power even more
acute. In large part, this is because a "Beijing consensus" has emerged as an
alternative to the American model of political and economic development.[34]
China has become increasingly adept at developing its own soft power based
on its culture and diplomacy and the attractiveness of its own system as an
alternative to the American model of political and economic development.[35]
As a 2007 report by the Center for a New American Security noted,

> Rather than seeking to weaken or confront the United States directly, Chinese
> leaders are pursuing a subtle, multifaceted, long-term grand strategy that aims
> to derive as many benefits as possible from the existing international system
> while accumulating the economic wherewithal, military strength, and soft
> power resources to reinforce China's emerging position as at least a regional
> great power.[36]

If, as seems to be the case, China weathers the economic storm better than the United States has, it will be in a position to expand its role in the developing world.[37] Even before the meltdown, China was taking advantage of America's preoccupation with the War on Terror to project its soft power into East and Southeast Asia.[38] China also is making inroads in Latin America, Africa, and Central Asia, by providing no-strings-attached aid and development assistance and through weapons sales.[39] Similarly, it is using its financial clout to buy up huge quantities of raw materials and natural resources worldwide and thereby bringing states into its political orbit. Unlike the United States and EU, China now is in a "position to assist other nations financially and make key investments in, for example, natural resources at a time when the West cannot."[40] Finally, China's willingness to extend economic assistance to other states without interfering in their internal political arrangements is beginning to affect change in prevailing international norms based on the U.S. preference for liberal interventionism.[41]

THE COMING CONTESTS FOR REGIONAL HEGEMONY

If the era of U.S. primacy indeed is winding down, what are the implications for international politics in the coming decades? Two things seem likely. First, as American power is perceived to erode, space will be open for other players to pursue their own international political agendas. Lapp argues that Brazil has taken a more assertive role to reduce conflict and promote democracy in South America since the 1990s. Second, as a declining United States retrenches strategically, America's extraregional hegemony in key parts of the world will give way to intense competitions for regional hegemony between key local powers. For example, in Chapter 11 of this volume Sitaraman chronicles the simmering rivalry between Pakistan and India.

Since the Cold War's end, states have tended to react to U.S. hegemony by trying to find instruments for restraining American power rather than by directly confronting the United States. As U.S. primacy withers, however, rather than taming American power, great and regional powers will tend to ignore it and pursue their own interests even when these conflict openly with America's. Simply put, U.S. preferences increasingly will be defied rather than complied with, and the United States will find it more difficult to persuade others to follow its lead. Indeed, it already is possible to see this trend beginning to take hold in international politics.

Here, one could cite a number of recent examples. For example, at NATO's April 2008 summit in Bucharest, France and Germany sidetracked the Bush administration's push to admit Ukraine and Georgia into the alliance. Notwithstanding the U.S. interest in Georgia, in August 2008 Russia ignored the United States and conducted a short, victorious war against Georgia. On the diplomatic front, the United States has found it ever more difficult to persuade the U.N. Security Council to impose effective economic sanctions on Iran to force it into giving up its program to enrich uranium. However, perhaps the most striking recent example of how other states are taking advantage of declining U.S. power to ignore American policy preferences is the recent joint initiative by Turkey and Brazil to bypass the United States and to reach their own agreement with Iran on the nuclear issue. Moreover, in defiance of the enhanced U.S. and EU economic sanctions on Iran, Turkey is making a concerted effort to expand its trade with Tehran.[42] Finally, at the November 2010 G-20 conference in Seoul, the United States, China, Britain, and Germany clashed on the issue of trade imbalances. As U.S. power is perceived to be continuing to diminish, we can expect to see more and more instances of major states defying U.S. preferences and pursuing their own interests even where these are at cross-purposes with Washington's.

If, as the late Speaker of the U.S. House of Representatives Tip O'Neill once said, all [domestic] politics is local, then it might equally be said that all geopolitics is regional. From 1945 onward, one of America's hegemonic functions has been to act as a "regional stabilizer" in Europe, East Asia, and the Persian Gulf. In this role, the United States has extended its security umbrella over these regions to prevent the major nations in these areas from "renationalizing" their foreign and security policies. If renationalization occurs, U.S. policy makers believed, it could set off a series of cascade effects, including arms races, intense security competitions, and possibly war. The U.S. role as regional stabilizer is the security component of hegemonic stability theory. And, just as in the economic sphere, the erosion of U.S. hegemony is bound to have important consequences as the United States downsizes its regional stabilizer role, the most important of which is that there will be an upsurge of competitions for regional hegemony.[43] As it pulls back its security umbrella from key areas, space will be created for major local powers to strive for regional hegemony.

In Eastern Europe, the Caucasus, and Central Asia, as discussed in Horowitz and Tyburski's Chapter 10 in this book, the coming decades will see a resurgence of Russia as a regional hegemon. Russia will seek to reassert its control over its "near abroad," try to maintain control over oil and natural gas pipelines, support ethnic Russian minorities in post-Soviet successor states, and resist ideological contagion. Russia has many tools to exert regional hegemony, including creating new security and economic institutions in its sphere of influence, using economic statecraft (especially energy) as both a carrot and a stick, using low-intensity forms of coercion (including cyber warfare), and using outright military force (as in Georgia). It is a good bet that as the United States adopts a policy of strategic retrenchment as a response to its relative decline, the American commitment to Europe and NATO will be the first major commitment to be jettisoned. For states that wish to resist Russian hegemony, therefore, a great deal will depend on whether they can find new security guarantors and economic partners to offset Russian power—the EU in Eastern Europe and perhaps China in Central Asia.

When it comes to future competitions for regional hegemony, China casts a huge shadow, not only over East Asia but over South Asia as well. China already is pushing hard for regional hegemony in East and Southeast Asia by using its economic power, through diplomacy (including playing the multilateral institutions game), and by building up its military power (including power projection capabilities). India is striving for regional hegemony in South Asia and the Indian Ocean. However, China and India are each potential counterweights against the other's quest for regional hegemony. They also are rivals for access to Middle Eastern energy and the control of the sea-lanes through which petroleum is shipped. In South Asia and the Indian Ocean, China is, arguably, attempting to encircle India by constructing its "string of pearls" naval bases in Pakistan, Sri Lanka, and Myanmar (Burma); cultivating close economic and security relations with Pakistan and Myanmar; using the so-called New Silk Road to enhance its political and economic sway in Central Asia; and challenging India on the Tibetan plateau both by building up its military capabilities and by enticing Nepal into its orbit.[44] As balance-of-threat theory would predict, because of geographic proximity the smaller states in South Asia feel more threatened by India's rise than by China's and hence are looking to China as an economic, diplomatic, and military counterweight to India.

East Asia (and Southeast Asia) looks to be theaters of especially intense competition because both China and the United States are competing against each other for hegemony (extraregional hegemony in the U.S. case) in the region. A rapidly rising China is following a geopolitical trajectory similar to that of the United States in the late nineteenth and early twentieth centuries.[45] As its economic power has grown, China has sought access to overseas markets and raw materials and also has sought to expand its diplomatic engagement to protect those interests. Having basically acquired the ability to deny the United States the ability to support Taiwan militarily, China is now turning its attention to acquiring the kinds of power projection capabilities necessary to protect its interests in Southeast Asia and along the lines of communication to the Persian Gulf. It has also been increasingly assertive in its claims to disputed territories, especially in the South China Sea, an area through which the trade routes to Northeast Asia pass and the seabed of which is reputedly rich in raw materials. As China has grown more powerful, like the United States a century ago, its ambitions and interests have expanded.

China's quest for regional hegemony is propelled by its economic power. China is the motor for regional economic development. It is a voracious consumer of Southeast Asia's raw materials and also an important market for its manufactured goods. In East and Southeast Asia, it is China, not the United States, that has the capacity to practice economic statecraft to enhance its political profile in the region. To be sure, smaller states in the region recognize that their economic dependence on China is a two-edged sword. At the same time, there is little they can do to escape the magnetic pull that China's economy exerts. Also, although there are concerns about Chinese hegemony, these are offset, at least to an extent, by China's soft power in the region, which is based on historical ties and cultural affinity. The bandwagoning of Japan and Taiwan to Chinese policy, as explained by Tan, is an example of the effectiveness of Chinese benign hegemony. Moreover, at least until 2010 China was very careful to avoid being seen as a threatening power. Hence, China has engaged in multilateral diplomacy and has been active in regional institutions. At some point, however, its power will loom so large in the region that its hegemonic threat will be impossible for others to ignore.

Ultimately, it will be America's ability to contest China's ambitions for regional hegemony that will determine East and Southeast Asia's future. Obviously, China's fast-rising power is one reason its regional influence has expanded so quickly. An equally important factor in China's rise, however, is that after 9/11 the United States largely ignored the region while it concentrated on the conflicts in Iraq and Afghanistan and the so-called War on Terror. China had a clear road to regional influence during the last decade.

However, as Secretary Clinton announced at the ASEAN Ministerial Conference in July 2010, the United States is "back" in Asia and intends to play an active role there. In the short run, the United States can contest China's drive for regional dominance.

By 2020, however, the United States is going to have real trouble sustaining that role. First, already the United States is at a disadvantage in the region because it no longer has the economic punch to offset China. With each passing day, the region's prosperity is tied more to China and less to the United States. Second, as China's military might grows, the credibility of America's extended guarantees to regional allies will become increasingly doubtful. As America's ability to compete for extraregional hegemony in East Asia wanes, the other major states in that region will have two choices. One option is to bandwagon with China. The second option is for states like Japan, Taiwan, Vietnam, and South Korea to build security and economic institutions—and military alliances that perhaps involve India and Russia—that would enable them to act as effective checks on China's ambition for regional hegemony. It's always hard to predict the future, but it is a safe bet that the struggle for hegemonic mastery in Asia will be the twenty-first-century arena for great power politics.[46]

CONCLUSION: HEGEMONY—QUO VADIS?

The era of the post–World War II *Pax Americana* is nearly over. From 1945 to 1991, the United States may not have been a global hegemon, but it surely exercised extraregional hegemony in Europe, East Asia, and the Persian Gulf. During this period, U.S. primacy was not always so eagerly embraced by its followers. Many of the great rows in the transatlantic relationship during this period resulted from the efforts of America's reluctant European followers to find ways to bind and constrain America's economic, military, and diplomatic preeminence. These efforts, however, were not notably successful because in its extraregional spheres influence the United States possessed overwhelming power.

With the Soviet Union's collapse, America seemed to bestride the global stage more powerfully than ever. The United States was, after all, as its leaders never tired of reminding the rest of the world, the sole superpower in a unipolar world, the indispensable nation. Almost from the moment the Soviet flag was lowered for the final time over the Kremlin, many of the world's follower states balked at being subjected to America's unchecked power. Yet, both because they benefited from the public goods provided by a hegemonic United States and because U.S. power was too overwhelming to challenge directly, the followers learned to live with America's unipolar power. With the option of engaging in hard balancing foreclosed, follower states rediscovered the tools of diplomacy in an attempt to tame American power. In retrospect, however, creative as they were in applying the techniques discussed in this volume (that is, soft balancing, binding, leash slipping) they were not notably successful in reining in the United States. In the end, what brought U.S. hegemony down was its own slow relative decline that began in the late 1960s—and was kicked into warp speed by the Great Recession—and China's astonishing rapid great power rise.

As the era of *Pax Americana* passes, the question of how followers could constrain a preeminent America is fast losing relevance. However, the issue of hegemons and followers will be as relevant as ever—perhaps more so—in the emerging twenty-first-century post–*Pax Americana* international system. As U.S. extraregional hegemony fades, space will be created for emerging powers (China, India, Russia, Brazil, and others) to compete for regional hegemony. In Eastern Europe, the Middle East, Central Asia, Latin America, and East and Southeast Asia, followers will be looking for techniques to restrain regional hegemons. The insights in this volume on the relations between hegemons and followers provide a framework for understanding the evolving international system.

NOTES

1. For the debate about whether great powers can be only regional hegemons or can attain hegemony beyond their region, see John J. Mearsheimer, *The Tragedy of Great Power Politics* (New York: W. W. Norton, 2001); Christopher Layne, *The Peace of Illusions: American Grand Strategy from 1940 to the Present* (Ithaca, NY: Cornell University Press, 2006); Layne, "The 'Poster Child' for Offensive Realism: America as a Global Hegemon," *Security Studies* 12, 2 (Winter 2002/2003): 120–164.

2. Charles Krauthammer, "The Unipolar Moment," *Foreign Affairs—America and the World 1990* 70, 1 (1990/91): 25–33.

3. See Christopher Layne, "The Unipolar Illusion: Why New Great Powers Will Rise," *International Security* 17, 4 (Spring 1993): 5–51; Kenneth N. Waltz, "The Emerging Structure of International Politics," 18, 2 (Fall 1993): 44–79.

4. On the historical pattern of counterhegemonic balancing, see Ludwig Dehio, trans. Charles Fullman, *The Precarious Balance: The Politics of Power in Europe, 1494 to 1945* (London: Chatto & Windus, 1963).

5. See Stephen G. Brooks and William C. Wohlforth, *World Out of Balance: International Relations and the Challenge of U.S. Primacy* (Princeton, NJ: Princeton

University Press, 2008); William C. Wohlforth, "The Stability of a Unipolar World," *International Security* 24, 1 (Summer 1999): 5–41; William C. Wohlforth, "U.S. Strategy in a Unipolar World," in *America Unrivaled: The Future of the Balance of Power*, ed. G. John Ikenberry (Ithaca, NY: Cornell University Press, 2002): 98–120; and Stephen G. Brooks and William C. Wohlforth, "American Primacy in Perspective," *Foreign Affairs* 81, 4 (July/August 2002): 20–33.

6. See for example, Michael Mastanduno, "Preserving the Unipolar Moment: Realist Theories and U.S. Grand Strategy after the Cold War," *International Security* 21, 4 (Spring 1997): 49–88. The seminal work on balance-of-threat theory is Stephen M. Walt, *The Origins of Alliances* (Ithaca, NY: Cornell University Press, 1987).

7. See Joseph S. Nye Jr., *The Paradox of American Power: Why the World's Only Superpower Can't Go It Alone* (New York: Oxford University Press, 2002); Nye, *Bound to Lead: The Changing Nature of American Power* (New York: Basic Books, 1990); Stephen M. Walt, *Taming American Power: The Global Response to U.S. Primacy* (New York: W. W. Norton, 2005); G. John Ikenberry, "Institutions, Strategic Restraint, and the Persistence of American Postwar Order," *International Security* 23, 3 (Winter 1998/99): 43–78. See also John M. Owen IV, "Transnational Liberalism and U.S. Primacy," *International Security* 26, 3 (Winter 2001/02): 117–152.

8. Joseph S. Nye Jr., *Soft Power: The Means to Success in World Politics* (New York: PublicAffairs, 2004). Also see Nye, *Bound to Lead*.

9. Craig R. Whitney, "France Presses for a Power Independent of the U.S.," *New York Times*, November 7, 1999.

10. Walt, *Taming American Power*.

11. Brooks and Wohlforth, *World out of Balance*; Michael Mandelbaum, *The Case for Goliath: How America Acts as the World's Government in the 21st Century* (New York: PublicAffairs, 2005); Fareed Zakaria, *The Post-American World* (New York: W. W. Norton, 2008).

12. Special Issue on Unipolarity, *World Politics* 61, 1 (January 2009).

13. Glenn Kessler, "Clinton Declares 'New American Moment' in Foreign Policy Speech," *Washington Post*, September 8, 2010.

14. J. O'Neill [Head of Global Economic Research, Goldman Sachs] (2008), Video Interview, February 2008, available at www2.goldmansachs.com/ideas/brics/index.html; Dominic Wilson and Roopa Purushothaman, "Dreaming with BRICs: The Path to 2050" (Goldman Sachs Global Economics Paper, No. 99), New York: Goldman Sachs, October 2003.

15. PricewaterhouseCoopers, "Convergence, Catch-Up, and Overtaking," January 2010, available at www:ukmediacentre.pwc.com/imagelibrary/detail.aspx? . . . 1626; Economist Intelligence Unit, April 20, 2009, all-country data set, available at http://store.eiu.com/products.html; "The World's Biggest Economy: Dating Game," *Economist*, December 16, 2010. China does not need to sustain double-digit growth rates

to overtake the United States in overall GDP later in this decade. For example, the *Economist's* forecast is based on the assumption that between 2011 and 2019 China's economy will grow at an average annual rate of 7.5 percent and U.S. growth will be 2.5 percent ("World's Biggest Economy"). Many economic analysts have predicted China's growth in 2011 and 2012 will slow to an annual rate of 8.5 percent. David Barboza, "China's Boom Is Beginning to Slow Cracks, Analysts Say," *New York Times*, June 21, 2011.

16. IMF, *World Economic Outlook Database* (April 2011). There is debate among economists about whether market exchange rate or PPP is the best measure of a state's GDP. Market exchange rate does a better job of capturing a state's international buying power. PPP, on the other hand, is a better measure of what a given amount of money can purchase in a state's domestic economy. PPP also does a better job of accounting for the role of service industries in contributing to a state's national wealth. For discussion of recent market exchange rate and PPP studies comparing the GDP's of the United States and China, see Gavyn Davies, "China May Be Bigger Than You Think," *Financial Times*, February 15, 2011. To the extent that most of the U.S. and Chinese defense expenditures—including weapons procurement—are domestic in nature, PPP may be a better measure of the long-run military potential of each nation's economy.

17. Arvind Subramanian, "How We Undervalue China," *Washington Post*, May 1, 2011. On the Peterson Institute for International Economics website, Subramanian explains his methodology in "Is China Already Number One? New GDP Estimates," available at www.iie.com/realtime/?p=1935.

18. William C. Wohlforth, "The Perception of Power: Russia in the Pre-1914 Balance," *World Politics* 39, 3 (April 1987): 353–381.

19. Charles P. Kindelberger, *The World in Depression, 1929–1939* (Berkeley: University of California Press, 1973); Robert Gilpin, *U.S. Power and the Multinational Corporation: The Political Economy of Foreign Direct Investment* (New York: Basic Books, 1975); Gilpin, *War and Change in World Politics*; Carla Norloff, *America's Global Advantage: U.S. Hegemony and International Cooperation* (Cambridge, UK: Cambridge University Press, 2010).

20. David E. Sanger and Mark Landler, "In Europe, Obama Faces Calls for Rules on Finances," *New York Times*, April 1, 2009.

21. Brooks and Wohlforth, *World Out of Balance*; G. John Ikenberry, *Liberal Leviathan: The Origins, Crisis, and Transformation of the American World Order* (Princeton, NJ: Princeton University Press, 2011); G. John Ikenberry, *After Victory: Institutions, Strategic Restraint, and the Rebuilding of International Order after Major Wars* (Princeton, NJ: Princeton University Press, 2001); Zakaria, *Post-American World*.

22. Ikenberry, *After Victory*. Also see Robert O. Keohane, *After Hegemony: Cooperation and Discord in the World Political Economy* (Princeton, NJ: Princeton University Press, 1984).

23. To make room for an enhanced role for emerging powers, in September 2010 the German government called on the United States to give up its veto over important IMF decisions in return for Europe agreeing to a reduced role in IMF decision making. Alan Beattie, "Germany Asks U.S. to Give Up its IMF Veto," *Financial Times*, September 14, 2010. The United States, however, successfully resisted this pressure and was able to persuade the Europeans to accept diminished voting power in the IMF so that the voting weight of the emerging market states could be increased.

24. Martin Wolf, "Seeds of Its Own Destruction," *Financial Times*, March 8, 2008.

25. Zakaria, *The Post-American World*: 234–235.

26. Ibid.: 234.

27. Altman, "The Great Credit Crash": 2.

28. See Joshua Kurlantzick, *Charm Offensive: How China's Soft Power Is Transforming the World* (New Haven, CT: Yale University Press, 2007).

29. National Intelligence Council, *Global Trends 2025: A Transformed World* (Washington, DC: 2008): 8–9, 87.

30. Ibid: 13–14.

31. See Quentin Peel, "EU Champion Takes Fright in Flight to Protectionism," *Financial Times*, February 27, 2009: 4; Steven Erlanger, "Impairing the European Union, Gibe by Gibe," *New York Times*, February 14, 2009; Bertrand Benoit, Nikki Tait, and Ben Hall, "Paris Support for Carmakers Draws Cross-Border Fire," *Financial Times*, February 11, 2009: 5; Tony Barber, "Czech Attack on Protectionism Exposes EU Rift," *Financial Times*, February 11, 2009: 5; Richard Milne, "Each to Their Own," *Financial Times*, February 5, 2009: 7; John Thornhill, "The Old Danger That Threatens New Model Europe," *Financial Times*, December 28, 2009: 7; Charles Grant, "Unilateral Germany Threatens to Weaken Europe," *Financial Times*, December 5, 2008: 11.

32. Wolf, "Seeds of its Own Destruction": 7.

33. Dennis Blair, director of national intelligence, warns that the political instability caused by the meltdown is the gravest current challenge to U.S. strategic interests. Mark Mazzetti, "Global Economy Top Threat to U.S., Spy Chief Says," *New York Times*, February 13, 2009; Walter Pincus and Joby Warwick, "Financial Crisis Called Top Security Threat to U.S.," *Washington Post*, February 13, 2009: A14; Greg Miller, "Global Economic Crisis Called Biggest U.S. Security Threat," *Los Angeles Times*, February 13, 2009.

34. David Brooks, "The Parent Model," *New York Times*, August 31, 2010.

35. Kurlantzick, *Charm Offensive*. See also Richard Armitage and Joseph S. Nye Jr., *Commission on Smart Power: A Smarter, More Secure America* (Washington, DC: Center for International and Strategic Studies, 2007): 25.

36. Kurt Campbell and Michele A. Flournoy, *The Inheritance and the Way Forward* (Washington, DC: Center for a New American Security, 2007): 17.

37. Altman, "The Great Credit Crash": 12.

38. See Guy Dinmore, Anna Fifield, and Victor Mallet, "The Rivals: Washington's Sway in Asia Is Challenged by China," *Financial Times*, March 18, 2005: 11; Jane Perlez, "Across Asia, Beijing's Star Is in Ascendance," *New York Times*, August 28, 2004.

39. See Isabel Gort and Jamil Anderlini, "China Puts Up $10bn for Central Asia Loans," *Financial Times*, June 17, 2009: 5; Simon Romero and Alexei Barrionuevo, "Deals Help China Expand Sway in Latin America," *New York Times*, April 16, 2009: A1; "Friends of Opportunity," *Economist*, November 29, 2008: 41–42; Tom Burgis, "Beijing to Boost Spending in Africa Fund," *Financial Times*, March 17, 2009; William McNamara, "China Eyes Developed Mines Assets," *Financial Times*, January 6, 2009.

40. Altman, "The Great Credit Crash": 3.

41. C. Fred Bergston, Charles W. Freeman, Nicholas Lardy, and Derek Mitchell, *China's Rise: Challenges and Opportunities* (Washington, DC: Brookings Institution, 2008): 225.

42. Daphne Strauss and David Gardner, "Turkey: The Sentinel Swivels," *Financial Times*, July 20, 2010; Daphne Strauss, "Turkey Seeks to Treble Trade with Iran," *Financial Times*, September 15, 2010.

43. There is something of a chicken/egg problem in trying to determine the effect a change in the U.S. global posture will have on regional security. Some would argue that U.S. withdrawal would be the cause of regional security competitions. However, it is more accurate to say that the relative decline of U.S. power, reflected in the rise of powerful regional states, is the variable causing an increased risk of security competitions. As other states realize that U.S. security guarantees are increasingly less credible, they have strong incentives to develop their own military capabilities. This is what raises the risks of arms races, instability, and even conflict. Whether the United States remains in these regions or withdraws from them, the geopolitical dynamics will be the same because decline casts a shadow of uncertainty over American staying power, and others will react accordingly.

44. Lydia Polgreen, "India Digs under Top of the World to Match Rival," *New York Times*, July 31, 2010; Vikas Bajaj, "India Worries as China Builds Ports in South Asia," *New York Times*, February 16, 2010; Banyan, "Himalayan Histrionics," *Economist*, October 31, 2009; James Lamont and Amy Kazmin, "Fear of Influence," *Financial Times*, July 12, 2009. Also see Robert Kaplan, *Monsoon: The Indian Ocean and the Future of American Power* (New York: Random House, 2011).

45. See John J. Mearsheimer, "China's Unpeaceful Rise," *Current History* 105, 690 (April 2006). On the United States's rise to great power status in the late nineteenth and early twentieth centuries, see Fareed Zakaria, *From Wealth to Power: The Unusual Origins of America's World Role* (Princeton, NJ: Princeton University Press, 1998).

46. See Aaron L. Friedberg, *A Contest for Supremacy: China, America, and the Struggle for Mastery in Asia* (New York: W. W. Norton, 2011).

INDEX

abandonment fear: in NATO European allies, 115, 116, 117–18, 118–19, 120, 124; public opinion in democracies and, 123–24

Abdelal, Rawi, 82

Abdullah II (king of Jordan), 86, 87, 88–89

Abkhazia, Russia occupation of, 165, 168, 169–70, 173

accommodation to hegemon, forms of, 13–14, 14t

Afghanistan: Indian rebuilding funds for, 181; Jordanian troops in, 91–92; and resistance to U.S. hegemony, 16; and SAARC, 177; Soviets occupation, U.S. response to, 130–32

Afghanistan War: and NATO threat perceptions, divergence in, 120; NATO troops, U.S. dependence on, 116, 120–21; and U.S. relationship with Pakistan, 177–78, 188

Africa, history of Cuban involvement in, 53–54

African Growth and Opportunity Act, 105

African National Congress (ANC), 209, 210, 211, 212, 215, 216, 219

African Renaissance, 208, 213

African Standby Force (ASF), 207–8, 213

African Union (AU), 207–8, 213, 215

Afrikaner National Party, 209

After Hegemony (Keohane), 4

agricultural trade, efforts to liberalize, 101–2, 103–4

Ahmed, Mahmud, 136

Akayev, Askar, 173

ALBA. *See* Bolivarian Alliance of the Peoples of the Americas

Alfonsín, Rafael, 146, 147, 149, 156

Algeria, Cuban involvement in, 53

Aliev, Heidar, 168, 171

Aliev, Ilham, 171

Allende, Salvador, 54

alliance security dilemma, 117–18

Alvor Accords, 55–56

American hyperpower, 225

Amsterdam Treaty (1997), 113

ANC. *See* African National Congress

Andean Pact, 146

Anglo-American Corporation, 208

Anglo–Irish Treaty of 1921, 66, 75

Angola: ANC and, 209; civil war, origins of, 55–56; DRC intervention by, 213; and SADC, 211; South Africa and, 208, 212–13, 214–15, 216, 217–18

Angola, Cuban involvement in: motives for, 49, 53, 54–55, 60–61; origins of, 56–57; Soviets' lack of influence on, 49, 57–58, 59; troop deployment, 49, 58–59

ANP. *See* Awami National Party

ANZUS (Australia, New Zealand, U.S. Security Treaty), 196

APEC. *See* Asia Pacific Economic Cooperation

Arab–Israeli War, Romania and, 40

United States trade concessions to Jordan: economic value of, 86; as effort to shift domestic balance of power, 81, 91, 93; internationalist coalition response, 86–88; King Abdullah's compensation of supporters, 88–89, 92; nationalist coalition response, 89–91, 92; opposition to, 81, 86, 89–91, 92; political goals of, 86, 91; QIZs and, 81, 86, 91–92; results of, 91–92; shortcomings of, as strategy, 92; theory of, 82–85; U.S.–Jordan Free Trade Agreement, 81, 86, 91–92

Uruguay: and agricultural trade policies, 104; and MERCOSUR, 147, 148, 149, 150; redemocratization of, 149; and WTO director-generalship, 154

Uzbekistan: soft balancing of Russia by, 170; U.S. military bases in, 170–71

Valenta, Jiri, 33

Vedrine, Herbert, 225

Velasco, Andrés, 103

Venezuela: Cuban involvement in, 54; hard balancing against Brazilian hegemony, 154–56; and MERCOSUR, 147, 149, 150, 156; relations with Colombia, 155; relations with U.S., 155

Vietnam, trade agreements, 106–7

Vietnam War: Cuban views on, 52; U.S. military timidity following, 60–61

Waever, Ole, 8

Walt, Stephen, 12, 13, 14, 18, 146

Waltz, Kenneth N., 4, 8, 11–14

War and Change (Gilpin), 6

War on Terror: and European fear of U.S. abandonment, 115, 120; Irish public opinion on, 74; Jordanian support for, 91–92; Pakistan as passive-aggressive malcontent in, 128, 130; and Pakistan–U.S. relations, 133; and U.S. neglect of Asia, 232, 235–36

Warsaw Pact (Warsaw Treaty Organization; WTO), as instrument of Soviet hegemony, 35–36

Warsaw Pact invasion of Czechoslovakia, 33; Castro on, 52; decision to invade, 37–38; as effective lesson to other nations,

42–43, 43–44; motives for, 38; Romanian refusal to support, 33, 38–43

Warsaw Treaty Organization. *See* Warsaw Pact

Washington Consensus, 230

Western European Union (WEU), 113

Wohlforth, William C., 3, 5, 229

World Bank: and Jordan debt restructuring, 81, 85, 88; and Mozambique, 217

World Economic Forum, 103

world order, hegemon's stake in, 24, 43

World Politics (periodical), 225

World Trade Organization (WTO): Brazil's bid for director-generalship of, 153–54; Doha Round, 102–4, 109; negotiations, Brazil and, 145; Singapore Issues, 103; support of secondary and tertiary states, 102; U.S.'s limited control over, 14

World War II, Irish neutrality in, 68, 71, 72, 73–74, 78n20

Wright, Thomas, 6–7

WTO. *See* Warsaw Pact; World Trade Organization

Yanukovych, Viktor, 173

Yeltsin, Boris: limited resistance to Western integration of Eastern European states, 165; regime of, 163; and Russian energy sales, 172; Russian territorial interests under, 167–68, 173

Yugoslavia: Soviet de-Stalinization and, 34–35; and Soviet invasion of Czechoslovakia, 40–41, 42

Yushchenko, Viktor, 173

Zaire: and Angolan civil war, 58; Cuban involvement in, 53–54

Zakaria, Fareed, 225, 229, 230

Zambia, 209, 216–17

Zardari, Asif Ali, 137, 139

Zelaya, Manuel, 145

Zilli, Aldo, 149

Zimbabwe: DRC intervention by, 213; and SADC, 211; South Africa and, 208, 210, 212–13, 214–15, 217–18

Zimmerman, William, 43

Zuma, Jacob, 214, 215

The authorized representative in the EU for product safety and compliance is:
Mare Nostrum Group
B.V Doelen 72
4831 GR Breda
The Netherlands

www.ingramcontent.com/pod-product-compliance
Lightning Source LLC
Chambersburg PA
CBHW030353270326
41926CB00009B/1089

* 9 7 8 0 8 0 4 7 7 1 6 4 1 *